A Practical Guide to Educational Research

Ward Mitchell Cates
Pittsburg State University

Prentice-Hall, Inc., Englewood Cliffs, New Jersey 07632

Library of Congress Cataloging in Publication Data

CATES, WARD MITCHELL (date)
A practical guide to educational research.

Bibliography: p.
Includes index.
1. Education—Research—Methodology—Handbooks,
manuals, etc. 1. Title.
LB1028.C29 1985   370'.7'8   84-15106
ISBN 0-13-690678-8

Editorial/production supervision and
interior design by Joyce Turner and Eva Jaunzems
Cover design by Wanda Lubelska Design/Filip Pagowski
Manufacturing buyer: Barbara Kittle

Printed in the United States of America

10   9   8   7   6   5   4   3   2   1

ISBN 0-13-690678-8   01

Prentice-Hall International, Inc., *London*
Prentice-Hall of Australia Pty. Limited, *Sydney*
Editora Prentice-Hall do Brasil, Ltda., *Rio de Janeiro*
Prentice-Hall Canada Inc., *Toronto*
Prentice-Hall Hispanoamericana, S.A., *Mexico*
Prentice-Hall of India Private Limited, *New Delhi*
Prentice-Hall of Japan, Inc., *Tokyo*
Prentice-Hall of Southeast Asia Pte. Ltd., *Singapore*
Whitehall Books Limited, *Wellington, New Zealand*

*This work is dedicated to
Pearl White Massey and Howard Braxton,
who demonstrate clearly that
true service is perfect freedom.*

CONTENTS

3

Questions, Statements, and Hypotheses Used in Research Studies

4

Organizational Plans for Research Proposals and Reports

5

The Literature Search

6

Analysis and Evaluation of the Work of Others

7

Probability and the Normal Curve

18

Interpretation of Results   191

19

Preparation of Research and Reports   197

References   238

Appendix:

PREFACE

It is my contention that competent researchers do not memorize vast quantities of information about research designs, research methodologies, and statistical procedures; rather, they seek to gain an understanding of the basic parameters of carrying out research studies and then consult a variety of reference works to identify designs, methodologies, and analytical procedures.

In conducting my own research and in supervising my students' studies, I often needed a reference from one work, an exposition on a different topic from a second work, and a description of a statistical procedure from yet another work; at times I felt stretched in several directions simultaneously. Often, too, I have felt myself and my students at the mercy of fate as books disappeared, microform records became misplaced, and unknown assailants employed razor blades to remove crucial articles from volumes of bound periodicals.

In support of these contentions and in response to these problems, I undertook the writing of this book. While this work will not eliminate the need to consult other references, it will serve as a handbook—a quick guide—to remind researchers and would-be researchers of some of the salient elements of conducting research studies and to supply them with information concerning designs, methodologies, and procedures appropriate to a variety of research problems.

In keeping with my intentions, this book often employs outlines or listings of steps instead of long explanatory passages. References are used only when necessary.

From time to time, this book suggests that researchers consult their advisors. An *advisor* in this context may be an academic advisor, an instructor, or a knowledgeable friend or colleague.

W. M. Cates

ACKNOWLEDGMENTS

I would like to acknowledge the legacy of the many writers and researchers who have preceded me and in whose debt I remain. In scientific endeavor one must always recognize that one stands on the broad shoulders of those who have gone before.

I would also like to express my appreciation to the students who helped me in the design and revision of this work. Special thanks go also to those whose research proposals are critiqued in the book.

I would like to express my particular appreciation and debt to Dr. Grover Baldwin who assisted me in preparing the first copy of this book, who supplied an intelligent and understanding foil for my first efforts, and whose interest in research and in the needs of novice researchers made his advice invaluable.

I am grateful to the Literary Executor of the late Sir Ronald A. Fisher, F.R.S., to Dr. Frank Yates, F.R.S., and to Longman Group Ltd., London, for permission to reprint extracts from Table III in their book *Statistical Tables for Biological, Agricultural, and Medical Research* (Sixth Edition, 1974).

Last, but most important, I wish to express my gratitude to my wife, Anne Sniffen Cates, whose patience and understanding have seen me through years of a dissertation, through the writing of seemingly innumerable journal articles, and through the years it has taken to write and revise this book. Were it not for her gentle understanding and impeccable typing, there would be nothing here to read.

ONE

RESEARCH AND COMMON SENSE

Chapter 1 discusses the scientific method and how it aids researchers in arriving at objective and defensible conclusions. This chapter also defines some frequently used terms in educational research.

Teachers, administrators, trainers, coaches, psychologists, and counselors seek answers to a variety of questions every day: Will some students do better using one technique than another? Which training methods work best? What therapies are effective? Often they try to use ''common sense'' to answer these questions. But what exactly is ''common sense''?

In general, ''common sense'' seems to be what appears reasonable to us. Sometimes it is truth derived from experience, as in ''Fire burns.'' Other times it is a generalized statement about human behavior based on observation, as in ''People tend to avoid that which causes them physical pain.'' Still other times it is a misconception based on a limited viewpoint or on limited information, as in the belief that the sun and planets revolve around the earth (a belief which survived for over a thousand years, even in the face of contradictory evidence).

Common sense more often than not is simply an attempt to bring to bear upon a situation the sum of our own personal experiences and those which others have shared with us. Limited personal experience, limited information or misinformation (often supplied by others), and the excessive influence of our own opinions all act to reduce the utility of common sense, which sometimes leads us to conclusions which are extremely inaccurate.

How then are we to use our intelligence, experiences, and observations to find answers? The *scientific method* is designed for this purpose. It enables us to minimize the role that rumor, opinion, and questionable interpretation often play when common sense fools us.

Common sense can be a valuable starting point, however. Our common sense ideas often supply us with beliefs about which one of two things is better or about what will happen in a given situation. The scientific method enables us to test our beliefs in ways that can be repeated by others and helps to minimize some types of misinterpretation.

In the scientific method we seek to control as many aspects of the situation to be examined as possible in order to isolate the influence of individual elements. This calls for objectivity in analysis of the results of any research study designed to examine the situation. Objectivity in analysis does not require neutrality or an absence of interest or concern on the part of the researcher. It requires instead that the researcher standardize the conditions of observation or measurement and do his or her best to be aware of and control any prejudices, biases, or possible "blind spots." As Kerlinger wrote, "The main condition to satisfy the objectivity criterion is, ideally, that *any* observers with minimal competence agree in their observations" (1979, p. 9).

This book shows you how to apply this scientific method to educational research. It helps you to set up and conduct educational research studies and to become a knowledgeable consumer of the research studies of others.

DISCUSSION OF TERMS

There is usually some confusion about the terms used in educational research. The term *educational research* itself is open to a variety of definitions. In elementary school we were assigned "research reports," which entailed our consulting a reference work (usually an encyclopedia) and preparing a report. In high school many of us were asked to write "research reports" or "research papers," which required us to go to the library, consult a variety of reference works, and produce a paper which incorporated what we had learned. While such library work is a major element of all research studies, it is not *educational research*. Educational research involves the identification of a specific problem, library research to expand and refine one's understanding of the problem, the setting up and carrying out of a research study using appropriate procedures and measurement instruments, the gathering and statistical analysis of data, and the drawing of logical conclusions based on this analysis. This book will discuss these steps in some detail.

To prepare you for this discussion, we will now examine the meanings of a few terms which will be used frequently in this book.

> **Hypothesis:** A statement about what will happen in a given situation. This statement contains certain elements which make it clear to a reader immediately what is being studied, with whom, and how results will be measured. When a hypothesis states what we believe will happen, we call it a *research*

hypothesis. Types of hypotheses and how they are generated will be discussed in detail in Chapter 3. The plural of hypothesis is *hypotheses*.

Subjects: The individuals (human or animal) involved in a study.

Population: A group of subjects who are considered as a group because of some criterion or set of criteria employed by the researcher.

Sample: A group of subjects selected from a population. Chapter 8 will discuss methods by which samples may be drawn from populations.

Variable: Any aspect of the study which varies. In practice, a variable is generally a score or measurement which varies because of characteristics of the subjects or as a result of a treatment administered to the subjects. If the variable is supposed to change as a result of a treatment administered to the subjects, it is called a *dependent variable*. An *independent variable* is a variable which is supposed to influence the dependent variable. Independent variables are therefore sometimes called *treatment variables*. Variables are usually represented by letters (e.g., A, B, X, Z, Y), sometimes with a *subscript* (number or letter below the line) to indicate variations of a single variable (e.g., X_1, X_2, X_3).

Statistically significant: Having a low probability of occurring by chance alone. We employ levels of probability which reduce the probability of our accepting a finding which occurred by chance alone. Probability is often represented by the letter p, and the probability levels of .05 and .01 (a probability of 5 chances in a hundred and of 1 chance in a hundred, respectively) are frequently employed by researchers.

Practically significant: A difference between treatments which is not only unlikely to have occurred by chance but also represents a meaningful difference in everyday application of the study's findings to actual practice.

Generalizability: The extent to which a study's findings can be applied to other populations in other situations. Researchers conduct studies using the populations which they have available to them. The findings of their studies are generally applicable to similar populations under conditions similar to those which existed in the study.

Do not spend long hours trying to memorize these terms word by word. Read them over until you feel you basically understand them. They will be used frequently, and soon you should feel comfortable with their use. Other terms will be defined and discussed as they appear in text.

TWO

SELECTION OF A RESEARCH PROBLEM

This chapter addresses ways in which researchers can locate research problems, evaluate them, select appropriate problems for their own investigations, and then consider the ramifications of their study.

IDENTIFYING A RESEARCH PROBLEM

There is no shortage of problems to be studied in education. The difficulty is in selecting from among the many available. Many beginning researchers have a hard time getting started. Where do you look? How do you choose? How can you be sure the problem that you select is appropriate and manageable? This chapter will help the beginning researcher answer these questions.

The procedure for selecting a research problem which is outlined in this book consists first of identifying research topics of interest, generating a variety of types of questions, investigating the feasibility of researching the topic, and then using a variety of statements and hypotheses to narrow your choice to a single research problem.

There are many approaches to selecting a topic. Some of those more commonly used are described below.

Exploring or Expanding Theories

Theories sometimes seem a bit nebulous and hard for educators to grasp. Often one hears comments like ''That's just theory; it doesn't really work that way.'' Such a comment is unreasonable. For a theory to be valid, it must apply in greater or lesser degree to all situations in which it claims to account for the occurrences. One of the author's colleagues used to say, ''There is nothing more practical than a good theory.'' If the theory is valid, then, indeed, ''Things *should* work that way.''

Ary, Jacobs, and Razavieh have suggested four characteristics which a theory must have:

1. It must be able to explain why a phenomenon occurs in the simplest and most direct wording possible.
2. It must reconcile new observations with the established theoretical evidence of the past.
3. It must provide for its own verification by clarifying how this theory purportedly accounts for the phenomemon.
4. It must stimulate further work. (1979, p. 17)

These last two characteristics are of particular interest to the researcher. When educators question the validity of a theory, usually they do not see how the theory accounts for the phenomenon. A potential research problem might be to determine the way in which a theory does indeed account for the phenomenon observed. This type of research is known as *basic research* or *pure research* and has as its goal the advancement of theoretical understanding and the formulation of new theories (thereby fulfilling the fourth characteristic listed above).

Applying Theories to Practice

Another use of theories as a source for research problems is to pursue applied research or action research. *Applied research* involves applying theories to actual practice in order to see which theories and practices are most effective. *Action research* is a more specific form of applied research which focuses on examining ways to improve the conditions in a specific setting. Let's consider for a minute how such types of applied research might derive from an examination of theories.

One theory of motivation suggests that individuals strive to earn rewards and avoid punishments. It follows therefore that in most situations individuals will seek to earn available rewards, provided that the rewards are appropriate to their psychological or physical needs (a proviso based on another theory of motivation). Still another theory suggests that individuals can receive so much reinforcement that it ceases to stimulate further effort or so little reinforcement that they cease to try because the likelihood of reward is so small. Consider for a moment the implications of these theories for students. Some questions come readily to mind: How much reward is too much? Which rewards work longest? How frequently does reinforcement need to be received? Are some students motivated by different rewards? Which students? Which rewards? Are some students not motivated to seek rewards?

It would be possible to replace the word "students" in these questions with "athletes" or "clients" without changing the nature of the research problem. Management, psychology, and other disciplines offer myriad theories which seek to explain and account for human behavior. Even the strangest sounding theories, based on studies of learning in infrahuman subjects (usually rats and monkeys), can often be applied to school situations.

The author encountered two learning theory corollaries ("Never try to teach the learner when he is fussy, cranky, sleepy, tired, or otherwise avoiding the learning situation," and "Learning occurs even when the learner is not attempting to learn and when such learning is visible neither to the learner nor the teacher") which seemed difficult to apply to everyday classroom instruction. Both statements led to questions which led in turn to research problems and finally to two research studies which produced new instructional techniques (Cates, 1978; 1982). Often a theory which is hard to apply to everyday practice inspires a variety of questions about its application which can produce research studies to answer them.

Resolving Conflicting or Contradictory Findings of Previous Research Studies

In pursuing a topic of interest through a review of the literature, researchers often find research studies which disagree on the correct course of action. Sometimes two researchers study the same problem and come up with diametrically opposed findings. Who is correct? One way to find out is to conduct a research study of your own. The original research studies may also have omitted some element which you feel is important to the findings. It is also possible, therefore, for your research study to expand on the previous research. If you are merely repeating the original study to confirm its results, your study is a *replication study*. A replication study is an effective way to confirm that a technique will work with your population. Replication also helps confirm that a finding from the past is still valid.

Correcting Faulty Methodology in Previous Research Studies

Sometimes in reading a research study one discovers that the researcher has used the incorrect methodology. He or she may have omitted or overlooked the influence of an important variable, used the wrong design, selected subjects in a way which produced the results obtained, or made any of a variety of other errors. If these errors were corrected, the results might be different. Thus, you might wish to correct the errors and reconduct the study. While beginning researchers are not apt to find many published studies with methodological flaws which they can spot easily, experience in carrying out research studies and analyzing published studies makes this source of new studies more fruitful with time. Chapter 15 discusses in detail some of the more serious methodological flaws which might warrant conducting a corrected version of a previous research study.

Resolving Conflicting Opinions

The majority of articles published in professional journals are not reports of research studies or articles based on research studies. They are, instead, expressions of the authors' opinions and beliefs. Sometimes the opinions and beliefs expressed are unfounded or show little understanding of either theory or practice. Other times, authors will express a variety of seemingly sound but conflicting opinions. Often the topics of disagreement will be discussed extensively, yet no one seeks to use the scientific method to resolve the conflict. From time to time, an authoritative pronouncement from one source will dominate the literature, supported by little or no evidence. These situations offer fertile areas for research studies designed to resolve the disagreements.

Studying Actual Practice

For the practicing educator, everyday experience is by far the most prolific source of research problems. Such problems lead to *action research*: the researcher looks at the current situation and asks what could be done to make it better. Usually this entails formulating both interest and comparative questions, a process discussed in the next chapter. The researcher seeks answers to questions concerning organizational plans, instructional or therapeutic treatments, or training and conditioning materials or methods. While some problems from actual practice may be too narrow in scope for research, many questions about improving practice can lead to interesting research studies of personal significance to the researcher.

An area of practice which is often a fertile source of research problems is the way in which new technologies, such as computing or drug therapies, are affecting current practice. What changes do such new technologies necessitate? How are clients or students affected? How are teachers, therapists, or coaches affected? Is the new technology more beneficial for some individuals than for others? Once again, questions lead to research studies. The process by which a researcher can move from an interest question to a hypothesis and a research study is discussed in detail in Chapter 3.

Unresearchable Topics

In order for a topic or problem to be researchable, there must be some observable and measurable variable. There must also exist currently an instrument capable of measuring these variations, or the researcher must be capable of designing one. Some problems do not satisfy these requirements. Consider the questions: "Is man good?" "Is there life after death?" "What is truth?" How will a researcher observe and measure the abstract concept of "good" with its numerous subjective interpretations? Philosophers and theologians have debated these questions for thousands of years without resolution. Problems of philosophy and religion do not fit the constraints of research design and the scientific method. Such problems are by definition, therefore, not researchable.

DEVELOPING THE RESEARCH PROBLEM

Having identified one or more possible problems for study, the researcher next needs to develop it into a well-defined research problem. To do this, the researcher undertakes a review of the literature related to the problem under study, seeking to analyze the problem, to identify relevant factors, variables, and assumptions, and to gain a complete and up-to-date knowledge of writings and research about the problem.

Analyzing the problem. Through careful examination and observation, the researcher begins to define the various parts of the problem. Parts may be added or deleted as this process continues. In addition to reviewing the literature, the researcher may derive benefits from talking with others or from just thinking about the possibilities. The researcher needs to identify as many aspects of the problem as possible. The more widely and deeply informed the researcher is about the problem under study, the more easily he or she will be able to limit it at a later date.

Identifying factors, variables, and assumptions. The researcher begins to examine the problem by looking for all possible factors, variables, or causes that might affect its outcome. The assumptions that are generally held about cause-and-effect relationships should also be considered. Eventually, the researcher needs to list these factors and variables in terms of their roles in the study as independent variables, dependent variables, or confounding/extraneous variables. While the researcher may be able to identify some relevant factors, variables, and assumptions on the basis of practical experience, interviews, or observations, the most fruitful process is usually the review of the literature.

Searching the literature continuously. Few activities help the researcher develop the research problem as much as working in the library and searching the relevant literature. While a shortcut method like an Educational Resources Information Center (ERIC) search may make a good starting point for a study, it is not a substitute for a comprehensive examination of books, periodicals, and microform references in the library. As the researcher seeks out pertinent materials, he or she develops some expertise in the problem area. Sometimes an avenue of research proves a dead end. This does not, however, make the effort a wasted one. Knowing where *not* to look is sometimes as valuable as knowing where to look. Further, a researcher cannot always tell what information will be of most value later in the study. A wide, thorough, and continuous search of the literature is the most effective method of developing research problems (and studies).

SOME CRITERIA FOR DETERMINING
IF A RESEARCH PROBLEM
IS AN APPROPRIATE ONE

Having identified one or more related research problems in a problem area, the researcher should evaluate each one and decide if it is appropriate to his or her interests, skills, and situation. The researcher will also wish to consider the merits of any study which would be based on the identified research problem. A set of criteria for determining the appropriateness of a research problem is provided below.

Is the problem of interest to the researcher?   Researchers spend long hours working on their studies. If the problems they examine are of little interest to them, they have little motivation to put forth the necessary effort. If a research problem does not interest you, you would be foolish to pursue it when there are equally researchable problems available in which you could have a genuine interest.

Does the researcher have the necessary resources (especially time and money) to complete the study?   Some research problems require great amounts of money for forms, computer time, or observers. Some studies require the researcher's attention almost every waking minute. In selecting a research problem, you need to consider whether you can spare the time required to pursue it and whether adequate funds are available. It is wiser to decide in advance that the necessary resources are lacking and to select an alternative research problem than to fail to take resources into consideration and discover partway through a study that the resources for completing it are unavailable.

Does the researcher possess the ability, knowledge, and training to carry on the study?   As a researcher explores a topic, he or she becomes increasingly expert in that subject area. Very few researchers are experts, however, in all areas of a study. Researchers must therefore decide if they have adequate skills to carry out the study. Review of the literature, consultation with advisors in particular fields, and experience in previous research studies go a long way toward helping you become more nearly adequate, but you must know when a problem is too large.

Does the study make a contribution to Education in general?   When working on a master's thesis, most researchers do not seek to be pioneers. They usually seek to develop necessary expertise and gain experience. Master's candidates usually, therefore, seek to explore topics of local or limited interest. In contrast, Ed.S. candidates and doctoral candidates seek to examine new areas of general value to Education as a field. In determining if the work you are considering is worth doing, you should consider whether it would benefit Education in general. Would the study have wide implications and generalizability, or would it be of use only locally?

Is the research problem actually researchable?   Any problem must be amenable to the collection and analysis of data. If data cannot be collected and analyzed, the problem cannot form the basis of a study. In order to determine the researchability of a problem, the researcher normally formulates a research question, a purpose statement, a set of procedural statements, and a statistics sheet. The preparation of research questions, purpose and procedural statements, and a ''stats'' sheet will be discussed in the next chapter. Researchers usually then consult their advisors for advice and guidance.

Is the research problem trivial or overworked?   A study to determine what flavor of milk is most popular with first-graders may be easily carried out, and a particular school system may be interested in knowing the answer, but it is not a fitting subject for a research study. It is *trivial*. Trivial subjects and problems are to be avoided. Some other subjects or problems have been examined so frequently and over such a long period that there is little reason for further study. These subjects are *overworked*. The relationship of IQ to achievement is an example of an overworked subject. Overworked subjects and problems are to be avoided.

Review of the literature should alert the researcher to overworked subjects and problems. Serious consideration and dialogue with knowledgeable colleagues should alert the researcher to trivial subjects and problems. If you are going to invest a part of your life in a study, it makes sense to insure that the work will be something to take pride in and perhaps even something which will make a real difference in Education.

SOME FURTHER CONSIDERATIONS
IN SELECTING A RESEARCH PROBLEM

In seeking a research problem there are some pitfalls into which beginning researchers often fall. For this reason, a few pieces of advice are in order at this time.

Don't just select the first problem you find as your research problem.   There is a temptation to settle on the first one that comes to mind. Experienced researchers seldom select research problems for certain until they have done at least a preliminary review of the literature. It is better to continue to narrow the focus of your study as you read on, until you have a manageable problem, than to start with an unchangeable problem and work desperately to find enough material related to it. Sometimes, as you read in pursuit of the answer to one question, the answer to another question will begin to appear. If you find the new question more interesting, you may wish to pursue it instead. Many a researcher has begun the hunt for the answer to one question only to end up doing a superb and comprehensive job of answering another question which his or her review of the literature uncovered. With very little change or addition, the same research base may be used to answer several different questions.

Begin with a research problem, not a procedure or a sample.   You don't take an aspirin to get a headache. Likewise, don't start with a statistical procedure that interests you or a classroom of students and then search for a problem to fit it. Rather, start with a perceived problem or a gnawing question and work to evolve it into an interesting research problem. Once the problem is defined, then seek out appropriate groups and procedures.

Be systematic and complete in reviewing the related literature.   This does not mean just having an ERIC search conducted or reading *Psychological Abstracts*. It means that all the time the research project is being planned, you should be reading, studying, examining, and looking for facts, explanations, causes, and relationships that will lead to a further delineation of your problem. The review of the literature ends only when the final research report is submitted. Until then, the researcher attempts to discover every possible piece of useful information.

Be exact and complete in defining the research problem.   An inexactly stated problem seldom leads to a well-done study. It leads to confusion and disarray. The more complete the statement of the research problem is, the more exactly it states groups, instruments, and comparisons, the more likely you are to have few troubles completing the study. Completion of the process of moving from interest questions to alternative hypotheses, which is presented in the next chapter, can help you define your problem exactly.

Plan ahead and take your time.   Sometimes the pursuit of a degree or the requirements of work tend to press heavily. At such times, researchers long to have their studies more nearly complete. Resist the pressure. A good study takes time to conduct. It requires a thorough research base founded in the review of literature. It requires careful gathering and analysis of the data. Try to plan the sequence and time requirements of the parts of your study. Such a scheduling plan helps remove some of the pressure. Remember that a well-done study is a source of pride and a symbol of your ability; a poorly done study is just a record of time wasted. Often the difference is the patience and perseverance of the researcher. Research is like a fertilized egg: you let it incubate and then hatch; you don't just crack it open because you're impatient.

THREE

QUESTIONS, STATEMENTS, AND HYPOTHESES USED IN RESEARCH STUDIES

Chapter 3 discusses—with examples—the types of questions, statements, and hypotheses which researchers use in identifying, narrowing, and defining their research problems.

In seeking to identify the research problem, to plan the research study and prepare a proposal for it, and to carry out the study and report its findings, the researcher uses a variety of types of questions and statements. Each type serves a different purpose in helping the researcher complete the task. As a general rule, your understanding and the statement of the research problem evolve as you move from one type of question to another, to statements, and to hypotheses. This process usually occurs in the sequence in which these questions, statements, and hypotheses are presented below.

TYPES OF QUESTIONS USED IN IDENTIFYING THE RESEARCH PROBLEM

Interest Questions

These questions express the interest of the researcher in a particular topic or problem but do not address how that interest relates to actual school settings or to comparing groups of students.

EXAMPLES:

1. Are special reading programs worth the cost?

2. Can schools cure behavior problems?
3. Are there ways to improve flexibility?

Such questions often form the basis of research. Researchers usually begin thinking in this vein and often list dozens of interest questions on a variety of topics before selecting one topic of interest.

Comparative Questions

These questions occur as natural extensions of interest questions. Once the researcher has identified a topic of interest, he or she seeks next to pose questions which explore how the topic of interest might be addressed in an educational setting. Comparative questions ask about specific individuals (subjects) and about specific teaching methods or treatments. Whenever possible, such questions state or imply comparison groups if the study involves comparison among groups.

EXAMPLES:

1. Do special reading programs benefit some students more than others?
2. What types of classroom management programs tend to bring about the greatest change in student behavior?
3. Is there a relationship between flexibility and basketball injuries?

Comparative questions begin to suggest to the researcher the nature of what it is that he or she wishes to determine, to compare, or to evaluate. Such questions help the researcher identify comparison groups and types of behavior, attitude, or achievement to be measured.

TYPES OF QUESTIONS AND STATEMENTS USED IN STATING THE RESEARCH PROBLEM

Research Questions

This type states succinctly the question which the research study seeks to answer. It differs from the comparative question in that it is specific in defining the population involved in seeking the answer to the question, gives a general description of the circumstances under which the researcher will seek to answer the question, and *always* states the comparison group if a comparison among groups is involved.

EXAMPLES:

1. Do reading programs in which third-grade students are removed from the regular classroom for individual or small-group work daily benefit such stu-

dents more than a comparable period of instruction by the regular teacher in the regular classroom?

2. Are behavior modification programs conducted by the regular teacher within the regular classroom more effective with fifth-grade boys or fifth-grade girls?

3. Do male high school basketball players who participate daily in a program designed to increase flexibility have fewer injuries than comparable players who do not participate in such a program?

Research questions often appear in research proposals and reports in the introductory text which identifies the research problem and describes how others have addressed it. Such questions prepare the reader for later statements and hypotheses. In studies designed to identify characteristics of the present (see Chapter 11) researchers sometimes use research questions instead of hypotheses or research objectives (discussed later in this chapter).

Purpose statements

A purpose statement tells the reader exactly what a study intends to do and how such actions will assist the researcher in answering the research question presented earlier. By convention, such statements in research reports are written in the past tense, since by the time they are read, the study has presumably already been conducted. The exception to the rule of using the past tense is in preparing research proposals, where the present tense should be used. To avoid the use of excessively long sentences, the researcher may use two or more sentences to complete the purpose statement. A study may also have more than one purpose and, thus, more than one purpose statement. (The first two examples below are written in the present tense, as they would be in research proposals. The third example is written in the past tense, as it would be in a research report.)

EXAMPLES:

1. It is the purpose of this study to examine the extent to which daily instruction in reading in special classes benefits third-grade students who have been identified as needing special instruction.

2. This study explores the influence of behavior modification programs conducted by classroom teachers in the regular classroom on the behavior of fifth-grade students. This is done with the purpose of determining if such programs are more effective in terms of behavior change when used with boys or girls.

3. This study had as its purpose to explore the relationship between flexibility and injuries among male high school basketball players. This exploration involved a comparison of the frequency and severity of injuries sustained by players who participated in a program of stretching activities designed to increase flexibility and by comparable players who did not participate in such a program.

Procedural Statements

These statements evolve naturally from purpose statements. Procedural statements tell the reader in brief what procedures or actions were undertaken by the researcher in order to attain the purpose(s) of the study.

In the case of research proposals, procedural statements describe the procedures which the researcher *plans* to undertake to accomplish his or her stated purpose(s) and are expressed in terms of the future ("The researcher *plans* to . . ." or ". . . *will be* examined [compared, explored, tested]"). These procedural statements often are organized in a *procedural outline* which lists them in more or less chronological order (roughly the order in which the researcher will execute them in carrying out the study). Procedural statements do *not* address statistical analysis procedures.

Researchers use a variety of phrases to introduce procedural statements. Some frequently employed introductory phrases are

"In order to attain the purposes of this study the researcher undertook the following procedures:" (usually followed in research proposals by numbered procedural statements).

"The researcher addressed this purpose through a variety of procedures." (if the purpose statement has just been stated).

"The researcher identified (or delineated) a number of procedures which helped him or her to attain the purposes of this study."

EXAMPLES:

The examples below are in the form which might be used in a research proposal. They would be in the past tense and discussed in greater detail in several separate sections if you were writing a research report. These separate sections will be outlined in the next chapter.

1. The researcher will confer with the reading specialist, the principal, and appropriate members of the central administration concerning the nature of her study and its purpose.
2. The researcher will draw a random sample of 30 third-grade students who are eligible to receive special out-of-class reading instruction.
3. The researcher will contact the parents of the 30 students so identified and explain both the nature and purpose of the study and will obtain written consent for each child to participate in the study, be the child assigned to regular class or special class instruction.
4. The researcher will pair subjects according to their scores on the Reading Aptitude Test (RAT), their IQ scores as determined by the California Test of Mental Maturity, and their scores on the Informal Diagnostic Reading Inventory (IDRI) administered in the first week of school. She then will randomly assign one of the two subjects in each pair to either the regular or special class group.

5. The researcher will then . . . .

The statements continue until the researcher has presented the reader with a clear outline of the basic procedures used in the study.

A reminder: Do not describe statistical procedures and analyses. This is not the place for them. Instead, if your study employs statistical analyses (the vast majority of studies do), list as the last statement in your procedural outline that you will "use appropriate statistical analyses to determine the significance of the findings."

Hypotheses

A hypothesis is a statement of what the researcher believes will be the relationship between two or more variables in a study. There are three types of hypotheses: research hypotheses, null hypotheses, and alternative hypotheses.

Research hypotheses. A *research hypothesis* states what the researcher believes that he or she will find as a result of the study. Hypotheses always identify the *populations* and any *comparison groups* involved, and always specify the *nature of any difference* to be tested and *how it will be measured* (unless the measurement is automatically indicated by the frequency with which some behavior occurs).

EXAMPLES:

1. Third-grade students who are removed from the regular classroom for 15 minutes each day in order to receive individual and small group reading instruction from a certified reading specialist will show significantly more growth in reading skills than will comparable students who remain in the regular classroom for instruction under their regular teacher. Growth in reading skills will be measured using a pretest-posttest comparison of scores on the Multiple Level Reading Skills Test (MLRST), Form LP.
2. Fifth-grade girls who are exposed to a behavior modification program conducted within the regular classroom by the regular teacher will exhibit greater behavior change in the desired direction (as measured by prestudy teacher objectives and comparison of baseline and poststudy observations) than will comparable fifth-grade boys exposed to an equivalent program.
3. Male high school basketball players who participate in a flexibility program will suffer significantly fewer injuries than will comparable players who do not participate in the program. The flexibility program consists of each subject completing 15 minutes of specific stretching exercises designed to increase flexibility prior to and immediately following each day's practice session.

Some researchers state research hypotheses in mathematical terms using symbols: O_1 stands for a score for the group expected to do better by the researcher; O_2

stands for the group expected to do less well. Thus, the three preceding examples might be written

$$0_1 > 0_2$$

where . . . (and the researcher then states what the scores represent, how they were measured and derived, and any ways in which they have been adjusted). This approach has one major shortcoming: Scores are not actually important variables in a study. Their importance is that they represent supposed measurements of important variables. A hypothesis should state the important variables and then state that a certain score was used as a measurement of that variable. Hypotheses help guide researchers. If a researcher uses hypotheses which state scores as if they were the important variables, he or she may lose sight of the fact that these scores are merely supposed (and perhaps invalid or inaccurate) measures of the actual variables under study.

Many researchers formulate research hypotheses but do not state them in writing. They prefer to let their earlier discussions of the problem, the presentation of research questions, and the statements of purpose guide the reader to infer the research hypothesis. They then state the null hypothesis, since dealing with it is logically and statistically easier. If, however, the researcher is *quite* certain that he or she knows in what direction the performance of the subjects will head or which of the treatment groups will demonstrate higher performance, the researcher will use research hypotheses instead of null hypotheses. Since research hypotheses predict a direction for the results of a study, they are also known as *directional hypotheses.*

Notice that research hypotheses use the present tense to describe what the subjects receive ("who *are* removed," "who *are* exposed," "who participate") and the future tense to describe the expected result ("*will* show," "*will* demonstrate," "*will* suffer). This same use of *present tense* for *treatment* and *future tense* for *results* is exhibited in null hypotheses (see the next section).

Note also that a hypothesis must use the word "significantly" coupled with a comparison word (e.g., "more", "greater", "fewer") or some other phrasing which expresses the concept of a statistically significant difference between the groups or quantities being compared. The word "comparable" (or a related word such as "equivalent") is used in a hypothesis to show that the researcher has made certain that subjects receiving the treatments are comparable and that the comparison of performance or behavior is, therefore, valid.

Null hypotheses.   The *null hypothesis* (sometimes written as "the $\varnothing$ hypothesis") is merely the statistical and logical equivalent of the opposite of the research hypothesis. Whereas a research hypothesis states that there will be a statistically significant difference between groups in favor of one group or the other, a null hypothesis states that there will be no statistically significant difference between the groups. Like the research hypothesis, the null hypothesis always identifies the *population* and *comparison group* involved, and always specifies the *nature of the difference* to be tested and *how it will be measured.*

EXAMPLE:

1. There will be no significant difference in growth in reading skills (as measured by a pretest-posttest comparison of scores on the Multiple Level Reading Skills Test) between third-grade students who are removed from the regular classroom for 15 minutes each day in order to receive individual and small-group reading instruction from a certified reading specialist and comparable third-grade students who remain in the regular classroom for instruction under their regular teacher.

Why not see if you can write the other two research hypotheses as null hypotheses? As with research hypotheses, remember to word the treatment in present tense, results in future tense and remember to include the concepts of "comparability" among subjects and "significant" comparison between treatments.

After you've given them your best shot (or two), you can find the author's versions in the Appendix (page 240). Remember, however, that there is more than one "right" way to write a hypothesis, and the important thing is to include all the necessary parts. Remember, too, that writing concise hypotheses is a skill which develops with practice. Almost everyone has trouble at first. The secret is to work toward adequacy by being careful to include all the parts and by being patient. Elegance comes with further practice. A further piece of advice: You can use more than one sentence to write your hypothesis if it begins to get long and cumbersome and would be easier to understand in shorter sentences.

Null hypotheses can also be written in mathematical terms:

$$O_1 = O_2$$

where . . . (and the researcher states what the scores represent, how they were measured and derived, and any ways in which they have been adjusted). Once again, be alert that you do not mistake a score for the variable which it represents.

The examples above may appear to suggest that all hypotheses are designed to disclose differences among *groups*. This is not true. A hypothesis in a *characteristic study* (see Chapter 11) might compare actual responses to theoretical expectations. A hypothesis in a *relationship study* (see Chapter 10) might postulate that the relationship to be studied would be a statistically significant one.

EXAMPLES:

1. There will be no significant difference between the distribution of responses among categories on a researcher-designed questionnaire of social preferences and the theoretical distribution which chance might produce. Respondents will be walk-in clients at a publicly supported safehouse for women.

2. There will be no significant relationship between standardized academic achievement (as measured by scores on the Metropolitan Achievement Test) of high school students and their actual academic performance (as measured by cumulative grade point averages in high school).

3. There will be no significant difference among the frequencies with which specific off-task behaviors occur among third-graders and what chance might produce. Specific off-task behaviors include sitting and staring out the window during question-and-answer sessions, walking around the room during times when assigned seatwork is to be completed, and talking with fellow students during oral presentations by the teacher. Off-task behaviors will be measured through observation.

Since null hypotheses predict no difference between or among treatment groups, they are also known as *nondirectional hypotheses*. Null hypotheses are easier to deal with statistically, because it is easier to state within predictable limits of certainty that evidence that two groups are different did not occur by chance than it is to state that one particular group's scoring higher than another did not occur by chance. This is based on the concepts of probability and the normal curve, which will be discussed further in Chapter 7. The null hypothesis is a logician's and mathematician's device. Trust it and use it. It makes life easier.

Research objectives.   Researchers sometimes use *research objectives* instead of research or null hypotheses—most frequently in studies designed to identify characteristics of the present (see Chapter 11). Research objectives should specifically identify the characteristic, perception, response, or opinion to be examined by the research. In a research proposal a list of research objectives is usually introduced by a phrase such as " The objectives for this study are." In research reports this phrase is usually worded in the past tense ("The objectives of this study were").

EXAMPLES:

1. To determine if administrators of public schools in this district have similar perceptions of the needs of students enrolled in their schools.

2. To determine if administrators and teachers in these schools who were given a list of priorities would order the list similarly.

3. To determine if a pattern of characteristics and perceptions exists among teachers who have retired early from teaching in schools of over 500 students in the state of Kentucky.

4. To determine which factors influence high school students' selection of elective courses and to determine which of these factors are most salient in those choices.

Alternative hypotheses (or *alternate hypotheses*).   Whether the researcher uses a research or null hypothesis, he or she is still assuming that the independent or treatment variables involved in that hypothesis accounted for the significance or nonsignificance of the findings of the study. (You will recall that an *independent variable* is a variable which is manipulated to produce a change in a *dependent variable*. Since treatments are independent variables, these variables are often called *treatment variables*.)

If the results indicated a nonsignificant difference, the researcher needs to consider whether some other variable might have prevented (or obscured) a significant finding. (Such variables are known as *extraneous variables*.) If the results indicated a significant difference, the researcher needs to consider carefully whether the independent variables considered in the hypothesis accounted for (or explained) the difference, or whether alternative hypotheses (involving extraneous variables) might account for the difference more accurately. Perhaps the researcher failed to consider some influence other than the treatment mentioned in the hypothesis, and perhaps this extraneous variable accounts more readily for the observed difference between groups.

To discover alternative hypotheses, the researcher needs to consider carefully the factors and influences in the educational setting. Examination of other studies and a skeptical, suspicious approach to problems can prove helpful. Researchers do well also to use observation and practical experience to alert them to forces in educational settings which may influence findings. Using a jaundiced and suspicious eye and a pernicious nature, a researcher might come up with the following alternative hypotheses for our examples:

EXAMPLES:

1. ALT. HYPO.: Any significant difference (or the absence of a significant difference) in growth in reading skills might be due to whether special reading classes are considered negatively by the involved students and their peers.

   CONTROL: This will be determined using an attitude inventory.

2. ALT. HYPO.: Any significant difference (or the absence of a significant difference) in behavioral change in the desired direction between fifth-grade boys and girls might be due to whether the ''rewards'' for desired behavior are perceived as ''masculine'' or ''feminine.''

   CONTROL: This will be determined through the use of an attitude survey.

You have probably noted that alternative hypotheses are abbreviated forms of hypotheses. That is because they are written after the researcher has already generated very specific research and null hypotheses, and the purpose of alternative hypotheses is merely to identify possible extraneous variables. In most studies there will be one or two null hypotheses, but it is not uncommon to generate five or more alternative hypotheses for a study.

You have probably also noted that each alternative hypothesis is followed by a statement of how the researcher seeks to evaluate or *control* the influence of that variable. These *controls* are designed to help the researcher eliminate any question about whether the treatment variables or some extraneous variables account for the finding.

Now, why don't you take a shot at writing an alternative hypothesis for our third research problem? Consider what besides flexibility might reduce injuries among those in the program and those not. Consider, for example, how the players might have been chosen to participate, the attitudes of the trainers and players, or anything else which you think might influence the findings. Once you have written a sample alternative hypothesis, try to write a control statement telling how you will find out if the extraneous variable you identified did influence the findings or telling how you would *prevent* it from influencing the findings. Several plausible alternative hypotheses and controls for this third example are presented in the Appendix, page 241, but give it a try on your own first.

Researchers attempt to think of as many alternative hypotheses as possible *before* beginning their studies. Such hypotheses alert them to influences which they will wish to examine and, if possible, control. If they waited until after their studies were completed and then determined if the extraneous variables were causal, many studies would have to be discarded because of uninterpretable results. That would mean a lot of wasted time and effort. It is wiser to control as many of these extraneous variables as possible and thereby strengthen your confidence in the hypotheses you originally proposed.

Formulating alternative hypotheses is also useful in evaluating the research reports of others, since it alerts the reader to possible explanations and influences which the researcher might have overlooked. Often an alternative hypothesis will suggest a fruitful area for a new study (see the discussion in Chapter 2 on "Correcting Faulty Methodology in Previous Research Studies").

FROM INTEREST QUESTIONS
TO RESEARCH PROPOSAL

The previous sections of this chapter have described various types of questions, statements, and hypotheses which researchers need to consider in identifying research problems, carrying out studies to explore these problems, and reporting their findings. In a typical study, a researcher will formulate a large number of *interest questions* to identify a topic of interest. He or she will generally then generate between three and a dozen *comparative questions*, from which the researcher usually selects one or two which are then translated into *research questions*.

Following the formulation of the research question(s), the researcher will write out one or two *purpose statements* for the study. The researcher next generates a *research hypothesis* which states the nature and direction of the expected difference, attributing it to the influence of a specific treatment variable. Unless the researcher has strong reason to expect the results to go in one direction, in order to facilitate later conclusions based in statistics he or she rephrases the research hypothesis as a *null hypothesis*, which will later be accepted or rejected on the basis of the study's findings. If the researcher is working on a *characteristic study* (see Chapter 11), he or she may use *research objectives* or *research questions* instead of a hypothesis (or as well as a hypothesis). Researchers consider *alternative hypotheses* to alert them to possible influences which might account for later findings and which they should seek to control if possible.

Finally, once this process has been completed, the researcher turns to preparing the outline of procedural statements, incorporating the controls which were necessitated by his or her alternative hypotheses. This leaves to be included only the introductory section, which presents the research problem and reviews what others have said and found about the problem (see Chapter 19), and the "stats" sheet (see page 24) in order to complete the research proposal.

As you work your way through this process, you would be wise to have your advisor examine your questions, statements, and hypotheses (if he or she is willing) and to give you guidance and advice. Going through this process not only helps you clarify your thinking, but it also helps others (particularly your advisor) observe how you identified and developed your research problem.

FOUR

ORGANIZATIONAL PLANS FOR RESEARCH PROPOSALS AND REPORTS

Although some of the sections contained in research proposals and reports have not yet been discussed, often beginning researchers feel more comfortable at this point if they can see a brief outline of what a research proposal contains and what a report of a research study is supposed to report. This chapter presents a sample organizational plan for each. These are merely two possible plans. In general, the guidelines of the advisor or agency to whom a proposal is to be submitted dictate its organizational plan. Similarly, one should use the organizational plan guidelines of the agency or journal to whom a research report is to be submitted.

AN ORGANIZATIONAL PLAN FOR A RESEARCH PROPOSAL

1. Introductory section. Always contains *Introduction to the problem*, often contains *Need for the study*, sometimes contains *Statement of the problem*. Usually untitled unless one or more of these three titles is used:
   a. *Introduction to the problem*. Incorporates the research question and a brief review of related literature.
   b. *Need for the study*. Demonstrates the researcher's personal interest and the need for the study in the specific educational setting, and uses references from the review of the literature to support the need for the study.
   c. *Statement of the problem*. Usually a statement or set of statements in which the writer presents his or her argument or summation of the problem to be studied. Ordinarily necessary only if there is some disagreement as to what exactly the problem is; a statement of the problem may not be necessary if the introduction to the problem identifies the problem

clearly. When included, it generally comes before the discussion of the need for the study.

2. *Statement of purpose*. (Written in the present tense.) See Chapter 3 for guidelines on writing purpose statements.

3. *Procedural statements*. (Written in the future tense.) A brief outline which describes *sampling procedures*, the *nature* and *design* of the study, the *treatments* to be administered and *how*, any *training* or *conditions involved in using observers*, and the *measurement instruments* to be used (if such instruments have been identified—and many advisors require this) or the *type of measurement instruments* to be used (if specific instruments have yet to be identified).

4. *Hypothesis statements*. Usually expressed in null form. *Research questions* or *Research objectives* may be used here instead (or in addition) in some types of studies.

5. *Definition of terms*. Optional. Meanings of any terms with which the reader is unlikely to be familiar or which are used with special meanings.

6. *References*. Use one bibliographic form *consistently*. A listing of the references actually mentioned in text.

7. *Alternative hypotheses and controls* or *Probable threats*.

8. *Statistics sheet*. (Also called ''stats'' sheet.) A listing of the types of statistical analyses to be employed in carrying out the study. Along with the name of each procedure, the researcher lists the data to be analyzed using that procedure.

EXAMPLES:

1. *t*-test for correlated means to determine if there is a significant difference between the pretest and posttest scores on the Witfer Achievement Test for the experimental or control group.

2. Covariance of posttest social studies scores using pretest social studies scores and IQ scores to adjust for initial differences between groups.

A complete sample research proposal is presented and several sections of sample proposals are analyzed in Chapter 19.

AN ORGANIZATIONAL PLAN
FOR A RESEARCH REPORT

The Introduction

(Always written in the past tense.) Always contains *Introduction to the problem* and *Statement of purpose*; often contains *Need for the study*; sometimes contains formal *Statement of the problem*. This section may be untitled unless it uses one or more (or a combination) of these titles.

1. *Introduction to the problem/Statement of the problem area/Need for the study.*
   a. What is the problem?
   b. How does it relate to Education in general?
   c. How does it relate to a specific area in Education?
   d. How have others approached the topic? What have other researchers found? (*References.*)
   e. What is the *theory* underlying the approach that this study takes to addressing the problem?
   f. Often contains the *research question.*
   g. Often contains the *Need for the study*: How is this a problem for researchers or educators?

2. *Statement of purpose.* (May be followed by a *brief* procedural outline.)

Hypotheses

Usually in *null* or *nondirectional* form unless before beginning the study the researcher was *quite* certain of the direction in which the results were most likely to head and, therefore, used *directional* or *research hypotheses*. In studies other than those designed to disclose differences (see Chapter 9), *research questions* or *research objectives* instead of hypotheses are often included in a section entitled *Research Questions* or *Research Objectives*.)

Method (*or* Procedures)

(Always in the past tense.)

1. *Discussion of the sample.* (Sometimes this is a separate section called *Description of sample* or *Subjects* which precedes the *Procedures* section.)
   a. A complete definition and description of the population from which the sample was drawn.
   b. Age range of subjects, proportion of males and females, division of sample by race, IQ distribution, scores of subjects in all groups on relevant variables, whether it is an urban or rural population, educational level of parents, etc.
   c. A detailed description of the sampling procedures employed (particularly if matching was used).
      (1) If matching was used, include *criteria for matching* and *why those criteria were used, number of subjects for whom an acceptable match could not be found and why, possible effects of losing these subjects*, and *any evidence that matching produced equivalent groups.*
      (2) If stratified sampling was used, include *criteria used to divide the population into those strata* and the *method of selecting subjects from those strata.*

(3)   If subgroups were used, include *criteria used to divide sample into subgroups*.

d.   A description of the educational setting from which the sample was drawn, including *program description; socioeconomic status (SES) and racial balance of group served; experience level, racial, SES, and any other relevant characteristics* of the teacher, therapist, or staff involved; *scores on appropriate standardized tests*; and *local, regional, or geographic characteristics* which help define the setting.

2.   Discussion of the research procedures employed.
   a.   Description of the nature of the study and the research design employed.
   b.   How the design or method was applied (in enough detail to permit replication of the study). Include descriptions of:
      (1)   Treatments administered.
      (2)   Data collection methods.
      (3)   Steps taken to establish controls or reduce errors.
      (4)   Flaws in methodology and threats to the study's results being accurately interpreted.

3.   Description of measures used to collect data. (Sometimes this information is reported in a separate section entitled *Instrumentation*.)
   a.   With *standardized, well-known instruments*: Type of score produced, variables measured, evidence of validity and reliability, and relationship of each measure to the research hypotheses or objectives.
   b.   With *new or infrequently used measures*:
      (1)   Description of types of items included.
      (2)   Reliability data.
      (3)   Evidence of validity (particularly construct validity).
      (4)   Findings of other studies in which instrument was used and other useful information on instrument.
      (5)   How scored.
      (6)   Relationship to hypotheses or objectives.
   c.   With an instrument that was developed for this study (often this will constitute a separate section of the report):
      (1)   How developed.
      (2)   How standardized.
      (3)   How scored.
      (4)   Relationship to hypotheses or objectives.

Results (*or* Findings *or* Analyses and Findings)

1.   Usually organized around hypotheses or objectives.

2.   Data usually reported in the form of tables, to which the the writer refers. It is not necessary to list the data in the text.

3.   All tables contain enough information and suitable headings and references to stand alone.

4.   Major findings are identified and interpreted.

a. Why results occurred.
b. How findings fit in with previous research findings.
c. How findings could be used.
d. How findings fit in with the conceptual foundation on which the study was based.

Conclusions and Discussion

(Sometimes two separate sections.)

1. Brief restatement of the research problem.

2. Description of the basic methodology used.

3. Brief description of the findings in terms of their relationships to the hypotheses or objectives.

4. Detailed discussion of the conclusions.

5. Discussion of methodological limitations of the study, possible threats to the study, and ways in which the researcher controlled for those threats.

6. If implications are presented, include speculations on applications, interpretations, or extensions of the findings.

Definition of Terms

(Optional.)

References

(Use one bibliographic form *consistently*.)

FIVE

THE LITERATURE SEARCH

This chapter describes some research tools which the researcher may find useful in identifying and developing his or her research problem through a search of the literature; then it presents some guidelines on using these tools.

Library facilities vary greatly in the extensiveness of their research resources. One library may contain all the reference works described in this chapter and may have access to a wide variety of computer searches, while a less affluent facility may have only one or two of the resources described. Fortunately, interlibrary loans enable researchers at less well equipped facilities to obtain access to many of the services available at larger research libraries, although often at the price of a two- to three-week waiting period and a limited period of time during which to use the loaned material. Computer transmission of data over telephone lines from a larger facility to a printer at your facility eliminates the time lag, but usually at a cost of from $5 to $100.

Guided tours of the libraries that will be be used, examination of the reference works shelved there, and consultation with both reference librarians and advisors will help the novice researcher identify which works are available there. Since there is some redundancy among many of the reference works described, the absence of one or more of them may not be severely limiting. If you employ a computer search and utilize interlibrary loans, any restriction on the breadth of your search of the literature should be negligible.

The two sources most frequently employed for finding materials to examine in the search of the literature are *published indexing volumes* and *computer searches*.

Both produce listings of references to be examined to determine their relevance to the researcher's research problem. The next section will describe briefly a few of the more commonly used indices and computer searches.

INDICES

Education Index each month contains full bibliographic listings of articles concerning education published in a broad selection of professional journals. Articles are listed by subject headings and by authors' names. The monthly issues for March, June, September, and December are cumulative indices for the four quarters of the year. Additionally, at the end of the periodical year, most libraries purchase a bound cumulative index for that year.

Current Index to Journals in Education (CIJE) is an ERIC (Educational Resources Information Center) monthly publication. Listings are by author and subject heading. The June and December issues are cumulative for the six-month periods preceding them. In addition to supplying full bibliographic listings for articles published in a broad spectrum of professional journals, this index also supplies brief abstracts and code numbers for ordering reprints through ERIC. Reprints of the articles may be ordered in microform (microfilm, microfiche) or as printed sheets (called "hard copy").

Psychological Abstracts is similar to *CIJE* and is published monthly. It covers articles relating to various aspects of psychology in professional journals. Listings are by author and by subject heading. Every sixth issue is an integrated index for the preceding half year. Annual cumulative indices to *Psychological Abstracts* are published by subject heading (*Cumulative Subject Index to Psychological Abstracts*) and by authors' names (*Cumulative Author Index to Psychological Abstracts*). Most libraries will have these large hardbound volumes shelved beside current and bound volumes of *Psychological Abstracts*.

Physical Education Index is similar to *Education Index*. It restricts its listings to articles relevant to physical education and is published quarterly with a hardbound annual cumulative index.

Completed Research in Health, Physical Education, Recreation and Dance is published yearly. It gives full bibliographic listings for relevant articles published in selected journals in the previous year. Additionally, this work lists abstracts of master's and doctoral theses completed during that year at 71 institutions.

Child Development Abstracts and Bibliography is published three times a year, and its author and subject listings for articles concerning child development published in professional journals are cumulative to the date of each issue. Each issue also includes a brief abstract of the articles listed.

Sociological Abstracts is similar to *Psychological Abstracts*. This work is published five times a year, and each issue gives author and subject heading listings for professional journal articles relevant to sociological concerns as well as brief abstracts for each article listed. A cumulative annual index is also published.

Reader's Guide to Periodical Literature is similar to *Education Index* except that it presents subject and author listings (and not abstracts) for articles in non-professional magazines on a variety of topics.

Abstracts of Instructional and Research Methods in Vocational and Technical Education is similar to *CIJE*. Six issues and an annual cumulative index are published each year. It lists and abstracts professional journal articles related to vocational and technical education.

Exceptional Child Education Resources also is similar to *CIJE* except that it concentrates on professional journal articles dealing with the education of exceptional children. It is published quarterly with the December issue containing a cumulative index for the year.

Educational Administration Abstracts is published three times a year. It reviews and abstracts articles in professional journals which relate to educational administration. While each issue supplies author and journal listings, no subject index is supplied.

Comprehensive Dissertation Index lists titles, authors, universities, and the volume and page numbers of abstracts of doctoral dissertations in *Dissertation Abstracts International*.

COMPUTER SEARCHES

The *ERIC search* is one of the most frequently used computer searches in education and one of the least expensive (usually $20 to $50). To have a search performed, one identifies one or more key words from the *ERIC Thesaurus of Descriptors*. It is necessary to narrow your focus as much as possible to avoid excessively broad and extensive (not to mention expensive) listings. The thesaurus supplies a variety of key-word labels which enable the user to expand or contract the breadth of the topics to be searched. If two or more key words can be used simultaneously in the search, the number of bibliographic listings and abstracts returned will be smaller, and those listings and abstracts should be better suited to the problem under study.

An ERIC search will return listings and abstracts of the type in *CIJE* and also descriptions which would normally appear in *Resources in Education* (which is described later in this chapter). The reference librarian or the computerized database search librarian (if your library has one) should have forms for this and other computer searches and should be able to help you get started.

Psychological Abstracts Search and Retrieval (PASAR) is similar to the ERIC search. It will return listings and abstracts from *Psychological Abstracts* on the topic you identify. As with ERIC, one uses key words (preferably cross-referenced for simultaneous searching). These key words are found in issues of *Psychological Abstracts* and in the cumulative index volumes. Forms for this search are available in issues of *Psychological Abstracts* and are probably available in your library in the same location as ERIC search forms. These forms allow you to limit the population considered (human or infrahuman and by age group) and the recency of the article (by publication date). Additionally, you can state a preference for how the listings or abstracts will be printed (alphabetically by authors' names or chronologically by publication date). Searches normally cost between $40 and $60.

Direct Access to Reference Information (DATRIX) will report titles, authors, universities, and the page numbers and volume numbers of abstracts in *Dissertation Abstracts International* on the topics you specify. One then goes to the identified volume to read the abstract of the work. The dissertation (on microform or in printed form) can be ordered from University Microfilms if so desired. As with the two previous searches, the user specifies key words, preferably cross-referenced for simultaneous searching. A search costs $15 for 150 titles, with an additional fee of 10 cents for each title reported over 150.

OTHER RESOURCES

In addition to indices and computer searches, researchers use several other resources to help search for relevant materials. These include dissertations, unpublished professional works, and specialized dictionaries, encyclopedias, and handbooks.

Dissertations and Unpublished Professional Works

Dissertation Abstracts International lists dissertations with their abstracts for the year in which the dissertation was completed. The yearly volumes are divided between the sciences (volume B each year) and the arts and humanities (volume A each year). Dissertations in education are listed in volume A. Necessary information for ordering microform or "hard" copies of dissertations abstracted is included.

Resources in Education (RIE) is a publication of ERIC which lists abstracts or summaries of unpublished work and presentations at meetings of national and international professional organizations. While this means that you can find material in *RIE* which is unavailable anywhere else, it is important that you evaluate what you find, since it is included with little or no evaluation or quality control. What you find may be very valuable or of little or no value to your study. RIE supplies an accession number in one section, and the user then goes to the Document Resumé section for the summary.

Specialized Dictionaries, Encyclopedias, and Handbooks

Since reference works of this type can assist researchers in exploring their research topics, a few of them are listed below. You should familiarize yourself with the works available in the facility you will be using and with what each contains.

Buros Mental Measurement Yearbook

Encyclopedia of Educational Evaluation

Encyclopedia of Educational Research

Handbook of Research on Teaching (vols. 1 and 2)

Handbook of Special Education

National Society for the Study of Education Yearbook (2 per year)

Personality Tests and Reviews

Research Guide for Psychology

Review of Research in Education (annual volumes)

Scales for the Measurement of Attitudes

Tests and Measurements in Child Development: Handbooks I and II (vols. 1 and 2)

Tests in Print

Yearbook of the American Association of School Administrators

SOME GUIDELINES FOR SEARCHING THE LITERATURE

In identifying, planning, and executing a research study, a researcher performs not simply a single search of the literature, but several searches: a prestudy search to identify areas of concern and general trends in opinion and research; a search in the early stages of the study to identify possible research problems, to refine them, and to explore some of the writings and research pertinent to them; and a larger, more comprehensive search to identify and examine the multitude of writings and research studies which bear on the specific problem the study seeks to explore.

Prestudy Search of the Literature

One of the general responsibilities of a professional is staying current with the literature in his or her field. This responsibility becomes exceedingly important when the professional seeks to conduct a research study. A researcher who is unaware of the areas of concern for writers and researchers, of the problems under their consideration, and of the general trends in both opinion and research in the field is unlikely to be competent to interpret what he or she reads. Without a frame of reference, the researcher is hard pressed to relate findings and contentions to theories or beliefs, or even to one another, with any semblance of coherence.

Many would-be researchers have kept current with at least one or two journals. Reading these journals has helped them maintain some acquaintance with what writers have said on a topic. If, however, none of the journals deals with research studies, then such would-be researchers are unlikely to be familiar with recent research findings. Unsubstantiated opinion (belief without research to support it) is useful in alerting a researcher to the nature and direction of arguments, but it is of little value in supporting the researcher's later arguments. Another problem with reading issues of only one or two journals is that editorial policy may have narrowed the topics and focus of articles in these journals, thus producing a one-sided view of some topics while ignoring others.

When a would-be researcher begins a prestudy search of the literature, he or she seeks to sample widely rather than deeply. You should attempt to examine a large number of professional journals, to examine what popular magazines (e.g., *Time, Newsweek, Parents*) have written on topics of interest, and to examine a variety of books. Such a search is designed to give you a feel for the flow of the diverse popular and professional literature. It is a kind of intellectual snorkeling in which you skim just below the surface of the literature, diving only after something of particular interest. Most useful at this stage are the reference works to periodical literature (e.g., *Reader's Guide, Education Index, CIJE, Psychological Abstracts*), the card catalog in the library, and examination of recent popular magazines.

Search of the Literature in the Early Stages of the Study

Once the researcher has become conversant with the flow of the general literature, he or she needs to begin to seek to identify possible problems and to explore the practical and conceptual foundations on which writings and research studies about the problem are based. This requires you to apply the criteria for identifying a research problem suggested in Chapter 2 (see pages 8-10). It also requires that you delve more deeply into the literature pertinent to each possible research problem. This is more like intellectual scuba diving than snorkeling: you explore in greater depth and continue to work in depth until you have a firm understanding of what others have said about each problem and what studies of that problem have found. In addition to continued use of the reference works employed in the prestudy search, reference works such as *Dissertation Abstracts*, the *Encyclopedias of Educational Research*, and the *Handbooks of Research on Teaching* are useful now. These works supply only direction, however. You must read copiously and explore the work of others.

You should be able in a single sentence to state what the problem is. You should be able to discuss thoroughly previous research studies on the problem. In accomplishing the latter goal, you will wish to apply the standards for evaluating research which are presented in the next chapter. You should also begin formulating appropriate questions, statements, and hypotheses as suggested in Chapter 3.

The More Comprehensive Search of the Literature

If the two previous searches were analogous to first snorkeling and then scuba diving, this larger search is similar to deep sea diving. As a result of the previous searches and the process of formulating questions, statements, and hypotheses, you have now identified a single problem to be studied. You seek to immerse yourself in the literature, to explore any work which relates directly or tangentially to the problem under study. You seek to relate studies and writings to one another and to the concerns and concepts which unify them. This is a time for synthesizing the literature. At this stage you should be able to dissect the problem, talk about its conceptual parts, discuss the theory underlying it, and analyze and evaluate both writings and research findings on the problem. You should be fast becoming an expert on the problem. It should be unusual for you to come across a previous study of which you were not aware. Few, if any, major writers on the problem have escaped your examination. A researcher at this stage speaks about the problem with the knowledge, understanding, and authority born of nearly complete mastery of that particular problem area.

The need to acquire such a level of expertise precludes exploring too broad a problem area. It requires that you identify and explore a problem of manageable proportion. While consultation with an advisor can help in identifying a manageable problem, only a thorough examination of the pertinent literature can enlighten you to the breadth and depth of previous work. At this point, only complete and systematic reading and careful analysis, evaluation, and synthesis of what is read can satisfy the need for expertise.

SOME ADVICE ON SEARCHING THE LITERATURE

1. Be open to all opinions and approaches. Try not to judge their worth until you are fully informed about the bases for the opinions and the rationales and practical concerns behind the approaches. There is a temptation to read only opinions which agree with your own or with those of one writer whose work seems to offer a basis for your study. Don't give in to this temptation. The review of the literature is designed to expand your horizons. Let it do so. Read conflicting opinions; examine opposing arguments objectively. Even if you do not change your position, you will be better equipped to discuss opposing positions. In your later report, presentation of conflicting arguments and findings coupled with an articulate discussion of their conceptual and practical weaknesses will confirm your expertise and strengthen your own arguments.

2. Don't just explore ''scholarly'' publications. It will soon become apparent to you that some publications are afforded a greater measure of respect by scholars than others. Some scholars feel that *Psychology Today* is appreciably less scholarly than the *Journal of Experimental Psychology*. Likewise, *Parents Magazine* is likely to be considered a much less scholarly source of information on schooling than, say, *The Journal of Reading*. Even within the realm of professional journals, some are considered more rigorously scholarly than others. One soon becomes aware of the relative status of each. Some researchers explore only those journals with reputations for extreme scholarship. This is not only a form of intellectual snobbery, it also can lead to a failure to gain an understanding of the concerns of the public, which play such a large role in all aspects of education. A comparison of the size of readerships of popular magazines such as *Parents* and professional journals such as *Psychometrika* quickly points up the disparity in potential influence. Popular magazines may influence hundreds of thousands of readers. They may also reflect in their writings the beliefs of large numbers of readers. If a researcher is to say that he or she has a broad grasp of writing on a topic, that grasp must encompass also popular magazines where appropriate. Newspapers may also offer sources of information on public opinion and the level of public knowledgeability on a topic.

3. When beginning a search of the literature, a researcher may have only a handful of subject headings or descriptors related to a subject. Upon reading more widely and more deeply, he or she becomes aware of new avenues to explore. Pursue many of these avenues. Often they prove more fruitful to a study than the original area in which you were searching. Read bibliographies at the end of articles and books. Track down and examine references. Bibliographies have often proved the most useful sources for further research and writing in a given topic area. The author of an article or book includes a bibliography for the very purpose of enabling others to retrace all or part of the search which produced the article or book.

4. In general, in searching the literature, start with the present and work backward chronologically, identifying potentially appropriate works to examine in detail. Remember also that if a work has a promising title but on examination readily evidences itself to be of little worth to your study, don't read it all. Use your time wisely; go on to other materials of greater relevance.

5. Don't just read abstracts. Search out and examine the promising articles.

6. Consider the advantages and disadvantages of published books. One advantage is that a published book often reflects a long period of writing and therefore is on a higher level than some articles. Another advantage is that its length permits it to be more comprehensive and divergent in addressing its topic. One disadvantage is that a book may take two years or more to make the trip from the author to the shelf. This means that, unlike journal articles, which are usually six months to a year in publication, published books seldom report the latest trends or the most recent findings of research.

7. There is a tendency sometimes to be persuaded by an articulate writing style instead of by the content of a piece of writing or by the validity of a study's findings. While talented researchers and thinkers often are capable writers, do not assume that a less well written article or book is the product of unsound reasoning or incompetent research. Evaluate content over style. Don't buy the sizzle; buy the steak.

8. Don't confuse writings/opinions with studies/research findings. A research study seeks to test theories through hypotheses and methods. Articles filled with unsubstantiated ''common knowledge'' abound. Be cautious of such articles. Use them to make you aware of trends; cite them to demonstrate opinion or contention; but do not refer to them as if they *confirmed* any belief or opinion. When you find agreement among opinions, say that you discovered agreement or that one writer supported another. In general, a research finding is a more powerful piece of support than the agreement of writers (provided that the study is properly conducted and the findings both appropriate and generalizable to your problem area).

9. When using material from *Resources in Education*, remember to be critical of its value. Most of the important or significant presentations at professional meetings are later published in the professional journal of that organization. This does not mean that material presented in *RIE* cannot be of value to a researcher. Sometimes *RIE* lists the current status of uncompleted studies which will later be published and thereby enables the researcher to identify and examine material prior to its publication. Even when the researcher finds a number of summaries of presentations at meetings on his or her topic which seem to be of questionable worth, this information can still prove valuable. Consider, for instance, the use of such information to document that the topic is receiving considerable attention from educators by showing that a large number of presentations on the topic have been made or that the topic has been addressed frequently at professional meetings.

10. Don't hesitate to write or contact authors of research articles. They are often able to apprise you of their latest findings or to answer questions you might have about the original published research. Allow several weeks for a reply to a mailed request, include a self-addressed stamped envelope, and be specific in your queries. If time is a problem, don't hesitate to use the telephone, but recognize that these authors are usually busy people.

11. Identify and define your research topic fairly specifically before you perform a computer search. Otherwise you will spend a lot of time (and money) examining irrelevant materials. Ignoring this piece of advice is like buying a gallon of every flavor of ice cream available in order to find one of which you'd like a single scoop.

12. Often in your search of the literature, you will come across one author's work quoted or described in the writings of another. Do not use the later author's version of the quotation or his description. Go back to the original work and confirm for yourself what the author said or found. Many a researcher has been confounded by inaccurate quotations, misleading descriptions, and even incorrect crediting of a quotation or a study.

13. Get to know the reference librarians in the libraries where you plan to search. They can help you develop expertise in using the materials housed there. In learning to use library facilities well, two rules apply: (1) never hesitate to ask for help; (2) there is no substitute for frequent use.

14. Make certain that your review of the literature is up-to-date. Make sure that it contains recent references, and, if your study covers an extended period, do not let your review fall behind. Continue to read and incorporate appropriate recent references.

15. Most researchers find that it helps to establish a consistent format for recording both data from materials you examine and your comments and evaluations of these materials. Ofttimes your advisor can suggest a suitable format. Don't hesitate, however, to adapt that format to your preferences. Many researchers use index cards. The author likes 5 × 7″ cards; a colleague of his uses 4 × 6″ cards. Avoid 3 × 5″ cards, which give too little space for notes and encourage overabbreviation, a bad practice. Use a few, standardized abbreviations.

Some researchers write their notes in longhand on paper and then type them onto cards. For a study which covers a long period and has no pressing deadlines, this is a fine practice, but for studies with tighter limitations, neater writing of your notes directly on index cards is more economical of time.

The consistent format you choose should have methods for indicating the type of material (book, article, presentation), the nature of the material (dissertation, opinion article, research study), and the topic or subtopic (usually a one- or two-word descriptor, often from your computer search). Always record the full bibliographic reference (in the appropriate bibliographic form).

16. When recording data from a research article, be sure to list population, sample, hypotheses, basic procedures and statistical analyses used, and the findings and conclusions. Even when on initial reading you are uncertain what some of these pieces of data mean, you will need them later if you decide to use the reference. Remember also that the more research articles you read, the more you will come to understand such data.

17. If you can get access to an institution's computer or to a microcomputer, consider using it to maintain your "data base" (the information which you gather from your reading indexed by important terms or *key words*). *Data-base management* programs are usually fairly easy to learn to use, and they permit rapid retrieval of information; you can use one of these key words to call up all articles and information relative to the topic indexed by that key word. The use of microcomputers to serve this function becomes increasingly possible and convenient with the advent of smaller "transportable" computers (weighing about 30 pounds) and "briefcase portable" computers (weighing around 8 pounds).

SIX

ANALYSIS AND EVALUATION OF THE WORK OF OTHERS

Beginning researchers often wonder how to evaluate the printed materials to which reference works and computer searches direct them. This chapter explains briefly how to analyze and evaluate published opinion articles, chapters in books, monographs, and research reports. It discusses what to look for in an opinion article, presents such an article, and then reproduces a brief evaluation of the article as recorded on an index card. The chapter next discusses what to look for in a published research report, presents such a report, and reproduces a typical index card which might be prepared in evaluating this published report of a research study.

EVALUATING OPINION ARTICLES

The term *opinion article* refers here to articles which express the beliefs or contentions of their writers. The writer of the article evaluates, analyzes, and makes assertions on the basis of his or her beliefs and experiences and not on the basis of a research study reported in the work. This does not mean that the evaluations, beliefs, contentions, and analyses are incorrect, nor that many readers might not have similar opinions based on similar experiences. The label ''opinion article'' is not pejorative; that is, it does not express either praise or disdain. It merely describes the nature of the work's content. Opinion articles differ from research studies. Opinion articles do not report the results of research studies, nor do they report the findings of a number of research studies in an attempt to consolidate related studies by a number of researchers. Opinion articles do not merely present and discuss bibliographies, nor do they report or discuss research methodology without expressing beliefs about which method is best suited to a particular situation. An opinion article may be an article in a newspaper, magazine, or professional journal, or it may be a chapter in a book, a monograph, or a report produced by an organization, institution, or agency.

In evaluating opinion articles, the researcher needs first to try to identify which of the writer's statements are merely restatements of fact and which are assertions of the writer. It is not important at this point for you to decide whether you agree with the writer's opinions; first you must identify those opinions. In doing so, look for some of the words which often (but not always) signal the presence of a statement of opinion. Some of these "opinion words" are listed below.

agree	disagree	ought
agreement	disagreement	prefer
always	disapproval	preferable
approval	disapprove	propose
argue	good	right
argument	has to	should
assert	inferior	suggest
assertion	maintain	suggestion
bad	must	superior
best	needs to	support
better	never	undesirable
certainly	obvious	undoubtedly
claim	obviously	worse
contend	only	worst
contention	oppose	wrong
desirable	opposition	

Once the researcher has identified the writer's major contentions, he or she needs to decide if the writer has presented any evidence to support the opinions expressed. Related to this decision is your evaluation of whether the writer seems competent and credible. That is, do you believe that the writer has the appropriate experience and intelligence to draw valid *inferences* (conclusions based on experience)?

At this point you need to consider external evaluation of the writer's assertions. Have other writers made similar assertions? Are there authorities in the writer's discipline who support the opinions expressed? You need also to consider your own evaluation of the writer's opinions. Ask yourself: Do I agree? Do these assertions seem reasonable? Do I trust and believe this writer?

Once you have made these decisions, you need to record all the relevant data and comments on an index card for later use. Researchers often include what they consider to be important or salient quotations from the article for possible use later in the introductory sections of their research proposals or reports.

In order to help the beginning researcher see how this process of evaluation works with an opinion article, this chapter next presents a short sample opinion article and a sample evaluation on an index card (Figure 6-1). The novice researcher should recognize that the guidelines presented above and applied below are simply some of the many which could be used in evaluating an opinion article. Beginning researchers should consult their advisors to ascertain what types of approaches they employ.

A SAMPLE OPINION ARTICLE

ARE YOU TEACHING THE WRONG GRAMMAR?
by C. M. Ward

Most English teachers hate to teach grammar. It seems dry and students seldom react to grammar sessions with anything akin to enthusiasm. With everything else that a teacher has to teach, she may find it easier to avoid teaching grammar altogether and go on to other more enjoyable topics.

I argue that this is a mistake. I recognize that many teachers have unpleasant memories of their own experiences with grammar when they were students. I certainly do. I remember with discomfort parsing sentences and learning all the various parts of speech. I recognize further that there is a tendency to teach grammar to our students in the same ways in which we were taught. Herein lies the problem for most teachers.

The grammar that most of us were taught is merely one type of grammar. It is known as "traditional grammar" and reflects trying to apply rules which governed Latin to the English language. Since these grammar rules were designed to govern Latin, they do not apply to English very well. English draws a large number of its words from the Roman language, Latin, but it is not identical to Latin and it contains words, phrases, and constructions from other languages.

In recent years linguists have been working on developing grammars whose rules fit English better. Instead of trying to make English fit the grammar rules, they have been trying to make the grammar rules fit English. This certainly makes sense to me.

One of the more promising and teachable grammars which have appeared recently is "transformational grammar." Transformational grammar is designed to explain how people "transform" what they want to say into ways to say it. It deals with "propositions" (units of meaning) and how we add propositions to sentences to enrich them. It also examines how we use different types of sentence structures when we wish to express different sentiments.

It is not my intention in this article to describe in great detail all of the mechanics of transformational grammar. There are many books available on the market which do a fine job of explaining and describing transformational grammar. A teacher ought to examine in particular the excellent books on grammar available from the National Council of Teachers of English (1111 Kenyon Road, Urbana, Illinois 61801).

I suggest that teachers need to be teaching transformational grammar instead of traditional grammar. Unlike the meaningless sentence parsing of traditional grammar instruction, transformational grammar actually helps students learn to write. My students write longer more polished sentences now than they ever did during the years when I taught traditional grammar. They also don't seem to mind grammar instruction as much, and I know that I find it more enjoyable.

The sentence combining activities help my students learn to avoid "run-on" sentences and sentences stuck together with commas. My students use "and" and "but" much more effectively and frequently. Likewise, my students have learned to use the "W" connectors—who, when, where, while, which—much more effectively as a result of sentence combining exercises which specifically address the use of these words.

The sentence expanding exercises have helped my students learn to use modifiers (adverbs and adjectives) much more effectively. Their sentences are longer and more interesting. There is more detail in their writing.

I don't teach traditional grammar anymore. You should drop the parsing as well. Traditional grammar isn't worth it.

About the author: Mr. Ward teaches 8th grade language arts at Foosbaum High in Colander, Michigan. He has his master's degree in secondary teaching from Heidegger University and has taught language arts from grades 7 through 9 for the past nine years.

FIGURE 6–1:   Index Card for the Sample Opinion Article

Front

Grammar instruction   Opinion Article
Ward, C. M. Are you teaching the wrong grammar? *Journal of Understanding*, 1983, *12*, 62–64.
   Summary: Traditional grammar is what most teachers teach because it's what they were taught. It is boring and not of much value. It is based on Latin and rules for Latin don't apply well to English. Transformational grammar is newer and tries to explain how English is actually spoken. There is little description of transf. grammar but suggests consult books. Recommends Nat. Council of Teachers of English (1111 Kenyon Rd. Urbana, Ill, 61801). Transf. grammar helps his students' writing (longer sentences, more detail, fewer run-on and comma splice sentences, better clause connections). Contends that teachers shouldn't teach trad. grammar but instead teach transf. grammar.

Back

Eval.: This is an OK journal. He has 9 yrs. experience (7-9th grade). Teaches in Colander, Mich. Writers disagree on transformational grammar's effectiveness (see Mitchell article). Traditional grammar isn't just "parsing." He uses terms from traditional grammar (adj., adv.) to describe transformational grammar's activities. Should some parts of trad. grammar be retained? Other writers say so (see Reid; Dumphries; Cumberland). How does "sentence expanding" (transformational grammar) differ from "adding detail" (traditional grammar)? This is a testimonial to how transformational grammar helps writing. No valuable quotes. Article needed a bit more detail on what he does with each grammar.

FIGURE 6-1 (cont.)

EVALUATING PUBLISHED RESEARCH STUDIES

In analyzing published research studies, readers need to consider the constraints of the publication process. Unlike research proposals and unpublished research reports, published studies usually do not contain extensive reviews of the literature. They seek, rather, to discuss some of the more pertinent studies and to present a sampling of relevant findings. Most published studies do not contain copies of materials or instruments used in the studies. The common practice is for interested readers to write the author or authors of the published study for more complete information. Likewise, data supplied in the article may be abbreviated. Such absence of material and data may cause a concern about the validity (see Chapter 15) of a published study, but should not be described as a threat unless the author has failed to discuss a number of relevant concerns.

A published research study should present the reader with a sufficient quantity of information to enable him or her to outline clearly:

1. The *conceptual bases* of the study (the theory behind the study).
2. The *nature of the research* and the *design* employed.
3. The *hypotheses* tested.
4. The *samples* used and the *procedures by which they were drawn*.
5. The *characteristics* of the *experimenters* or *teachers, therapists, or staff* involved.
6. The *treatments* administered.
7. The *measurement instruments* employed.
8. The *statistical analyses* performed.
9. The *findings* of the study.
10. The *implications* of those findings.

The reader should also evaluate whether he or she believes that any conclusions drawn by the researcher were warranted by the methodology and findings of the study. As part of this evaluation, the reader needs to look for forms and expressions of bias on the part of the researcher/author of the article. Usually such bias evidences itself in an article when the author:

1. States as *fact*, conclusions or statements from other writers or researchers which are open to argument and should be identified as *contentions* or *beliefs* and not facts.

2. Presents only one side of an argument or presents only supporting research when opposing research is available.

3. Selects a sample which is, in some ways, more likely to produce a desired outcome (as usually expressed by a research hypothesis).

4. Accepts research findings of marginal significance ($p > .10$) as if there were no question about the treatment's producing those findings.

5. Fails to discuss plausible alternative hypotheses.

A sample published research report follows: Figure 6-1 shows two sample evaluations of this report on an index card.

A SAMPLE PUBLISHED RESEARCH REPORT

WHICH APPROACH TO GRAMMAR INSTRUCTION IS MOST EFFECTIVE IN DEVELOPING WRITING SKILLS?: A COMPARATIVE STUDY
by W. C. Mitchell

Teachers often find themselves frustrated in teaching students the mechanics of writing. "Traditional grammar" (based on Latin grammar) has gone out of vogue in many systems, despite the fact that many teachers were trained in the use of "traditional grammar" and feel most comfortable with its divisions and prescriptions. Other teachers who were trained in structural grammar (based on the function of words and phrases) find themselves faced with teaching the more recent transformational grammar (based on changing form to retain meaning in various uses). Curriculum planning committees in school systems find themselves faced with a choice: do they want to legislate that one of these three "grammars" be taught in this system or to legislate that a combination of two or more be taught?

Montay (1950) found that there appeared to be no measurable improvement in student writing when traditional grammar was taught. This finding was confirmed in later studies by Janeros (1958), Touster (1962), and Februsco (1969). Additionally, the Februsco study (1969) found that there was no significant difference among the writing skills of eighth graders who were given "traditional," structural, or no formal grammar instruction. In contrast, Wednesday (1971) found that the teaching of structural grammar did appear to produce a significant difference in writing ability among tenth grade students when compared with tenth graders who had received no formal grammar instruction. The literature exhibited extensive disagreement on the benefits of teaching transformational grammar in terms of improved student writing. While Meels (1971), Tenlenst (1974), and Anvil (1978) found significant gains in writing ability made by students who had received instruction in transformational grammar, Fidelo (1970), May (1973), Joor (1977), and Snelling (1980) found no significant difference in writing ability between students who received transformational grammar instruction and those who received either "traditional" grammar instruction or structural grammar instruction.

When the researcher examined language arts textbooks, she found that most contained a combination of approaches to grammar instruction which employed aspects of all three "grammars" (e.g., *Albatross & Aardvark Language Series*, 1980; *Art of Language*, 1979; *Language Systems*, 1980; *Reptile & Revolver*, 1980). Surrel (1979) examined the influence of eclectic approaches to grammar instruction on seventh graders' writing skills, but her findings were inconclusive. Auller (1979) also explored an eclectic treatment which utilized sentence combining exercises and traditional parts of speech exercises. Although Auller found that there was a statistically significant difference between the mean scores of students in the eclectic treatment and the "traditional" approach, she discounted the practical significance of her findings, attributing them to the use of a large sample.

In light of the fact that many elementary teachers rely heavily on language arts textbooks for their students' grammar instruction, this study sought to examine the relative effectiveness of the eclectic approach employed in these books as opposed to "traditional," transformational, or structural approaches to grammar instruction. Since a large number of curriculum planning committees cite "improved ability in writing " as the main objective of grammar instruction (Sealream, 1976), the study used pretest and posttest measures of writing complexity (Oldmoan, 1978; Nesterey, 1980) to determine the relative gains in writing ability among the four treatments: eclectic, "traditional," structural, and transformational.

The hypothesis for the study (stated in null form) was

> There will be no significant difference in application of grammar skills to writing (as measured by scores on the Donnlevy test of writing complexity) among fifth grade students instructed in grammar using an eclectic, "traditional," structural, or transformational approach.

Description of the Sample

This study was conducted in a school system of 12,000 students in upstate New York. Of those 12,000 students, 6800 were enrolled in grades K–6. The researcher chose to work with only fifth grade students. This decision was based on logistic concerns since she felt that data collection on the 1206 fifth graders presented a more manageable collection task, and because writing complexity measures and comparison scores for this grade level were readily available.

The 1206 students were enrolled in nine schools. These schools served the communities surrounding a city of 750,000 persons. Metropolitan, suburban, and rural communities all fed students to these schools, and an extensive federally approved and enforced busing system insured a proportional balance of black and white students. The average racial balance for the nine schools was 65 percnt white/35 percent black, with schools ranging from 62 percent black/38 percent white to 70 percent white/30 percent black.

Since the distribution of students to these nine schools was based on a combination of residential patterns and a federal busing plan, the researcher chose to perform random assignment to treatments within each school. The distribution and assignments are presented in Table 6–1.

Since this study was conducted with the complete cooperation of the school district, random selection of students for each class (treatment) was possible. As Table 6–1 indicates, the researcher was able to insure that the numbers of students and classes assigned to each of the four treatments were approximately equal.

Of the 1200 students, 732 (61 percent) were female and 468 (39 percent) were male. Within treatments, this proportion remained relatively stable with the eclectic treatment having the highest percentage of males (43 percent) and the structural treatment having the highest percentage of females (63 percent). All fifth graders in the school system take the California Test of Mental Maturity in September of the school year. Scores for the 1200 students tested ranged from 69 to 139 with a mean IQ score of 102.5. Due to absences, six students failed to take the California Test of Mental Maturity in September and were therefore not included in the study. The distribution, range, and means for pretest scores are presented in Table 6–2.

Procedures

All 1200 students were pretested using the Donnlevy Sentence Combining Exercise (Donnlevy, 1966) during the first week of school. They were then posttested using this same exercise three weeks before the close of the school year. The Donnlevy exercise asks the student to combine 37 simple sentences, each of which expresses a single thought, into as many or as few sentences as the student "feels makes it read better." The teacher admin-

TABLE 6–1 Distribution of the Sample Among Schools, Classes, and Treatments

SCHOOL	NUMBER OF STUDENTS	NUMBER OF CLASSES	NUMBER OF STUDENTS ASSIGNED TO TREATMENT*			
			ECLECTIC	TRADITIONAL	STRUCTURAL	TRANSFORMATIONAL
A	215	8	53(2)	54(2)	54(2)	54(2)
B	213	8	53(2)	53(2)	53(2)	54(2)
C	162	7	46(2)	46(2)	46(2)	24(1)
D	106	5	21(1)	21(1)	21(1)	43(2)
E	108	5	22(1)	44(2)	21(1)	21(1)
F	50	2	25(1)	0	25(1)	0
G	127	6	21(1)	42(2)	43(2)	21(1)
H	116	6	20(1)	19(1)	38(2)	39(2)
I	103	3	34(1)	34(1)	0	35(2)
Totals	1200†	50	295(12)	313(13)	301(13)	291(12)

*The numbers in parentheses indicate the number of classes of students assigned to each treatment.
†This number reflects the absence of 6 students from the pretest session.

TABLE 6–2   Ranges, Distribution, and Means of Scores of Sample on California Test of Mental Maturity

TREATMENT	N	LOW SCORE	HIGH SCORE	MEAN SCORE
Eclectic	295	69	139	102.6
Traditional	313	69	139	102.8
Structural	301	70	138	102.1
Transformational	291	71	136	102.4
Totals	1200	69	139	102.5

istering the exercise is cautioned not to communicate to the student any preference for the number of sentences the student uses. The resultant paragraph which incorporates the ideas presented in the original exercise is then analyzed for the number of words and sentences employed and the average length of each "*t*-unit." A *t*-unit is a main clause including any clause it subordinates or any nonclausal expression which it contains or to which it is attached (Hunt, 1965). The figures produced by this analysis can then be compared to a table of figures based on use of the exercise with several thousand fifth graders in school systems across the country.

The researcher held training sessions for the teachers in each treatment. The twelve teachers in the eclectic approach were instructed in the use of the Reptile and Revolver (1980) textbook. The thirteen teachers in the traditional approach were instructed in the use of the *Basics Alone Language Series* (Lean, 1980). The 13 teachers in the structural approach were instructed in the use of the *Surface and Below Grammar Text* (1980). The twelve teachers in the transformational approach were instructed in the use of the *Decade Language Series* (1980). Each of the textbooks chosen employed the approach to grammar instruction appropriate to the treatment in which it was to be used. All other instructional materials used in the system were identical by board policy. Teachers were cautioned not to use the textbooks used in treatments other than their own. Supervisory staff and systemwide curriculum specialists continued to assist all teachers in the system using the same techniques for classes regardless of treatment.

Findings

The researcher gathered posttest scores on 1145 students. The fifty-five students for whom posttest scores could not be obtained because of absence or withdrawal represented a loss of students from all four treatments. Thirteen students in the eclectic treatment, fifteen students in the traditional treatment, fifteen students in the structural treatment, and twelve students in the transformational treatment lacked posttest scores. No one class lost more than three students. In order to prevent these students from being lost to the study, the researcher used the mean score for the treatment to which each was assigned as the posttest score.

The pretest scores for the sample and the range and means for the pretest are reported in Table 6–3. Posttest scores, their range and means are reported in Table 6–4.

The researcher used an analysis of covariance to compare the mean writing complexity scores of the four treatments. IQ scores on the California Test of Mental Maturity and writing complexity pretest scores were used as covariates. The analysis of covariance showed differences among groups which were significant at the .05 level. This led the researcher to reject the null hypothesis.

The researcher then compared the means of the various treatments using Scheffé's method (as described by Ferguson, 1976, pp. 295–297). She found that there was a significant difference among treatments ($p < .05$) in favor of the transformational grammar treatment. None of the other three treatments differed significantly in resultant scores on the Donnlevy Writing Complexity Exercise.

TABLE 6–3   Distribution, Range, and Means of Pretest Scores on The Donnlevy Sentence-Combining Exercise for Fifth-Graders

TREATMENT	N*	LOW SCORE	HIGH SCORE	MEAN SCORE
Eclectic	295	.6	2.0	1.1
Traditional	313	.5	1.8	1.2
Structural	301	.3	1.9	1.2
Transformational	291	.8	1.7	1.3
Totals	1200	.3	2.0	1.2

*Totals given reflect use of treatment mean scores for the 55 students who failed to take the posttest.

TABLE 6–4   Distribution, Range, and Means of Posttest Scores on The Donnlevy Sentence-Combining Exercise for Fifth-Graders

TREATMENT	N	LOW SCORE	HIGH SCORE	MEAN SCORE
Eclectic	295	.8	3.1	1.3
Traditional	313	.6	1.9	1.4
Structural	301	.5	2.3	1.4
Transformational	291	.9	3.2	1.6
Totals	1200	.5	3.2	1.42

*Totals given reflect use of treatment mean scores for the 55 students who failed to take the posttest.

Discussion

The findings of this study appear to support the findings of earlier studies by Meels (1971), Tenlenst (1974), and Anvil (1978). Fifth grade students who received grammar instruction using the transformational approach made significantly greater progress in writing complexity as measured by the Donnlevy instrument. The researcher feels that the findings represent both statistical and practical significance. The criteria used to evaluate the Donnlevy instrument—length of expression, average number of ideas contained in each expression, and use of subordinate expressions— are the criteria normally mentioned by teachers and writers as indications of mature writing style. The findings of this study suggest that teachers whose major objective in teaching grammar is to increase the maturity of their students' writing would be best advised to use transformational approaches to grammar instruction. Recognizing that differences in instructional materials may influence the nature and strength of the findings, the researcher suggests that similar studies involving other commercially produced instructional materials be conducted. She also suggests that studies comparing the relative effectiveness of commercially produced materials using each approach and teacher-produced materials using each approach be conducted.

Front

Grammar instruction   Research Article
Mitchell, W. C. Which approach to grammar instruction is most effective in developing writing skills?: A comparative study. *English Researcher*, 1982, *16*, 136-144.

Theory: Curric. committees identify improved writing as objective of grammar instruction. Writers & researchers disagree on which grammar approach fulfills this obj. best. Commercial textbook publishers use an eclectic approach. Many teachers rely on textbook.

Nature & design: Disclose differences: True experimental--Factorial.

Hypothesis: There will be no significant difference in application of grammar skills to writing (as measured by scores on the Donnlevy test of writing complexity) among the fifth grade students instructed in grammar using an eclectic, "traditional," structural, or transformational approach.

Sample: 1200 5th graders (of entire 5th of 1206) drawn from 12,000 student school system. Nine schools involved. 750,000 person urban, suburban, rural area of upstate NY. Race = 65(W)/35(B)%. S's randomly assigned within schools. Classes randomly assigned to treatments. Sex = 6l(F)/39(M)%. IQ = 69-139 w/102.5 mean (Cal. Test of Ment. Mat.).

Back

Experimenters: #'s only, no characteristics. Eclectic (12), trad. (13), structural (13), transf. (12).

Treatments: eclectic = (Reptile & Revolver,1980); trad. = (Basics Alone Lang. Series, 1980); struct. = (Surface & Below Grammar Text, 1980); transf. = (Decade Lang. Series,1980); other materials identical

Measurement: Donnlevy (1966) Sentence Combining Exercise (1st wk & 3 wks before close of school).

Stats: analysis of covariance using IQ & pretest scores to adjust; 55 absent (evenly distributed) replaced by treatment means. Scheffé's test.

Findings: transf. higher ($p < .05$); others NS

Implications: transf. more effective in producing improved writing.

Eval.: Is grammar instruction the only way to learn to write? What about other treatments? Who & how scored Donnlevy tests? Differences among textbooks? What about characteristics of teachers? How good is the Donnlevy test? More info on treatments? In general, there are too many undiscussed threats for complete confidence in findings even though no bias and generally well done.

SEVEN

PROBABILITY AND THE NORMAL CURVE

This chapter does not attempt to cover all aspects of probability theory nor to teach statistics. It seeks instead to make the beginning researcher familiar enough with the terms and mathematical reasoning of research that he or she will feel neither bewildered nor intimidated. Beginning researchers who have a desire to learn more about probability theory should consult one of the many fine books available on the topic.

STATEMENTS OF PROBABILITY

Each day the weather bureau issues a statement telling what the probability (or chance) of precipitation is for that day. This prediction does not, however, influence the weather (as evidenced by days when, despite the favorable forecast, we get soaked). What, then, does the prediction do? It indicates what the chances are that the weather conditions that actually occur will be the same as those that were predicted. If the probability of rain is 30 percent, then the weather bureau believes that there are thirty chances in 100 (or three in ten) that it will actually rain.

If you flip a coin, it can come up either heads or tails. The probability of its coming up heads is one in two (since heads is one of two possible results). One in two is ½ or .50 or 50 percent probability. Mathematicians often use the letter p to indicate probability. Thus, for our coin flip, the probability of the result's being heads might be expressed as $p = .50$.

Neither our weather forecast ($p = .30$) nor our coin flip ($p = .50$) leaves us with much confidence that what will actually happen will be the same as the predicted result. In evaluating the findings of a research study, we don't wish to leave this much room for simple chance variation to produce our results.

While it is difficult to predict what the result of an individual coin flip will be and our prediction will often be incorrect, it is much easier to predict the cumulative outcome of a large number of coin flips and our cumulative prediction will usually be accurate. In general, the more times the coin is flipped, the more accurate is likely to be our prediction of the distribution of the results between the two possible outcomes (heads or tails). It both seems logical and proves out mathematically that, over a very large number of coin flips, approximately one-half of the time the result will be heads and one-half of the time the result will be tails. Therefore, our initial probability calculation of $p = .50$, while not very reliable for predicting individual coin flips, is extremely reliable for predicting the distribution of results of a large number of coin flips.

In most studies, however, a researcher is faced not with two but rather with a number of possible outcomes. Consider, for example our earlier sample research problem which dealt with a treatment to help third-graders improve their reading ability. This improvement was to be measured using a standardized reading test. It is not difficult to envision thirty subjects receiving thirty different scores on that standardized test. How then do we use a knowledge of probability to help us interpret these scores? This leads us to statistics and the normal curve.

STATISTICS

A *statistic* is a score (number) which in some way describes a sample or a population. Consider our thirty third-grade students. We might use the average of these thirty scores on the standardized test to tell us something about the performance of the class. This average (known to statisticians as the *mean*) would be a statistic of the group's performance. In most situations the mean would be a pretty good predictor of what score any of the thirty students got on the standardized reading test. The problem is that, like a prediction of the result of an individual coin flip, it is accurate for large numbers of subjects but not very accurate or reliable for predicting individual performance. The scores would *in most cases* vary around the mean. Some scores would be higher, some might be the same as the mean, and some would be lower. If we were to try to compare the performance of groups merely by comparing their means, we would make mistakes from time to time, since some groups' means would be more accurate indicators of the group's performance than others.

STANDARD DEVIATION
AND THE NORMAL CURVE

The *variability*, or the extent to which the scores differed from the mean, could tell us how reliable an indicator the mean is of the performance of the group. The *standard deviation* (usually abbreviated *sd* or *s*), or the average amount that each score differed from the mean, would be one statistic of variability which could help us determine how reliable an indicator the mean is. Just as we were able to predict the distribution of coin-flip results with some accuracy on the basis of what occurs naturally when a large number of coin flips are considered, we can make a similar prediction of the distribution of scores around a mean based on the way in which large numbers of various naturally occurring scores (statistics) vary around population means. For example, height and weight are characteristic values of a population which vary around their means (average height, average weight).

Examination of the distribution of these population values (statistics) will show that they tend to be symmetrically distributed around the mean. Generally about 34 percent of these values will be between the mean and one standard deviation above the mean and about 34 percent of them will be between the mean and one standard deviation below the mean. Thus, for population values (variables) which occur as typical characteristics of a population, about 68 percent would be located within plus or minus one standard deviation of the mean.

Further examination will show that approximately 13.6 percent of the population values will be located between one standard deviation below the mean and two standard deviations below the mean. Likewise, about 13.6 percent will be located between one standard deviation and two standard deviations above the mean. This means that a little over 95 percent of the population values would be located within plus or minus two standard deviations of the population mean.

This symmetrical distribution further shows that another approximately 2 percent of the population values will be between two and three standard deviations below the mean and approximately 2 percent will be between two and three standard deviations above the mean. Thus, for naturally occurring variables typical of populations, about 99 percent will be located within plus or minus three standard deviations of the population mean.

What has just been described is known as the *normal probability curve* (or just the *normal curve*). It is illustrated in Figure 7–1.

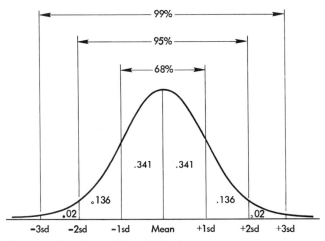

Fig. 7–1   **The Normal Probability Curve**

What the normal probability curve illustrates is that most naturally occurring characteristics among humans are distributed symmetrically according to a predictable (or highly probable) pattern. This predictability (or probability) makes it possible to compare the variability of a group's scores around the group's mean to the variability of the normal curve. This ability to compare group values to a theoretical or probable curve makes it possible for researchers to compare the performances of groups to one another and to determine if the differences among their performances differ significantly from what the normal probability curve would lead us to expect.

Researchers use *probability levels* to help them decide if any differences among groups are *statistically significant* (see Chapters 17 and 18). The two probability levels most frequently employed by researchers are $p < .05$ and $p < .01$.

You may observe that in the normal curve approximately 95 percent of the values are located within plus or minus two standard deviations of the mean. You may also observe that approximately 99 percent of the values are located within plus or minus three standard deviations of the mean. Further, you might note that only 5 percent of the values are located more than plus or minus two standard deviations from the mean and that only 1 percent of the values are located more than plus or minus three standard deviations from the mean. It is no coincidence that the two probability levels most frequently employed by researchers are .05 (the percentage of values more than plus or minus two standard deviations from the mean) and .01 (the percentage of values which are more than plus or minus three standard deviations from the mean). Without going into detail about why and how these probability levels were derived, suffice it to note that they are based upon the normal curve and relate to the the variability of values in relation to their mean. Probability levels are also known as *significance levels*, since they are used to help researchers determine if differences among group performances are significant.

EIGHT

DRAWING SAMPLES FROM POPULATIONS

This chapter discusses some of the more frequently employed methods of drawing a sample of subjects for a research study. The techniques described here apply equally to selecting individuals to include in a survey, selecting the time periods during which to observe an activity, or selecting subjects for groups in an experimental study designed to disclose significant differences in the effectiveness of various treatments.

SOME IMPORTANT TERMS

To prepare the reader for the rest of this chapter, it seems wise first to present a few brief definitions:

A **population** is a large group of individuals, objects, or events.

A **sample** is a smaller group drawn from a population.

Subjects are individuals in a sample. (For a more detailed definition, see Chapter 1.)

A **target population** is a large group of individuals, objects, or events to which we would like to generalize the findings of our study.

An **experimentally accessible population** is a population to which the experimenter has access and from which the experimenter may draw samples.

A **defined population** is a population which has been selected by the experimenter and which he or she has examined and described in terms of the traits, attributes, and characteristics of its members.

For ease in discussion and since most educational research studies involve humans or animals, this section on sampling will use ''individuals'' or ''subjects'' when speaking of samples instead of the more exact, but cumbersome, ''individuals, objects, or events.'' The reader should keep in mind, however, that whether we select periods of time to study (*time sampling*), or words to use on a test, or stimuli to present to subjects (*stimulus sampling*), or any other object or event from a larger number of available objects, items, events, or individuals, the process of selection falls under the heading *sampling*.

STEPS IN DRAWING A SAMPLE

1. The researcher must first consider the nature of the individuals to whom the research findings are to be generalized (the *target population*). What are their characteristics, traits, and attributes? (When sampling individuals, these characteristics, traits, and attributes are normally referred to as the *demographics* of the population and include such variables as age, sex, race, religion, education, geographic location, employment, and social and economic status.) The more specifically you are able to define the desired target audience, the more likely it is that you will be able to recognize an appropriate experimentally accessible population from which to draw a sample.

2. Next you examine the experimentally accessible populations. You then seek to identify and describe any pertinent differences between what you feel is the most appropriate experimentally accessible population and the target population. These demographic data will be useful later in preparing the research report, since you will wish to discuss these differences in order to alert readers to qualifications of the findings which may restrict their generalizability. These data are involved in determining the *population validity* of the study's findings. This will be discussed further in Chapter 15.

If you are unable to find an appropriate experimentally accessible population locally, you should seek to find one elsewhere rather than simply use the "best one available." If the experimentally accessible population is not sufficiently similar to the target population, you should not conduct the study until you are able to locate an appropriate one.

3. The researcher draws a sample from the selected experimentally accessible population using one of the sampling methods described below.

SAMPLING METHODS

Random Sampling Methods

Random sampling methods are preferable, since they enable the researcher to choose a sample which should resemble the defined population closely. Random selection generally breaks up patterns which might exist in other selection processes and increases your confidence that your sample is typical of the defined population. There are three frequently used random sampling methods.

Simple random sampling. This method selects subjects from the defined population using a random selection device, and every individual in the defined population stands an equal chance of being selected for the sample.

There are many random selection devices. One such device is a simple *lottery* in which names of all subjects in the defined population are placed in a hat and the necessary number of subjects for the sample are drawn out. This is generally used only when the population and sample involved are relatively small (fewer than 100 in the population and fewer than 50 in the sample).

Another device often used is the *table of random numbers*, which enables researchers to select subjects from their own numbered lists by choosing those whose numbers match those in the table.

Still another random selection device, which is related to the table of random numbers, is the computerized *random* or *pseudo-random number generator*, which is now available for many microcomputers. Using the random number generating properties of the computer's processor, these programs generate a listing of the numbers of subjects to be included in the sample. As was the case with the table of random numbers, you must have first numbered your defined population list in order to have numbered subjects to select. You need to be certain that each time the random number generator program is run, it uses a different *seed number* (the number from which the random numbers are generated). Otherwise, the sample will not be random; if the program uses the same seed number, it will always select the same subjects for the sample. Some recent random sampling computer programs get their seed numbers from the time of day when the program is run. This method is unlikely to produce the same seed number repeatedly.

Systematic random sampling.   This method is similar to simple random sampling except that each subject in the population does not have an equal chance of being selected for inclusion in the sample. The researcher first must obtain a random listing of all members of the defined population. If there is a pattern to this listing (listed alphabetically, by income, by residence, or using some other pattern), you should use simple random sampling instead. If there is no pattern to the listing, you then number the subjects on the list. You divide the total number of subjects in the defined population by the number of subjects you wish to have in the sample. This produces a dividend n. If the dividend is a fraction, you need to round it down to the next lower integer (whole number). You then select any number smaller than n and count this number of names from the top of the listing. The name on which you land is the first subject for the sample. You then take every nth name on the list after this first subject until you have selected the number of subjects to be included in the sample.

For example, if your listing contained 250 subjects and you wanted a sample of 50 subjects, you would divide 250 by 50 and get 5. This is your n. You decide to use 4 (a number smaller than n) to select your first subject. This means that the fourth subject on the listing is the first member of your sample. You now add 5 (n) to this first number (4) and get 9. You take the ninth subject, and the 14th ($9 + n$), and the 19th ($14 + n$), and so forth until the 249th subject (4 added to 49 times $n =$ 249). You now then have selected your 50-subject sample systematically. The method is called systematic because it relies on a system of selection which automatically eliminates from the sample all but the nth subjects (calculated from the first selected).

Stratified random sampling. This method is employed when the researcher wishes to insure that selected subgroups in the defined population will be represented in the sample in the same proportions as in the defined population. The researcher first identifies the appropriate *strata* (levels or divisions) of the population and divides the defined population into subgroups accordingly. The researcher next decides what is the size of the smallest subgroup with which he or she wishes to work. The size of this smallest subgroup is normally a function of protection against *attrition* (loss of subjects from the sample) and satisfaction of statistical analysis requirements. If this smallest subgroup contains too few subjects, even the loss of one or two may invalidate any conclusions about the subgroup based on the results of the study. (Remember the problem of making individual predictions based on a small number of cases.) Some statistical analyses also require a minimum number of subjects in order to draw valid *inferences* (conclusions based on the analysis of the data). In most cases, the larger the group of subjects, the more likely the results of data analysis are to be reliable. (Once again, this is a function of the greater likelihood that large numbers of scores will distribute themselves about their mean in an arrangement resembling the normal curve.)

Once you have identified the size of the smallest subgroup (*stratum*—singular of strata), you are ready to determine the size of each of the other required subgroups and the total number of subjects to be included in the sample. These calculations are derived from the size of the smallest stratum. In defining the population and identifying the appropriate stata, you need to determine what percentage of the defined population comprises each subgroup. You, therefore, must know these percentages. In order to use these percentages to determine the number of subjects to be sampled from each stratum, you must now calculate what quantity of subjects in the sample represents a single percent of the defined population. This is calculated from the size of the smallest subgroup using the formula:

$$\frac{sgs}{sgp} \times gp = gs$$

where

sgs = the number of subjects the research requires for the smallest subgroup in the sample

sgp = the percentage of the defined population which falls into this smallest stratum—omitting the percentage sign but not expressed as a decimal fraction

gp = the percentage of the defined population which falls into another stratum for which you would like to decide how many subjects to include in the sample—once again omitting the percentage sign but not expressed as a decimal fraction

gs = the number of subjects from that other stratum which shold be included in the study

Since you're unlikely to be a professional mathematician, since some people are uncomfortable with applying formulas (solving equations), and since this is the first formula (or equation) included in this book, let's try using this formula with a sample population:

Suppose that you have a defined population of 2000 people. On examining it, you decide that it contains four strata which you wish to use in obtaining a stratified random sample. The four strata are women over forty, men over forty, women forty and under, and men forty and under. You discover that 27 percent of the population are women over forty, 17 percent are men over forty, 32 percent are women forty and under, and 24 percent are men forty and under. This means that men over forty is the smallest subgroup (17 percent). You determine that for purposes of this study you want your smallest subgroup to be twenty-five subjects. Using the formula, you find:

$$\frac{25}{17} \times 27 = 39.7 \text{ subjects from women over 40}$$

$$\frac{25}{17} \times 32 = 41.1 \text{ subjects from women 40 and under}$$

$$\frac{25}{17} \times 24 = 35.3 \text{ subjects from men 40 and under, and}$$
$$25 \text{ subjects from men over 40}$$

You obviously can't sample parts of subjects, so you round any fractional amount of .5 or larger *up* to the next higher number of subjects and round any fractional amount less than .5 *down* to the next lower number of subjects. This leaves you with forty, forty-seven, thirty-five, and twenty-five subjects to be selected for the four subgroups which will produce a total sample of 147 subjects.

Once you have determined how many subjects are to be selected from each stratum (subgroup), you select them randomly using one of the random sampling devices described above.

Nonrandom Sampling Methods

While researchers prefer to use random samples because they provide greater confidence that the samples are typical of the populations from which they were drawn, often in education the researcher is unable to obtain a random sample because of administrative, legal, or ethical constraints. Two of the more frequently employed nonrandom sampling methods are described below.

Cluster sampling. This method is employed by researchers when it is more feasible to select *groups* of individuals than individual subjects to be included in the sample. The sampling unit is therefore a group of individuals instead of a single individual. In educational research this group is usually a therapy group, a team, a classroom of students, a staff of teachers, or some other group which exists in educational settings. When such a group is included as a sample, it is often referred to as an *intact group*, since the researcher takes the group intact, exactly as it exists, with all its inherent patterns of characteristics and behaviors.

The advantages of cluster sampling are that it is less expensive than other methods, requires less time to draw a sample from a population, and avoids administrative difficulties. It conforms to most of the legal, ethical, and administrative constraints of educational settings. One disadvantage is that it does not break up any of the pre-existing patterns among the sample, and therefore the researcher cannot discount the possibility that these patterns may introduce extraneous variables (see Chapter 1) which may make interpretation of the results of the study difficult. Another disadvantage is that you cannot be as confident that the sample is representative or typical of the defined population. You will have to gather demographic data to help in confirming such population representation and sample typicality. Another disadvantage is that the absence of random selection generally militates for the use of a set of statistical tests which tend to be less sensitive to differences among treatments. (This will be discussed in detail in Chapter 17.)

Volunteer sampling.   This method is often used when the researcher is forced by administrative or ethical constraints to ask subjects to participate, or when some subjects who are identified by random selection refuse to participate. The need to call for volunteers is not uncommon in educational research, particularly in the areas of educational psychology and counseling. Research has indicated, however, that volunteers differ from nonvolunteers in a number of ways.

Rosenthal and Rosnow (1975) studied the ways in which volunteers differ from nonvolunteers. They expressed considerable confidence in twelve of the conclusions of their study:

1. Volunteers tend to be better educated than nonvolunteers, especially when personal contact between the investigator and the respondent is not required.

2. Volunteers tend to have higher social-class status than nonvolunteers, especially when social class is defined by the respondent's own status rather than by parental status.

3. Volunteers tend to be more intelligent than nonvolunteers when volunteering is for research in general, but not when volunteering is for somewhat less typical types of research such as hypnosis, sensory isolation, sex research, small-group and personality research.

4. Volunteers tend to display a greater need for social approval than nonvolunteers.

5. Volunteers tend to be more sociable than nonvolunteers.

6. Volunteers tend to be more arousal-seeking than nonvolunteers, especially when volunteering is for studies involving stress, sensory isolation, or hypnosis.

7. Volunteers tend to be more unconventional than nonvolunteers, especially when volunteering is for studies of sexual behavior.

8. Females are more likely than males to volunteer for research in general, but less likely than males to volunteer for physically or emotionally stressful research (e.g., research involving electric shock, high temperature, sensory deprivation, interviews about sexual behavior).

9. Volunteers tend to be less authoritarian than nonvolunteers.

10. Jews are more likely to volunteer than Protestants, and Protestants are more likely to volunteer than Roman Catholics.

11. Volunteers are more likely to be less conforming than nonvolunteers when volunteering is for research in general, but not when subjects are female and the task is relatively "clinical" (e.g., hypnosis, sleep, or counseling research).

12. Volunteers tend to be more interested in the topic under investigation than nonvolunteers. (pp. 195–197)

In this same research report, Rosenthal and Rosnow discussed ways in which researchers might induce potential subjects to volunteer. Among those ways might be included:

1. Give the potential volunteer the impression that, if included in the study, he or she would be likely to be evaluated favorably by the researcher.

2. Emphasize to potential volunteers those aspects of the study which seem likely to be of interest to them.

3. Emphasize the importance or significance of the research study.

4. Attempt to make potential volunteers feel good about themselves or to make them feel competent.

5. Consider offering small gifts or gratuities to potential volunteers without any requirement that they participate (volunteer) in order to receive them.

6. If appropriate and feasible, offer rewards or incentives to potential volunteers for participating in the study. (p. 197).

If the researcher is considering using a volunteer sample, he or she needs to examine the relevant differences between the characteristics of volunteers and nonvolunteers. If some one of the characteristic differences is of a type likely to have a substantial influence on the study, the researcher should not use a volunteer sample. Researchers should also examine research reports of similar studies to see if those researchers identified and discussed any confounding influences introduced through the use of a volunteer sample. Such a check of other research reports should also enable the researcher to determine ways in which other researchers have addressed or controlled for the influence of characteristic differences between volunteer and nonvolunteer samples. Researchers should also compare the characteristics of volunteers, nonvolunteers, and members of the defined population who were not selected for inclusion in the sample.

DETERMINING SAMPLE SIZE

Although there are several rather complex formulas for estimating the size of samples necessary to produce statistically reliable results, the beginning researcher is generally not seeking such mathematical guidance but is rather asking for general guidelines. The author wishes to address this desire; however, beginning researchers must recognize that as their expertise develops with experience, they should consult statisticians or statistical reference works to learn of these valuable (although at times a bit complex) formulas.

Let's begin this discussion with a general rule: *Always use the largest sample you can afford and obtain.* (Increased sample size leads to increased normality and increased conformance to population values.)

Researchers disagree on guidelines for the *minimum* number of subjects required for a study. Gay (1981) suggested that for survey research (*characteristic studies*), the sample should constitute 10 percent of the population sampled. He suggested that if the population for the survey were small (probably less than 500), 20 percent of the population should be included in the sample. Borg and Gall (1979) went further and suggested that in a survey, the smallest major subgroup should contain 100 subjects, with minor subgroups containing between twenty and fifty subjects each. Williamson, Karp, Dalphin, and Gray (1982) suggested that thirty-five to forty subjects was a minimum for most research samples, while samples of 100 or more were much more desirable. Harrison (1979) recommended that most studies use samples of thirty subjects or more but was willing to suggest that twenty subjects per group might serve as a bare minimum. Gay (1981) has suggested a minimum of thirty subjects in each group in experimental and causal-comparative studies. (The types of studies mentioned in this section will be described in detail in Chapters 9, 10, 11, and 12.)

Recognizing that the typical class of students, team of athletes, homogeneous client load of a school counselor, staff of teachers, or class of special education students may well be unlikely to contain thirty subjects, the author suggests that such guidelines be weighed against practical restrictions. In special education, a researcher may have only a small population from which to sample. A need to use cluster sampling because of administrative or other restrictions may leave an educational researcher with two classes of students to serve as his or her samples with twenty-two students in one and twenty-five in the other. Provided that they are representative of the defined population, these samples are satisfactorily large enough.

In contrast to Gay's suggestion of thirty subjects for each group in the sample for experimental and causal-comparative studies, Borg and Gall (1979) suggested a minimum of 15 subjects per group for such studies. Marken (1981) suggested that his rule of thumb was to have a minimum of ten subjects in each group in a study.

It is more important to assure that the sample is representative or typical of the population than it is to have a large sample. As mentioned earlier, researchers should define their populations and samples as carefully and completely as possible in order to document this typicality. Use of random selection processes can also help assure sample typicality. Remember, a large sample cannot overcome the invalidity and uselessness of an atypical sample.

Researchers may also be able to overcome the problem of small sample sizes by *replication* (carrying out their studies several times with similar samples drawn from the same defined population) to confirm their findings. They may further strengthen studies which use small samples by randomly assigning subjects to treatments where possible. This is often difficult in educational research, because random assignment of students to classes or to counseling treatments (or counselors) may present administrative difficulties. If cluster sampling precludes random assignment of subjects to treatments, the researcher can still employ random assignment of *groups* to treatments (usually using a coin flip or the lottery method).

There are instances, however, in which the researcher would be wise to use a larger sample. Borg and Gall (1979, pp. 194–197) suggested five such instances:

1. *When many uncontrolled variables are present in the study.* (The researcher allows randomization and normal distribution to increase the likelihood of equivalence among any groups being compared.)

2. *When small differences between or among groups or small relationships (correlations) among variables are anticipated.* (Larger numbers of subjects here help to overcome some of the statistical difficulties which often accompany small samples and may obscure significant findings.)

3. *When groups must be broken into subgroups.* (Sometimes stratified sampling is used to ensure that there will be a sufficient number of subjects in each subgroup.)

4. *When the population is highly heterogeneous (dissimilar) on the variables to be studied.* (Once again, the researcher uses the normal curve to assist in establishing equivalency between or among groups.)

5. *When reliable measures of the dependent variables are not available.* (The researcher hopes to counteract a measure of low reliability's large *error of measurement* (the probable inaccuracy of the measure) with norming properties of the larger sample.)

COMMON ERRORS IN SAMPLING

Beginning researchers (and, unfortunately, some researchers with experience who should know better) make some fairly common errors in drawing samples for their studies. A few of these more common sampling errors are listed below.

1. Selecting subjects for a sampling because they are available and it is convenient for the researcher to use them instead of selecting subjects on the basis of appropriateness in terms of the target population: If the sample is inappropriate, the findings of the study cannot be generalized.

2. Selecting subjects for groups to be compared from different populations: If the comparison between groups is invalid, the study is invalid.

3. Selecting a sample which is not typical of the population.

4. Selecting too small a sample for the research design and statistical analyses to be employed.

5. Selecting a sample which fails to meet the needs of the research design: Is a random sample needed? Is a stratified sample more appropriate? Would cluster sampling suit the situation better?

6. Using volunteers but failing to determine whether they differ from nonvolunteers on some characteristic or ability crucial to the study.

7. Selecting a sample which does not make provision for attrition and may at the end of the study prove too small.

NINE

RESEARCH STUDIES DESIGNED TO DISCLOSE DIFFERENCES

Chapter 9 discusses studies which are designed to determine if there is a significant difference in the performance of an individual group or set of groups as a result of a treatment or set of treatments administered in a research study. This discussion touches on some of the problems inherent in using each type of design presented.

A major use of educational research is to identify which specific educational treatments are most effective in producing desired changes in which specific educational settings. Such studies seek to answer questions such as Which instructional method is more effective? Is behavior modification more effective with some students than others? Under which administrative organizations do teachers teach more effectively? Which types of training benefit which types of athletes? These studies examine the effects of one or more treatments on one or more groups. At the conclusion of the studies, the researcher seeks to discover if the treatment made a difference or to determine if there is a difference between or among the performances of the groups examined.

This type of research study is usually known as an *experimental study*. Experimental studies may be of two types: *true experimental* and *quasi-experimental*. A study is assigned one label or the other on the basis of sampling and treatment assignment procedures. That is, how the subjects were selected for the study and how they were assigned to the treatments they received determine whether an experimental study is true experimental or quasi-experimental.

Subjects for the sample in a *true experimental* study are selected randomly from the population and are generally assigned to groups randomly. Random assignment of treatments to groups is also employed whenever possible. In true experiments, the researcher seeks to control as many extraneous variables as possible by using the norming properties of the normal distribution to assure equivalency between groups.

In contrast, subjects for the sample in a *quasi-experimental* study are not randomly selected from the population. They may be volunteers or they may be part of some group or groups which are available to the researcher. Regardless, the researcher is unable to select them randomly. The researcher still assigns the treatments to the groups randomly where possible. It is also possible for the researcher to use matching in quasi-experimental designs. In that case, the researcher selects the subjects either randomly or from an intact group, then pairs them on the basis of some variable or variables, and then randomly assigns one subject from each pair to one group and one subject to the other. The most frequent reason for using a quasi-experimental design is that random selection of subjects to groups was not feasible. This is often the case when the researcher works with intact classrooms of children in public schools, when administrators conduct research with the staffs they employ, or when coaches and trainers study the influence of treatments on athletic teams.

This chapter's discussion of research studies designed to disclose differences is divided according to the number of subjects or groups and variables involved. The differences studied range from those in the performance or behavior of a single individual to those designed to disclose differences among the influences of a variety of independent variables on a large number of groups.

In order to help the beginning researcher identify the type of experimental design (*true* or *quasi-*), each design is labeled. To help the researcher identify possible problems in using a particular research design, each experimental design is followed by a list of probable threats to a study using that design. The author recognizes that beginning researchers may not understand what each of these threats entails (each is described in Chapter 15). The list of threats is included here to give the researcher a central location for rapid examination of this material. In keeping with this objective, beneath each design are listed the statistical analyses most frequently employed in analyzing data from studies utilizing that design. The author has also used an outline format and as little text as possible to facilitate quick later reference. The author assumes that beginning researchers will be guided by advisors when they are first exposed to these designs and that they will consult their advisors if they have questions concerning a design or threats to a study employing that design.

STUDIES OF DIFFERENCES USING A SINGLE SUBJECT

Single-subject designs (where the researcher works with a single individual or treats an entire group as if it were a single individual) may be considered as either true experimental or quasi-experimental, depending on how the subject was selected. In practice, however, researchers seldom use these labels, which are usually employed when the researcher is considering generalizing the findings of a study to other populations. In the case of single-subject designs, such generalization is usually not intended.

Single-subject designs are employed frequently in behavior modification studies and are sometimes referred to as *individual case studies*, although this label may not be completely accurate. Many individual case studies are more descriptive than experimental. That is, they describe the behavior prior to treatment, describe the treatment administered, and describe the behavior after treatment. In contrast, single-subject experimental studies document pretreatment behaviors using measures of verifiable reliability, administer treatments over a period of time, and document behavioral changes using these same reliable measures. Additionally, they attempt to identify and control extraneous variables, often through the use of designs which incorporate replication of the pretreatment and posttreatment conditions and measures. Individual case studies usually do not employ such rigorous methodology; they concentrate instead on describing behavior and performance in an attempt to shed light on the individual or setting under study.

When to Use Single-Subject and When to Use Multisubject Designs

Researchers use *single-subject designs* when the individual is considered more important than the group in terms of findings, when the findings are not intended to be generalized, and when the study can be replicated without contamination (usually this requires tallied behaviors). Most single-subject studies deal with psychomotor behavior (physical actions which can be observed).

Researchers use *multisubject (group) designs* when the group is considered more important than the individual in terms of findings and when they intend to generalize the findings of the study to other populations. Cognitive studies (concerned with mental or intellectual performance of the subjects) and affective studies (concerned with attitudes, interests, and values of the subjects) normally employ group designs because of the contaminating influence of repeating measures in these areas as often as is required in single-subject studies.

Types of Single-Subject Designs

(*B* represents a baseline measure of the subject's behavior over a period of time and *T* represents a treatment accompanied by measurement of the dependent variable, the behavior or response under treatment.)

Single-baseline designs.

1. *B–T:* A baseline followed by a treatment. This design has low internal validity (see discussion below).

2. *B–T–B:* A baseline followed a treatment followed by a second baseline (a period of time in which the dependent variable is measured without the

influence of the treatment). This design has higher internal validity but the removal of the treatment sometimes has an adverse effect on the subject's attitudes.

3. **B–T–B–T:** A baseline followed by a treatment followed by a second baseline without treatment followed by a reinstatement of the treatment. This design is in effect a replication of a B–T study. As such, it has strong internal validity and its findings are more reliable.

Multiple-baseline designs.   In these designs the researcher identifies two or more target behaviors (dependent variables) and reliable ways to measure them and establishes a baseline for these behaviors. A treatment is then administered with one baseline variable incorporated. Once the measurements have indicated that the treatment is influencing this baseline variable, a second variable is incorporated. A third variable may be incorporated once measurements have indicated that the treatment is influencing the second variable. See Figure 9-1.

Fig. 9-1.   A three-behavior multiple-baseline study.

In multiple baseline studies, the behaviors to be influenced by the treatment must be independent of one another. That is, the treatment must be able to influence one behavior without having an effect on another of the behaviors to be studied which has yet to be exposed to the treatment.

Validity in Single-Subject Designs

Internal validity.   In single-subject studies, internal validity is addressed through:

1. Attention to reliability of observations.
2. Repeated measurement (usually of one targeted behavior).
3. Use of standardized and reliable measurement instruments.
4. Exact descriptions of the conditions and treatments of the study.
5. Establishing baseline data on the frequency and stability of the occurrence of the targeted behavior at the beginning of the study.
6. Use of measures spaced throughout the study to permit accurate statistical analysis and interpretation.

External validity.   In single-subject studies, external validity is addressed through:

1. Designs which replicate baseline and posttreatment conditions and measures.

2. Careful description of treatments and of the characteristics of the subject.
3. Precise description of the procedures used to measure the behavior.
4. Discussion of extraneous variables and of their possible influence on the study's findings.
5. Replication of the study using comparable baselines.

(For a discussion of threats to a study's validity, see Chapter 15.)

Statistical Analyses Employed

1. Multiple *t*-tests for correlated means.
2. Time-series analysis.

(See Chapter 17 for descriptions of these analyses.)

STUDIES OF DIFFERENCES USING GROUPS

This section will first discuss studies which attempt to disclose a difference between the pretreatment and posttreatment performance of a single group. It will then examine true experimental (random selection of subjects) difference studies involving two or more groups and quasi-experimental (nonrandom selection of subjects) difference studies involving two or more groups. The next section will discuss difference studies which involve more than one independent variable.

In these discussions, O will be used to represent an observation (or measure) of a dependent variable and X will be used to represent a treatment. Thus $O \ X \ O$ would stand for a pretreatment observation or measure followed by a treatment, followed by a posttreatment measure or observation. $O \ O$ would represent two observations separated in time but with no treatment administered between them.

Single-Group Designs

Weakest Design: *One-shot case study:*

$X \ O$

PROCEDURE:

1. Randomly selected (true) or intact (quasi-) group of subjects.
2. Treatment followed by posttest.

COMMENTS:

This is a nearly worthless design, infested with more threats to validity than are acceptable to serious researchers. It is almost impossible to attribute the results of the posttreatment measure to the treatment because there is no way of knowing if there was any difference between the pretreatment and posttreatment performance of the group.

Weak Design: *One-group pretest–posttest*:

O X O

PROCEDURE:

1.   Randomly selected (true) or intact (quasi-) group of subjects.
2.   Pretest followed by treatment followed by posttest.

STATISTICAL ANALYSIS:

Comparison of pretest and posttest means using the *t*-test for correlated means.

MOST PROBABLE THREATS TO INTERNAL VALIDITY:

1.   History: Any change in mean scores may be due to the influence of events other than the treatment.
2.   Maturation: The change in mean scores might have occurred as a result of physical or psychological development even if no treatment had been administered.
3.   Testing: The subjects may have become better test takers as a result of taking the pretest.
4.   Instrumentation: Any change in mean scores may be a result of unreliable measurements or of changes in observers or measurement instruments.

THREATS TO EXTERNAL VALIDITY REQUIRING PARTICULAR ATTENTION:

1.   Experimentally accessible population versus target population.
2.   Interaction of sample and treatment.
3.   Multiple treatments.
4.   Experimenter effect.
5.   Pretest sensitization.
6.   Posttest sensitization.
7.   Measurement of the dependent variable.

COMMENTS:

Since there is no comparison group in this design, it is difficult to control for the influences of extraneous variables. This design is useful only in studying relatively stable variables which are unlikely to change without treatment. It should not be used where the variable under study is unstable or where maturational influences are present, since these factors might account for any changes measured. It is wisest to keep the interval between pretest and posttest short in order to minimize the influence of extraneous variables and the influence of history. If you can get a control group, you strengthen this design infinitely, since you can then use the pretest–posttest control group design described later in this chapter.

Stronger Design: Time-series design:

$$O \ldots O \; X \; O \ldots O$$

PROCEDURE:

1. Usually no random selection of subjects (quasi-experimental).
2. Only one group involved.
3. Dependent variable measured periodically.
4. Experimental treatment administered between two of these measures.
5. Same instrument or criterion used in each measurement.

MOST PROBABLE THREATS TO INTERNAL VALIDITY:

1. History: Any change in group scores may be due to events other than the treatment and might have occurred even if no treatment had been administered.
2. Testing: With such frequent measurement, subjects could become familiar with the measure employed, and this familiarity or experience could produce any findings.
3. Instrumentation: Unreliability in observation, measurement, or scoring could account for any observed differences in performance.

THREATS TO EXTERNAL VALIDITY REQUIRING PARTICULAR ATTENTION:

1. All three forms of *population validity*.
2. Multiple treatments.

3. Pretest sensitization.
4. Posttest sensitization.
5. Measurement of the dependent variable.

COMMENTS:

The time-series design is useful when it is not possible to form a control group and when it is possible to measure subjects' performance repeatedly using the same instrument. Observation proves a useful measurement device in such studies, particularly if it merely records the frequency of a behavior. In such a case, observations do not lead generally to pretest sensitization or testing threats, as would many forms of tests. Frequency-count observation is desirable because it can be performed with a very high degree of reliability.

True Experimental Control-Group Designs

In these designs the researcher uses a *control group* (or groups) as a standard against which to compare the influence of the treatment on the *experimental group*. The control group receives either no treatment or the treatment normally administered. The experimental group receives the treatment whose influence on the group's performance the researcher is seeking to determine. Researchers sometimes do not use a "formal" control group. They use several experimental groups as control groups for comparing the groups' relative performances to one another. The *R* which precedes representations (using *O* and *X*) of these designs indicates that subjects were selected randomly.

Pretest–posttest control-group design:

RO X O
RO   O

PROCEDURE:

1. Subjects are selected randomly and assigned randomly to groups.
2. Both experimental and control groups are pretested.
3. Experimental group receives new treatment.
4. Control group receives no treatment or the normal treatment.
5. Both groups are posttested.

STATISTICAL ANALYSIS:

1. Comparison of posttest means using the *t*-test for independent samples. This is the most frequently employed statistical analysis.

2. Analysis of covariance using pretest scores to adjust posttest scores (optional). Covariance is employed if the researcher finds or suspects significant initial differences between groups.

3. Comparison of mean pretest-posttest gains using a *t*-test for change scores. The analyses listed above are preferable to this one. (The reasons will be discussed in Chapter 17.)

MOST PROBABLE THREATS TO INTERNAL VALIDITY:

None.

THREATS TO EXTERNAL VALIDITY REQUIRING PARTICULAR ATTENTION:

1. Experimentally accessible population versus target population.
2. Interaction of sample and treatment.
3. Multiple treatments.
4. Experimenter effect.
5. Pretest sensitization.
6. Posttest sensitization.
7. Measurement of the dependent variable.

COMMENTS:

This is a strong design which uses randomization to control for the influence of extraneous variables, since researchers assume their influence on the two groups to be equivalent. With samples of 100 or more subjects (50 subjects in each group), random selection generally assures equivalence between groups. With smaller groups, the researcher can examine the groups for differences. If relevant differences are found, analysis of covariance can be used to control for initial differences. If concerned that the pretest may have influenced the experimental treatment, the researcher may use the *posttest-only control-group design* (see below) or the *Solomon four-group design* (see pages 75–76).

POSTTEST-ONLY CONTROL-GROUP DESIGN:

R   XO
R   O

PROCEDURE:

1. Subjects are selected randomly and assigned to groups randomly.
2. One group receives the experimental treatment while the other receives no treatment or the normal treatment.
3. Both groups are posttested.

STATISTICAL ANALYSIS:

Comparison of posttest means using t-test for independent samples. If more than two groups are involved, analysis of variance is employed.

MOST PROBABLE THREATS TO INTERNAL VALIDITY:

1. Experimental mortality: Having no pretest score for each subject, the researcher is unable to control statistically for subjects who drop out of the study. If more subjects in one group are lost than in another or if there is a pattern of the type of subject lost, this may be a serious threat.

THREATS TO EXTERNAL VALIDITY REQUIRING PARTICULAR ATTENTION:

1. Experimentally accessible versus target population.
2. Interaction of sample and treatment.
3. Multiple treatments.
4. Experimenter effect.
5. Posttest sensitization.
6. Measure of the dependent variable.

COMMENTS:

The posttest-only control-group design is often used when the researcher is unable to locate an appropriate pretest or when there is a concern that the pretest might sensitize subjects. There is some concern that if initial differences between groups still exist after randomization, they will go undetected and may actually explain any differences in posttest scores between the two groups. To control for this concern, the researcher should work with as large a sample as possible, since increased sample size increases normality of distribution and should minimize initial differences. Another concern is that without pretest scores, the researcher cannot form subgroups to examine differential effects of the treatment. Lastly, since the researcher does not have pretest scores, he or she cannot verify that experimental mortality (subjects dropping out of the study) drew comparable subjects from each group. If the researcher anticipates the possibility of substantial loss of subjects to attrition, he or she should avoid this design.

Solomon four-group design:

```
RO  X  O
RO     O
R   X  O
R
```

PROCEDURE:

1. Randomly selected subjects are randomly assigned to four groups.
2. Two of these groups are pretested and two are not.
3. One pretested group and one nonpretested group receive the experimental treatment.
4. The other two groups receive no treatment or the usual treatment.
5. All four groups are posttested.

STATISTICAL ANALYSIS:

The most frequently performed analysis is a 2×2 factorial analysis of variance of the posttest means of the four groups. Huck and Sandler (1973) suggested, however, that analysis of covariance is perhaps a stronger statistical tool.

MOST PROBABLE THREATS TO INTERNAL VALIDITY:

None.

THREATS TO EXTERNAL VALIDITY REQUIRING PARTICULAR ATTENTION:

1. Experimentally accessible versus target population.
2. Interaction of sample and treatment.
3. Multiple treatments.
4. Posttest sensitization.
5. Measure of the dependent variable.

COMMENTS:

This is a very powerful design which controls for most threats to validity. Its major drawbacks are the requirement of a larger-than-usual sample (generally, a minimum of fifteen subjects per group and a total sample of at least sixty subjects) and substantial coordination responsibilities for the researcher. Usually this design is used only when the researcher hypothesizes that the pretest has an influence on the treatment and wishes to test that hypothesis.

Quasi-Experimental Control-Group Designs

The dashed line which separates representations (using *O* and *X*) of the designs indicates that the design uses intact groups. In the case of the one design below which uses matching of subjects in groups, *MAT* is used in the representation to illustrate this fact.

STATIC-GROUP COMPARISON:

$$\underline{X}\ \underline{O}$$
$$O$$

PROCEDURE:

1. No random selection of subjects (intact groups).
2. Treatment to one group only.
3. Posttest to both groups.

STATISTICAL ANALYSIS:

Comparison of posttest means using a Mann-Whitney *U*-test.

MOST PROBABLE THREATS TO INTERNAL VALIDITY:

1. Differential selection: Groups may have differences at start of study which account for differences in posttest means.
2. Experimental mortality: Without pretest scores, the researcher cannot control statistically for lost subjects.
3. Selection interactions: If differences between two groups exist at start, these may interact with the treatment to produce misleading findings.

4. Interaction of previous testing and selection: What the difference in posttest means may measure is differences in testing experience which occurred prior to the treatment.

THREATS TO EXTERNAL VALIDITY REQUIRING PARTICULAR ATTENTION:

1. All three forms of population validity.
2. Multiple treatents.
3. Experimenter effect.
4. Posttest sensitization.
5. Measure of the dependent variable.

COMMENTS:

Without a pretest and without the "protection" of randomization, this design is open to a large number of threats. Employing a pretest for both groups, as described below, strengthens this design appreciably.

NONEQUIVALENT CONTROL-GROUP DESIGN:

$$\frac{O \; X \; O}{O \quad\;\; O}$$

PROCEDURE:

1. No random selection of subjects (intact groups).
2. Pretest both groups.
3. Treatment to one group only.
4. Posttest both groups.

STATISTICAL ANALYSIS:

Analysis of covariance using pretest scores to serve as adjustment for individual differences, permitting equivalent posttest mean comparison.

MOST PROBABLE THREAT TO INTERNAL VALIDITY:

1. Differential selection and selection interactions: Lack of randomization makes these interactions possible.

THREATS TO EXTERNAL VALIDITY REQUIRING PARTICULAR ATTENTION:

1. All three forms of population validity.

2. Multiple treatments.

3. Experimenter effect.

4. Pretest sensitization.

5. Posttest sensitization.

6. Measure of the dependent variable.

COMMENTS:

This is one of the most frequently used designs in educational research. It is often chosen because researchers can use intact classes of students, teams of athletes, or groups of counselees where randomization would be impractical or where educational officials would be unreceptive to the demands of randomization. Some researchers minimize *selection* threats by preliminary matching (somewhat helpful), by random assignment of classrooms to groups with the use of class means in later analysis (more helpful), and by use of covariance analysis to make posttest scores comparable (most helpful).

Pretest–posttest control-group design with matching:

MAT O X O
MAT O   O

PROCEDURE:

1. Administer the instrument (pretest) designed to produce scores to be used in matching.

2. Match subjects in pairs on the basis of the scores obtained on the matching measure.

3. Randomly assign one member of each pair to one group (usually by a coin flip) and assign the remaining member to the opposite group.

4. Administer the experimental treatment to one group and administer no treatment or the normal treatment to the control group.

5. Posttest both groups on the dependent variable.

STATISTICAL ANALYSIS:

Comparison of mean posttest scores using *t*-test for independent samples or Mann-Whitney *U* test. Analysis of covariance using pretest scores to adjust for initial differences may also be employed.

MOST PROBABLE THREATS TO INTERNAL VALIDITY:

1. Differential selection: If the matching results in differences between the two groups, any difference in posttest means may be attributable to these initial differences.

2. Selection interactions: If differences do exist between groups, these may interact differentially to produce misleading findings.

3. Interaction of previous testing and selection: Since test scores are used in matching, if some subjects have more experience with testing, this may result in differential measurement and inaccurate matching.

THREATS TO EXTERNAL VALIDITY REQUIRING PARTICULAR ATTENTION:

1. All three types of population validity.

2. Multiple interactions.

3. Experimenter effect.

4. Pretest sensitization.

5. Posttest sensitication.

6. Measurement of the dependent variable.

COMMENTS:

Matching is used in an attempt to insure that the two groups contain comparable subjects. Subjects are matched on scores received on a pretest measure of the dependent variable or of variables which correlate with the dependent variable. The researcher hopes that matching will reduce initial differences between subjects in the two groups. Matching is used here to replace the covariance analysis which would be used in the random-selection-and-assignment version of this design, which is described above. Matching is used most frequently when working with small samples and with small anticipated differences. It is also useful to researchers in helping them to make subsample divisions. Accurate matching calls for high correlations between the variable or (preferably) variables used in matching and the dependent variable. A concern here is the loss of subjects due to inability to find a match. One possible solution is to rank-order subjects, to pick the top two, to assign one randomly to one group and the other to the other group, to go on to the next pair of subjects, and so forth.

COUNTERBALANCED DESIGNS:

$$\underline{X_1O} \quad \underline{X_2O} \quad \underline{X_3O}$$
$$\underline{X_3O} \quad \underline{X_1O} \quad \underline{X_2O}$$
$$X_2O \quad X_3O \quad X_1O$$

(Subscripts indicate different treatments.)

PROCEDURE:

1. Nonrandom groups.
2. Same set of experimental treatments administered to each group but in different order of primacy, although sequence is generally retained.
3. Measure all groups on dependent variable after each treatment.

STATISTICAL ANALYSIS:

Modified analysis of variance.

MOST PROBABLE THREATS TO INTERNAL VALIDITY:

None.

THREATS TO EXTERNAL VALIDITY REQUIRING PARTICULAR ATTENTION:

1. All three forms of population validity.
2. Multiple treatments.

3. Measure of the dependent variable.

COMMENTS:

Interactive effects of multiple treatments are a major source of concern here. In order to employ this research design, the researcher must assure that one treatment does not affect performance in or after a successive treatment.

DIFFERENCE STUDIES INVOLVING MORE THAN ONE INDEPENDENT VARIABLE

The studies discussed to this point are designed to disclose a difference between two or more groups relative to a single independent variable (treatment). Sometimes researchers wish to compare more than two treatments. Other times they may wish to examine the influence of one or more treatments on different subpopulations (for example, examining how a treatment affects males as compared with its effect upon females). When researchers wish to make such comparisons, they use *factorial designs*.

Factorial designs are merely extensions of several of the designs presented earlier, principally the Solomon four-group, the random pretest–posttest control-group, the random posttest-only control-group, and the nonequivalent control-group designs. Whether a factorial design is true or quasi-experimental depends upon whether the sample was chosen using random selection methods. Factorial designs permit the researcher to test several hypotheses simultaneously. Factorial designs are described by the number of *cells* they contain (for example, "2 × 2", "2 × 3"). The first number in this numeric cell description for a factorial design represents the number of *rows*, the second the number of *columns*. Each example of factorial design presented below is labeled with its numeric cell description. Among the types of variables whose influence researchers might compare using factorial designs are included:

1. Various teaching, training, therapy, or organizational methods assigned by the researcher (for example, comparing the effectiveness of three teaching methods with males and with females).

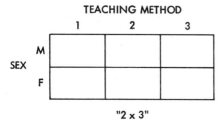

"2 x 3"

Fig. 9–A

2. Subject area or aspects of the educational schedule or organization which are manipulated by the researcher when the assignment of treatments is not random (for example, comparing business majors, education majors, and liberal arts majors on verbal and quantitative achievement).

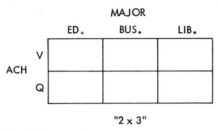

Fig. 9-B

3. Aspects of the educational setting or clientele [for example, community, school, socioeconomic status (SES)] which cannot be controlled by the researcher but which can serve as a basis for stratification and can be examined and "manipulated" statistically (for example, comparing high- and low-SES students on attitude change following a political speech either favoring or opposing a national welfare system).

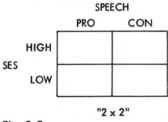

Fig. 9-C

4. Physical characteristics of the subject (height, weight, age, sex) which cannot in any real sense be manipulated, but which the researcher may examine ("manipulate") statistically (for example, comparing the attitudes toward exercise of people whose weight is above and people whose weight is below the national

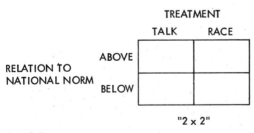

Fig. 9-D

mean for their sex, size, and age after half of each group of people have participated in a relay race and half have listened to a talk on the need for fitness).

5.   Responses or performances of subjects (test scores) which may be used to manipulate data and thereby "manipulate" variables statistically. In most cases above, the cells (squares) in the factorial designs would also be filled with such response scores. That is, subjects' performance on tests frequently serve as dependent variables as well.

For example, consider comparing the grade-point averages of students who have differing levels of anxiety as measured by a standardized test and whose IQ scores are rated as either high, middle, or low:

Fig. 9-E

Researchers must bear in mind, as discussed in Chapter 3, that studies should be designed not to determine if treatments influence *scores* but rather to determine if those treatments influence the *variables* which are *represented* by scores. When conducting research studies which use factorial designs employing test scores as both independent and dependent variables, researchers sometimes lose sight of this important distinction. Scores are *representations* of some variable and may or may not be accurate or reliable representations. The concept of instrument validity is discussed in Chapter 14.

Statistical Analyses Employed with Factorial Designs

1.   The most frequently employed statistical analysis is multiple analysis of variance.

2.   If the researcher wishes to control for possible initial differences between or among groups, he or she may employ multiple analysis of covariance.

3.   A variety of other multivariate analyses may be employed, including factor analysis, cluster analysis, and discriminant function analysis. Descriptions of these analyses are not given in this book but may be found in any good statistics textbook.

MOST PROBABLE THREATS TO INTERNAL VALIDITY:

If Quasi-Experimental:

1. Differential selection.
2. Selection interactions.

If True Experimental:

None.

THREATS TO EXTERNAL VALIDITY REQUIRING PARTICULAR ATTENTION:

If Quasi-Experimental:

1. All three forms of population validity.
2. Multiple treatments.
3. Experimenter effect.
4. Pretest sensitization.
5. Posttest sensitization.
6. Measurement of the dependent variable.

If True Experimental:

1. Experimentally accessible population versus target population.
2. Interaction of sample and treatment.
3. Multiple treatments.
4. Experimenter effect.
5. Pretest sensitization.
6. Posttest sensitization.
7. Measurement of the dependent variable.

METHODS OFTEN EMPLOYED IN STUDIES TO DISCLOSE DIFFERENCES

In order to infer that the findings of a difference study indicate the effect of a specific treatment, the researcher seeks to control a variety of variables to insure that the groups being compared differ as little as possible except in the treatments received. A number of methods are used in seeking this group and environmental equivalence:

1. The researcher seeks to select equivalent groups of subjects. He or she may use randomized selection, selection with precise matching, or statistical correction for initial differences among subjects to attain equivalence. Of these, by far the most reliable and effective method is randomized selection.

2. The researcher seeks to standardize the conditions under which the treatments are administered. This may entail controlling elements of the physical environment (for example, temperature, light, noise levels), or aspects of the administration of the treatment (for example, through use of tape recorders, printed materials as opposed to individually prepared materials, or staff training to help those conducting the study present the treatment more homogeneously).

3. The researcher seeks to attain equivalence in measurement of the dependent variable. This entails standardized procedures for observation and testing. If the study employs observers, it entails observer training and calculation of interobserver reliability coefficients. It entails also standardized procedures for recording and scoring measurements.

4. The researcher seeks to use statistical procedures which compare groups equivalently. Tests of significance and tests of homogeneity of variance may be employed to determine if groups are equivalent. Subdivision of sample groups, stratified analysis, or partial correlation may be used to identify and compare equivalent subsample groups. Differential analysis (see p. 93) may also be employed, as may analysis of variance or factorial analysis.

5. The researcher uses probability levels to insure against accepting conclusions of equivalence or of effect without consideration for the influence of chance. In practice, this means that researchers usually reject findings which have more than a five in one hundred probability of occurring by chance. They accomplish this by establishing the .05 level as their goal *before* beginning an experimental study.

TEN

STUDIES DESIGNED TO IDENTIFY RELATIONSHIPS OR MAKE PREDICTIONS

This chapter discusses studies which are designed to help researchers identify relationships among variables and, if desired, to use knowledge of the strength of those relationships to make predictions. Variables which share a relationship with one another are said to be *correlated*. Correlated variables vary in direct relation to one another.

The relationship between two correlated variables (usually referred to as their *correlation*) is expressed by a number known as a *correlation coefficient*. Correlation coefficients may be as large as +1.0 or as small as −1.0. The positive or negative sign indicates the nature of their relationship. If the coefficient is positive, that means that when one variable gets larger, so does the other variable. If the coefficient is negative, that means that when one variable gets larger, the other gets smaller.

A correlation coefficient of 1.0 (either positive or negative) is extraordinarily rare. Such a coefficient would indicate a perfect relationship. That is, if one variable increased by .00001, so would the other variable. In real life, such perfect relationships very seldom occur.

A correlation coefficient of 0 indicates that there is no relationship between the variables whose comparative variations it describes. This means that although the variables vary, there is no relationship among their variations. When one variable gets larger, the other variable stands equal chances of getting larger, getting smaller, or staying the same.

Many researchers describe correlational studies (to identify relationships or make predictions) as *descriptive studies*. They do so because it is not possible to say with any measure of certainty that two variables which are highly correlated (that is, have a large correlation coefficient) also have a *causal* relationship. Correlation does not insure that a causal relationship exists. While a correlation between two variables X and Y may suggest that variable X determines the size of variable Y or vice versa, it may also suggest that variable Z determines both variable X and variable Y *or that* variable X and variable Y share common elements which account for the correlation. This latter case is known as *artifactual causality*.

To illustrate, let's consider a pair or variables which which might be positively correlated: body weight and shoe size. Despite their strong positive correlation, we cannot say that body weight *causes* shoe size or that shoe size *causes* body weight. Both are caused by some other variable or variables (such as genes, diet, or health conditions as a child).

This does not mean that correlations cannot often *suggest* causality. There is most probably a high correlation between practice in playing tennis and the frequency with which a player who hits the ball gets it over the net and inside the appropriate boundaries of the opponent's court. The difficulty in attributing causality to a correlation lies not in whether causality exists, but rather in whether the researcher can demonstrate a scientific basis for attributing causality. In order to demonstrate such a scientific basis, the researcher generally must conduct a *difference study* (as described in the previous chapter) which illustrates that, if the highly correlated variable which the researcher considers causal were not present or were present to a smaller degree, the behavior, performance, or response which the researcher believes it causes would be influenced in a way indicated or predicted by the correlation. Similarly, in the case of predictions made on the basis of correlations, researchers usually conduct difference studies to confirm the accuracy and reliability of the predictions made.

Studies designed to identify relationships are often termed *prestudies* or *pilot studies*, since researchers frequently use the findings as a basis for later studies using difference-study designs. Similarly, correlation is often employed as a part of other types of studies to describe relationships among variables.

PROCEDURES IN RELATIONSHIP OR PREDICTION STUDIES

Theoretical Foundations

The researcher needs first to identify variables which may be causally related to the behavior or pattern of behavior to be examined or predicted. The researcher usually finds that the three sources most useful in identifying these variables are the review of the literature, personal experiences, and thoughtful reflection. Whenever possible, you should attempt to bring all three sources to bear on a problem. Avoid using the *shotgun approach*, which measures a wide variety of variables without a basis in theory but rather in hopes of getting lucky.

The shotgun approach may disclose significant relationships, but you are usually then at a loss as to how to explain them or consider causality, since you are not acquainted with their theoretical foundations. Working backward from findings to theoretical foundations is difficult and often unreliable, since knowledge of findings frequently compromises the researcher's objectivity in considering the relationship of findings to theory.

Sampling

Using one of the sampling procedures described in Chapter 8, the researcher next selects subjects for whom measures of the desired variables can be obtained. If you anticipate examining various subsamples to determine whether stronger relationships exist for these subsamples, then you may wish to employ stratified sampling procedures.

Collecting Data

Using measures of known reliability and validity, the researcher needs to collect quantifiable data on the selected subjects. Reliability and validity of measurement instruments are discussed in Chapter 14. Researchers frequently use standardized tests, questionnaires, interviews, or observational techniques to collect data on the subjects. In prediction studies you need to confirm that the measures you select measure the specific behavioral pattern or performance you hope to predict. You also need to insure that *predictor variables* are measured *prior to* measurement of the variables which they are purported to predict.

Analyzing Data

The researcher next analyzes the data using appropriate statistical analyses, as described in the next section. In general, in relationship studies this entails calculation of correlation coefficients and statistical testing of their significance. In prediction studies this often involves the additional steps of conducting *multiple-regression analysis* to determine which predictor variables may be combined to enhance their predictive power. Sometimes researchers also employ *moderator* or *differential analysis*, in which they examine correlations or predictive power of correlations among subgroups of the total sample.

Once you have calculated a correlation coefficient, you should determine if it is statistically significant. The formula for this calculation is supplied below (see p. 91). Many researchers then examine the *standard error of estimate, coefficient of determination*, and *coefficient of predictive efficiency* (if the study is a prediction study) for their correlation coefficients. The formulas for these calculations are also presented below (see pp. 93–94).

Interpreting Findings

Once data are analyzed using appropriate tests, researchers must consider how to interpret them. You need a clearly stated conceptual base to which to relate the findings. You need to consider whether the measures of the behavior or attitude were conceptually sound and what the conceptual base permits you to say about the findings. In prediction studies you must further consider the practical and ethical concerns involved in applying predictive results in the schools: Will a student be denied access to a program on the basis of predictive scores? Will such scores be used to determine assignment to specific classes, courses, or vocational programs? Will teacher or staff hirings or job assignments be predicated upon these scores?

The question of interpreting findings is made more difficult by the problem of causal attribution, which was discussed earlier. If a researcher wishes to attribute causality to a variable, that variable must meet certain conditions.

1. The variable must be related to the occurrence of the behavior or trait predicted or to a variable evidencing the behavior or trait in the subjects (variable X must be correlated with variable Y).

2. The variable suggested as the cause must precede the behavior or trait in time (X must come before Y).

3. There must be a reasonable theoretical and conceptual foundation for attributing causality to a variable.

4. Plausible alternative causes for the occurrence of the behavior or trait must have been considered and rejected. (*Alternative hypotheses* or *strong inferences* must have been evaluated and rejected.)

In evaluating statistically significant correlation coefficients, researchers employ a variety of criteria. The author has synthesized the suggestions of several researchers and his own experiences to create the following general guidelines for evaluating correlation coefficients. These guidelines apply equally to both positive and negative correlations, since the plus or minus sign merely indicates the nature of the direction of the relationship described. Note that the correlation coefficient is represented by the letter r. Statisticians often use the letter r to represent a correlation coefficient in calculations or findings. It may help to think of the r as standing for *relationship* among variables or for *reliability* of predictions or scores. A correlation coefficient of $+.72$, by whatever formula calculated, might therefore be represented as $r = +.72$. The r is sometimes subscripted. That is, sometimes there are letters or numbers written half a line lower and to the right of the r. Thus, r_{xy} might stand for the correlation between variables x and y, and $r_{1 \cdot 2}$ might represent a correlation between variables 1 and 2.

Guidelines for evaluating correlation coefficients:

$r < .20$ A very slight relationship which is of little use.

$.20 \leq r \leq .40$ A slight relationship which might be useful in prestudies to indicate more specific directions for later studies. Correlations of this size are almost useless in predictive studies.

$.40 < r \leq .65$ A modest relationship which is usually statistically significant. In prediction studies, correlations of this size are frequently used in multiple-regression analysis to ''add up'' to a reasonably reliable prediction. Taken individually for predicting *individual* performance, correlations in this range are not generally very useful. For predicting *group* performance, coefficients between .50 and .65 may serve as crude predictors.

$.65 < r < .85$ A marked, fairly reliable relationship which is useful for fairly accurate group prediction. As the correlation coefficient nears .85, the reliability of the relationship and its predictive power increase greatly.

$r \geq .85$ A very high, very dependable relationship, generally reliable in both individual and group prediction. It is unusual, however, to find coefficients of this magnitude in educational prediction studies.

STATISTICAL ANALYSES EMPLOYED IN RELATIONSHIP AND PREDICTION STUDIES

Correlation Coefficients

There are many types of correlation coefficients, and each employs a different set of calculations involving the data. The most frequently employed coefficient is the *Pearson product-moment correlation coefficient*, which is described in detail in Chapter 17. This coefficient is used when both variables to be correlated can be expressed as scores on continuous interval scales—that is, when the interval between any two adjacent scores on the measurement scale is the same (for example, in the metric scale for weight, where the difference between 1 and 2 kg is 1 kg and the difference between 524 and 525 kg is also 1 kg).

Another frequently employed correlation coefficient is the *Spearman rank-order coefficient*. It is used when the variables to be correlated are both expressed as rank-ordered (or *ordinal*) scores. If a researcher wished to correlate the top 10 scores on one test with the top ten on another, he or she would employ a Spear-man rank-order coefficient (also known as Spearman's *rho* coefficient).

A third correlation coefficient which researchers sometimes use is the *contingency coefficient* (sometimes called *C* coefficient). It is employed when the data are divided into three or more categories. This coefficient is used in a chi-square calculation (see Chapter 17).

Significance of a Correlation Coefficient

Researchers usually wish to confirm that the correlation coefficients they got differed significantly from a correlation coefficient 0 (no relationship). That is, chance sampling of scores did not produce the correlation coefficients they got when a correlation coefficient of 0 (no relationship) would have been more accurate. They determine the significance of the difference between the obtained coefficient and the no-relationship coefficient using a formula. Presented below is the formula for testing the significance of a Pearson product-moment correlation coefficient. The formula for determining the significance of a Spearman rank-order coefficient is presented on pages 174–75.

$$t = \frac{r \times \sqrt{n-2}}{\sqrt{1-r^2}}$$ where t = the test value to be compared to table values

r = the correlation coefficient

n = the number of pairs of scores which were correlated.

Assume that you calculated a Pearson product-moment coefficient for 18 pairs of subjects and got an r of $+.8$. Inserting those values into this formula would produce:

$$t = \frac{.8 \times \sqrt{18-2}}{\sqrt{1-.64}} = \frac{.8 \times \sqrt{16}}{\sqrt{.36}} = \frac{.8 \times 4}{.6}$$

$$= \frac{3.2}{.6} = 5.33$$

You would then consult a *t*-table using the formula $n-2$ to tell you which row of the table to use. (The results of this formula are often referred to as the *degrees of freedom* or *df* of the test.) You would compare your value to the values in that *row*. Researchers generally look under the .05 and .01 significance-levels columns in the table and locate the values listed in the intersections of these *columns* and the degrees-of-freedom *row*. If the value you got is equal to or larger than these values, you judge your correlation coefficient to be significantly different from zero.

In the example above, the degrees-of-freedom formula produces 16. At the intersection of the *16 df row* and the *.01* and *.05* significance-levels *columns*, you will find the values 1.746 and 2.583, respectively. The *t*-value that you got (5.33) is larger than either of these values, so you can conclude that your correlation coefficient is significantly different from a coefficient of no relationship.

It is important, however, to recognize that just as correlation does not confirm causality, statistical significance does not insure that a correlation is of any practical value in everyday applications. With large samples, a low correlation may prove statistically significant but be of little value in practical application. Concerns about practical applicability should always override statistical concerns.

Correlation Involving More Than Two Variables

Sometimes the researcher wishes to examine the relationships among three or more variables. This may involve a variety of types of calculations. A few of the more commonly used types are described below.

Multiple correlation.   Each variable is correlated with every other variable and coefficients are determined.

Multiple regression.   Each variable is correlated with the *criterion* (or *predicted*) variable and all other variables. Then the combination of predictor variables which makes the best prediction is selected. *Stepwise multiple regression* (the most frequently used form) selects the predictor variable which correlates most highly with the criterion variable, next selects the predictor variables which increase this correlation significantly, and finally lists them in order of the increase in predictive power which each contributes. In working with predictive measures with repeated sampling, researchers often observe the influence of *shrinkage,* the tendency of the predictive value of a test to be lower when used on samples other than the one on which it was originally calculated. Shrinkage is a normal occurrence and is, in fact, desirable, since it reflects the increased normality of the distribution of predictive values in relation to the target population.

Discriminant analysis.   This is a type of multivariate (more than one variable) analysis similar to multiple regression. Multiple regression is used when the criterion variable is a continuous score (on an interval scale—recall our earlier discussion of continuous scores and our example using measures of weight. For further discussion, see p. 146). Discriminant analysis is used when the predicted variable is one of several categories which identify discrete (separate) groups. The criterion (or predicted) variable in discriminant analysis is membership in a group of individuals with a similar characteristic (for example, sex, profession, level of achievement, age).

Factor analysis.   Variables are grouped on the basis of intercorrelations to form a limited number of factors which can then be examined and their relationships to the criterion variable explored. Factor analysis begins with the calculation of a *correlation matrix* which relates every variable in the study to every other variable in the study. Factor analysis then clusters variables which are intercorrelated and determines the *loading* (correlation coefficient) of each variable on that factor. *Factor scores* represent the combined score/performance of each subject on that cluster of variables (factor). Such factor scores may be compared and analyzed statistically, but only with extreme care.

Differential analysis.   *Subgroup analysis in relationship studies* involves creating subsample groups which are relatively homogeneous on one variable. The researcher examines whether the performance of these subgroups correlates more highly with the criterion variable than does the performance of the entire sample. If it does, you can draw inferences about the influence of the variable on which the subsample was homogeneous.

Moderator variables in predictive studies are identified and analyzed using a procedure similar to the one described above. To identify moderator variables which appear to influence the predictive value of a score in relation to the criterion variable, usually you first identify a characteristic of the subject or a score attained by the subject on some measure which seems to influence the predictive value of other variables, and then you use this knowledge to help you interpret the predictive validity of a measure involving those predictor variables.

Formulas Employed in Interpreting Correlation Coefficients

Researchers frequently use three formulas in determining their confidence in inferences based on correlation coefficients:

Standard error of estimate: $\sqrt{1 - r^2}$.   Used to determine the range within which will lie the actual value of a variable predicted on the basis of a correlated variable.

Coefficient of determination: r^2.   Used to determine what percentage of the variance in a variable is explained, predicted, or accounted for by the variance of another variable. For example, if the correlation coefficient for X and Y is .50, it can be said that variance in X accounts for 25 percent [$(.50)^2 \times 100\%$] of the variance in Y.

Coefficient of predictive efficiency: $1 - \sqrt{1 - r^2}$.   Used to describe the extent to which the correlation coefficient is a better estimate than chance in predicting the value of one or the other variable whose relationship r describes. The resultant figure is normally expressed as a percentage. Thus with an r of .50, one variable is 13.4 percent better than chance at predicting the value of its correlated variable. With an r of .87, that variable becomes more than 50 percent better than chance.

ELEVEN

STUDIES DESIGNED TO IDENTIFY AND DESCRIBE THE CHARACTERISTICS OF THE PRESENT

This chapter discusses the use of survey and observation to obtain information regarding the characteristics of a sample drawn from a population. It examines relative advantages of different techniques for gathering data, as well as possible areas of difficulty.

Another major purpose of educational research is to examine and describe individuals, groups, situations, or conditions of interest to the researcher. These studies seek to identify the specific *characteristics* which *describe* the topic under study, and so they are called *characteristic studies* or *descriptive studies*. Often they supply information which can help researchers set up *difference studies* designed to test hypotheses about the topic under scrutiny; for this reason, characteristic studies are also sometimes known as *prestudies* or *pilot studies*. The information they supply frequently contributes to the theoretical understanding of the ways in which individuals, groups, and situations operate.

The two data-gathering approaches most frequently employed in characteristic studies are *survey* and *observation*. This chapter will discuss both of these approaches as well as their specific techniques.

SURVEY

Generally researchers do not survey entire populations (such a survey is known as a *census*). Usually they use one of the techniques discussed in Chapter 8 to obtain a *sample*, which they hope will be representative of the population from which it was drawn. Researchers prefer to use *random* sampling methods and large samples, since the norming properties of the normal probability curve help assure that the sample is representative of the population.

As Williamson et al. (1982) put it, surveys seek to discover characteristics of a sample by substituting talk for action (p. 157). This substitution of response for actual observation is a two-edged sword. While it enables researchers to consider a broader range of data, it raises the possibility that some responses will be untrue. Respondents sometimes intentionally "lie" in the belief that a certain type of response will win the researcher's favorble opinion. Other times respondents "lie" because their self-esteem needs prevent them from evaluating themselves or their situations honestly (objectively). Still other times, respondents are not competent to respond, lacking either knowledge of the topic or training to make the required judgment. Such unintentional "lying" is particularly likely when respondents are asked to make judgments about events or issues about which they are uninformed or when they are asked to diagnose their own behaviors or beliefs.

Types of Surveys

Surveys are divided into two types, according to the length of time during which the researcher gathers data. If the researcher gathers data only once on a sample, such a survey is known as *cross-sectional*. If the researcher gathers data on the sample repeatedly over a period of time, the survey is known as *longitudinal*. Longitudinal surveys may be of three types: trend studies, cohort studies, and panel studies.

A *trend study* is a longitudinal survey in which the researcher draws samples repeatedly from a large general population over a period of time. You then analyze the data from each sample and compare the samples to one another to determine if there is a *trend* or pattern of change or stability in the data. Often researchers use trend studies to examine and compare changes in the beliefs, activities, levels of awareness, or demographics of the population over time. *Demographics* are characteristics of a population such as age, gender, level of educational attainment, occupation, socioeconomic status, and the like.

A *cohort study* is a longitudinal survey in which the researcher draws repeated samples from a smaller specific population over a period of time. Researchers seek in such studies to analyze the stability or change of characteristics and behaviors of this smaller group. One well-known example is the study of various samples drawn from a graduating high school class over a period of years, examining how the class' characteristics and behaviors change.

In a *panel study* the researcher gathers and analyzes data from all members of the *same* sample over a period of time. In such studies *attrition* (loss of subjects) can be a serious problem, since samples can become small and the remaining sample (panel) may no longer be representative of the original population from which it was drawn or even representative of the original complete sample of which it represents the remainder.

Tools Used in Surveys

Questionnaires.   The major *advantage* of using a questionnaire is that, if properly prepared, it can offer a reliably consistent presentation of items. The major *disadvantages* are that the respondent must be able and willing to read it; good questionnaire items are difficult to write; if questionnaires are sent through the mails, response rates are often low; and it is often difficult to interpret a questionnaire which employs open-ended questions. *Open-ended* questions, sometimes called *unstructured-response* questions, do not offer a choice among a limited number of responses, but rather leave space for the respondent to answer in any way he or she feels is appropriate. The opposite of the open-ended or unstructured question is the *forced-response*, *forced-choice*, or *structured-response* question, which is more difficult for the designer of the questionnaire to write, but which produces data which are more easily analyzed and interpreted. In such forced-choice questions the respondent must choose one or more responses from among a limited number presented.

Researchers employ a number of techniques to increase the response rate for questionnaires. They *always* include a cover letter which describes the purpose of the survey and offers to share findings with respondents. This cover letter assures the respondent that his or her identity will not be revealed and emphasizes the importance of the survey in terms of its objectives or the possible benefits of its findings. Some researchers go further and enclose "rewards" for potential respondents, as suggested by Rosenthal and Rosnow (see p. 61). Many researchers incorporate some of Rosenthal and Rosnow's other suggestions for increasing the rate of volunteering, since completing and returning a questionnaire may be viewed as a form of volunteering.

When conducting surveys by mail, researchers enclose stamped self-addressed envelopes for use in returning completed questionnaires. They also use follow-up mailings or follow-up telephone calls to increase the response rate. Many researchers consider a 60 percent response rate as the minimum acceptable. Regardless of the response rate, researchers examine the characteristics of respondents and try to ascertain how respondents differ from nonrespondents. This may involve comparing the characteristics of respondents to the known characteristics of the population surveyed. It may also entail identifying and contacting nonrespondents to determine their characteristics and the causes for their failure to respond. Such information is important in interpreting the findings of the survey.

Interviews.   The major *advantage* of the individual interview is that the interviewer can tailor it to the person being interviewed and can utilize both verbal and nonverbal cues in determining the responses. The major *disadvantage* is that data gathered through individual interviews may be unreliable or inconsistent because of differences in questions or methods employed by the interviewer or because of differing levels of perceptiveness and effectiveness among interviewers.

Researchers use extensive training of interviewers and careful supervision of the way in which interviews are conducted to minimize the unreliability of the data gathered. Interviewers are trained in how to use a nonjudgmental tone, how to present questions clearly, how to elicit further response from a respondent who is reticent or whose response is unclear, and how to record the data in a consistent manner.

Telephone interviews.   The greatest *advantages* of the telephone interview are that it requires little time to complete and enables the researcher to reach large numbers of subjects easily. Its *disadvantages* are that it may employ either geographically biased samples or small national samples, since researchers frequently use samples drawn from a limited geographic area or use small national samples in telephone interviews (because of long-distance telephone costs); that selecting only those who have telephones as a sample leads to a biased sample; and that telephone interviews frequently produce "shallow" data (seldom do they pursue any topic in detail). An additional problem with the telephone interview is that in order to be reliable, it must be a product of a mechanistic repetition of a prepared questionnaire. This, in turn, can discourage spontaneous response by interviewees. Interviewers need to be trained to present exactly the same questions in a fresh and spontaneous fashion each time.

Examining records.   The *advantages* of using records to supply research data are that all materials are in one location, they are generally complete, and there is no loss of respondents. The need for consent is the only major *disadvantage*.

Analysis of Data

Since the data gathered can be quantified, the findings can be displayed using descriptive statistics—mean, median, mode, and measures of variability (these types of scores are described in detail in Chapter 17).

Often the raw data are gathered in response to Likert-type scale questions which offer a five-point scale (usually in terms of agreement: *strongly agree* through *neutral* to *strongly disagree*, or, in terms of frequency: *always* to *never*). Other times the data are gathered through the use of multiple choice questions or true-false questions which permit the frequency of response to be plotted. Attitudinal scales are also quantifiably reported.

Researchers recognize that respondents may intentionally or unintentionally supply inaccurate information. For this reason, most researchers leave it to the judgment of the reader to decide if the responses given were truthful. Inept researchers overlook the possibility of inaccurate responses and might well report that "75 percent of the respondents earn between $20,000 and $40,000 per year" instead of stating that "75 percent of respondents indicated that they earned between $20,000 and $40,000 per year." The distinction is important. You should never confuse *responses* with *facts*. They may or may not be the same.

OBSERVATION

Researchers often use observation as a method of gathering data on the characteristics of situations, conditions, individuals, or groups. Observers may record three different types of observations: descriptive, inferential, and evaluative.

Descriptive observation.   The behavior recorded is either described in words or reported in terms of *tallies* (marks which record each time that a behavior occurred). The observer does not record anything except what he or she actually observed. The observer draws no inferences and makes no judgments. This type of observation is usually easily quantifiable, and observers are usually quite reliable in their recording.

Inferential observation.   The observer is required to consider what each observed behavior is indicative of and then record that behavior under a specified classification. This type of observation generally entails the use of a categorized recording system which requires the assignment of each behavior to one of a number of categories. Such categorical assignment is markedly less reliable than simple descriptive observation but often supplies more detailed and informative data. With thorough training, observers can learn to make consistent, reliable inferential observations.

Evaluative observation.   The observer must judge the quality of the behavior and then record this judgment as an ordinal rating. Of the three types of observations, evaluative observation is usually the most difficult, since observers frequently differ in evaluative judgments. One person's "good" may easily be another's "average." Fortunately, careful and thorough training of observers coupled with frequent exercises in which observers compare evaluative ratings can result in sufficiently reliable observations. Use of a few, clearly defined rank ordered-categories in which to record behavior can also assist in obtaining reliable evaluative observations. In general, the more ordinal categories among which the observer is asked to distribute observations and the finer the distinction among categories, the lower is likely to be the reliability of evaluative observations.

Approaches to Obtaining Observations

Independent trained observer.   An observer who has been trained to make observations and who is not a participant in the situation to be observed records his or her observations.

Trained participant-observer.   A trained observer who is also a participant in the situation to be observed is responsible for making the observation. His or her observations are most reliable if made on the spot while the behavior to be observed is occurring, but some observers find that this compromises their roles as participants. For this reason, participant-observers often record their observations immediately following completion of activities in which they are involved. This delay between observation and recording can reduce somewhat the reliability of the observation, but proponents of trained participant-observer research argue that this weakness is more than offset by the increased understanding of the dynamics of the behavior under observation which observers gain through participation. They argue that with adequate training observers can attain acceptable reliability and that the increased understanding gained through participation increases greatly the validity of later interpretation of the observations made.

Ethnographic.   The observer may be either a participant or a nonpartici- pant. Usually he or she participates in some activities but not in others. The observer seeks to record *everything* in as much detail as possible. Ethnographic research may be thought of as *observation through immersion.* That is, the observer goes into the situation with very few preconceived notions, and those few are based on rather general hypotheses derived from theories and observations of other social groups. The observer intends to learn about the situation as he or she observes it.

During the period of observation, the observer formulates hypotheses designed to help organize and explain that which is being observed. The observer then looks for *negative cases*—that is, observations for which the new hypotheses do not seem to be appropriate. Finding such cases, he or she then modifies the proposed hypotheses to reflect their presence. In short, the researcher seeks through observation, trial and error, and constant immersion in the situation to find a set of hypotheses which best fit the situation under observation.

A widely publicized example of ethnographic research was the study of Samoan life carried out by Margaret Mead. Some researchers label ethnographic research as *qualitative research* because they view its major objective as the description of the qualities of the situation as opposed to the quantification of behaviors occurring in the situation.

Unobtrusive-measures research.   Instead of observing the behavior of the group, the observer examines the influence of group behavior on the physical environment and then infers the behavior of the group itself. Often in educational research this may involve examining waste materials, furniture, quantities of con- sumable products used in educational settings, or the condition of textbooks or other equipment and supplies used.

Simulation and role playing.   Sometimes researchers simulate situations as a method of testing hypotheses about how groups and situations operate. They recognize that such artificial situations may supply only the most general data about the actual situation and that the findings may, therefore, be unreliable in applica- tion. For these reasons, many researchers use such simulations in *prestudies* to assist them in refining hypotheses and in designing appropriate systems of classification to be used to record observations later. Among the types of simulations used are included:

1. *Leaderless-group discussion:* The observer attempts to ascertain how informal networks of communication and leadership evolve in the absence of a declared formal leader.
2. *Team problem solving:* The researcher presents a group with a problem and observes ways in which they define, analyze, and attempt to solve it.
3. *Individual role playing:* The researcher presents a situation to an individual and helps him or her assume a role. Such help usually includes discussions concerning the experiences, attitudes, and beliefs which accompany the role. Once the individual appears comfortable at playing the role in the given situation, the researcher presents other situations and observes how the individual playing the role reacts.

Untrained observer: Sometimes educational researchers wish to use observations made by untrained observers such as principals, supervisors, other administrators, teachers, and staff. Researchers use such observations despite their questionable reliability because it is sometimes the only way in which to obtain the observations. Among the ways in which these observations are obtained are included:

1. *Anecdotal reports:* The observer describes the behavior of the subject without interpretation. Anecdotal reports may record ordinary, typical behaviors or unusual behaviors which are considered illustrative of a particular behavioral pattern.
2. *Sociometric techniques:* Members of the group under study assign others in the group either to roles or to categories of social status. Researchers then examine the patterns which operate within the social networks of the group.
3. *Supervisory ratings:* An individual in a supervisory capacity reports his or her regular observations.
4. *Critical-incident technique reporting:* Individuals in the group under study identify events or behaviors which they feel were critical to the behavior of another member of the group or to some situation in which the group was involved.

Content analysis. The observer analyzes the content of messages exchanged among and between members of a group under study and attempts to infer both the motivations of the individuals in the group and the effect of this content on the behavior of individuals in the group and on the behavior of the group as a whole.

Five Major Methods
of Recording Observations

1. *Duration recording*: Recording how long an observed behavior lasted.

2. *Frequency recording*: Recording the frequency with which an observed behavior occurred (usually recorded using tallies).

3. *Continuous recording*: Recording *everything* which occurred (insofar as is humanly possible). Continuous observation often entails extensive use of audio or video recording equipment or multiple observers in simultaneous observation.

4. *Interval recording*: Recording observations at specified intervals (as opposed to continuous recording.)

5. *Time sampling*: Recording observations only of what occurred during particular periods of time selected for study. These time periods are often randomly sampled so that an observer can obtain representative observations of a period of time too long for reliable observation or else not available in its entirety for observation due to administrative or budgetary limitations.

Concerns in Making Observations

Observer bias.   Do beliefs and attitudes of the observer create observational "blind spots"?

Observer influence.   Does the presence of the observer influence the nature of behaviors he or she is to observe?

Adequate training of the observers.   Have the observers been trained sufficiently well to be able to recognize the behavior, and can they work with sufficient reliability and technical proficiency?

Rating errors.   Do the observers have a tendency to make certain types of errors when required to distribute observations among categories or to make qualitative judgments? The most frequent rating errors are listed below.

Errors of central tendency occur when an observer who is having difficulty rating a behavior on an ordinal or categorical scale resolves the difficulty by assigning such behaviors to the central (or average) portion of the scale. This tendency restricts dramatically the range (or spread) of ratings and contributes noticeably to difficulty in later analysis of the observations.

Errors of leniency occur when observers tend to rate behaviors on evaluative scales higher than they should be rated because of a feeling that a lower rating might be "a bit hard on" the subject. Such "niceness" produces a limited range of evaluative observations which, like observations resulting from errors of central tendency, are of decreased potency in terms of helping researchers analyze the situation under study.

Errors due to the influence of the halo effect occur when the observer begins to allow earlier observations to cause the him or her to "expect" a certain type of behavior and rating. Such nonobjective observation is a "self-fulfilling prophecy." That is, once the observer begins to expect a certain behavior or rating, he or she generally produces observations which appear to confirm this expectation, but which do not conform to what an objective observer in the same situation would record. The best practice to follow is to ignore past behavior in interpreting, evaluating, and recording observations.

Interobserver (or interrater) reliability.   Can observers be counted on to record observations of the same event consistently? Interrater reliability is calculated using correlation analysis of the ratings given by observers and is expressed as a correlation coefficient. Researchers generally require a minimum interrater reliability figure (r) of $+.70$.

Validity and reliability of the measurement instrument.   Is the instrument adequately sophisticated to measure the behavior? Is the instrument too complicated? Is it valid? Is it reliable? *Validity* refers to the extent to which the instrument measures what it is intended to measure. *Reliability* refers to the extent to which the instrument can be counted upon to produce consistent observations when used by a well-trained, consistent observer. Reliability and validity of measurement instruments are discussed in some detail in Chapter 14.

Contamination of observations.   Does the observer know some piece of information which prevents him or her from being objective? Knowledge of pretest scores and active participation in analysis of data collected earlier are the most common causes of contamination. Observers need to recognize that opinions they hold about the subjects they are observing may influence their observations subtly, and they should seek to control this influence.

TWELVE

STUDIES DESIGNED TO EXPLORE THE PAST

This chapter examines the two types of studies designed to explore the past: historical research and causal-comparative research. It discusses sources of information for, and possible problems in, historical research as well as problems in attributing causality in causal-comparative research.

Researchers sometimes explore the past in order to gain a better understanding of the events and motivations which preceded the current state of affairs. Such explorations often help them in identifying a pattern of behavior of which the present merely represents a point on a continuum of development. If, through exploring the past, a researcher is able to identify such a pattern and continuum, that may help him or her in projecting or predicting the future. An understanding of the events and motivations which produced current events and situations can also assist researchers in understanding the ways in which current events and behaviors operate. Such studies of the past are usually referred to as *historical research.*

Researchers often find themselves wishing to study the influence of variables which, for administrative, physical, legal, or ethical reasons, they are unable to manipulate. By *manipulate* we mean that the researcher supervises the administration of the treatment to one or more groups while other groups of comparable individuals do not receive the treatment. It is not reasonable to manipulate some treatments. In a study to determine the effects of drug abuse, it would be unreasonable for the researcher to select one or more groups in the study to abuse drugs. It is unethical and illegal. Similarly, researchers wishing to study the effects of imprisonment on individuals could not imprison some individuals while letting other comparable individuals remain free. We have legal guidelines which determine imprisonment. How then is the researcher to study the influence of such treatments? The answer lies in use of a second type of study which explores the past: *causal-comparative research*.

In causal-comparative research, the researcher explores how exposure to a treatment has affected the individuals exposed in relation to comparable individuals who differ only in regard to that treatment (or differ as little as the researcher is able to attain). Researchers may use causal-comparative studies to examine the effect of any treatment which is already completed by the time the study is conducted.

While most researchers view *historical* research as *descriptive*, many associate *causal-comparative* research with *quasi-experimental (difference)* studies, since the researcher is able to employ some statistical measures to equate groups, the researcher is often working within the constraints of the actual situation in a conscientious attempt to analyze differences, and in many cases, owing to the ethical, physical, legal, or administrative difficulties involved, no more appropriate or effective method for carrying out a difference study exists.

This chapter will discuss both types of past-exploration studies: historical and causal-comparative.

HISTORICAL RESEARCH

In historical research, the researcher systematically investigates and analyzes documents and other sources of facts about a given problem, behavior, or event in the past. You do so principally to determine how such history influenced current practices, to predict future trends, or to suggest ways in which current practices should be modified in light of the events of history. Modern historical research tends to emphasize *interpretation* over mere reporting.

A major concern of researchers who wish to conduct historical research is whether they will be able to obtain information from a sufficient number of reliable and informed sources. There are two types of sources of historical information: primary and secondary.

Primary sources are individuals who were present at an event about which they are reporting. The more informed and competent the primary sources were at the time of the observation, the more reliable and valuable to the historical researcher are their observations.

Secondary sources are individuals who were not present at the event about which they are reporting, but are rather reporting what other people have told them. The person who reported the event to the secondary source may have been present at the event or may be a secondary source. The more intermediaries that are involved (the further removed from a firsthand report the secondary source is), the less reliable become the data reported by that secondary source. *Hearsay* or *rumor* represents information which is sufficiently removed from firsthand reporting to have obscured the identity of the primary source and to have severely restricted the researcher's ability to determine its reliability. In many cases, the reliability of rumor or "common knowledge" cannot be confirmed, and you are able to use such data only to identify common beliefs instead of to confirm actual occurrences.

Sources in Historical Research

Documents.   Documents may be handwritten or printed materials which report on an event. Researchers use two types of documents in historical research: intentional and unintentional.

Intentional documents were produced with the intention that they serve as records of actions, ideas, or events. Examples are legal records of business transactions, legislative and judicial records, minutes of meetings, and personal diaries.

Unintentional documents were intended for immediate, short-term use and not as permanent records. Examples are letters, memos, notes, and ordinary bills of sale.

Quantitative records.   Numerical data which have been collected in the past often serve as sources for historical researchers. Typical quantitative records are census records, attendance figures, and test scores.

Oral records.   Historical researchers frequently conduct personal interviews of individuals who were present at past events or who are secondary sources of information. Such interviews supply much information which was not written down or recorded in any other fashion. Other forms of oral records include video and audio tape recordings of such accounts.

Relics.   Relics are objects from the past. In educational research they may include measurement instruments, school furniture, learning devices, or other objects used in education.

Steps in Historical Research

1. Identify your research objectives.   Researchers frequently formulate research objectives based on noncomparative research questions and purpose statements (as outlined in Chapter 3). Such questions and statements help them define the problem under consideration and narrow the area of study to a manageable one.

2. Identify and examine sources of information.

3. Evaluate the reliability of the information supplied by these sources.   In evaluating sources of information in historical studies, researchers employ two types of evaluation or *criticism*: external and internal.

External criticism addresses questions about the authenticity of the document, record, or relic. Among the questions it examines are included:

Is it genuine or a forgery?

Is it the original or one of a set of copies? (Copies often vary and for this reason often constitute *variant sources.*)

Who wrote, recorded, or said it? *or* Who made the relic?

When and where was it created?

How was it originally used, or under what conditions was it created?

Internal criticism deals with sources other than relics. It assumes that the source being examined is authentic and seeks then to analyze the source's perceptiveness and reliability. Internal criticism asks such questions as:

Can the source be trusted?

Was the individual present at the event described, or did he or she hear about it secondhand?

Was the writer or speaker a capable observer at the time of the events?

Was the source sufficiently well informed to make appropriate judgments?

What were the apparent biases of the person describing the event?

Could the events described have occurred as described?

Are the souce's descriptions of the actions of the people involved reasonable?

Are the figures used reasonable (*quantitative reliability*)?

4. Organize the relevant information in terms of an interpretive approach to the events which occcurred.   In organizing such information and interpreting the events, the researcher must be aware of concerns which other researchers examining his or her interpretation will have. Those concerns might be expressed as a series of questions:

Is the researcher biased in a way which leads him or her to overlook or minimize information and interpretations which are dissonant with this bias?

Has the researcher used an excessively narrow perspective on history in making his or her interpretation (*one-schoolism*)?

Has the researcher interpreted past events in light of much more recent concepts and perspectives (*presentism*)? This does not mean that you cannot use knowledge which was not available to the participants in the past event, but rather that you should not interpret past events in a way which assumes that those participants were aware of information and perspectives which became available after the event under study.

Has the researcher failed to state the assumptions on which he or she based causal inferences in interpretation? If you do not make clear in the presentation of your interpretation the bases on which that interpretation is founded, other researchers will almost certainly have difficulty determining if your reasoning and the resultant interpretation are sound.

5. Present the interpretation for analysis and evaluation by other scholars.   One of the most effective methods of validating historical research is to present the results of the study to the scientific and scholarly community for examination, analysis, criticism, and evaluation. If your interpretation is sound, it should stand close scrutiny by competent scholars.

CAUSAL-COMPARATIVE RESEARCH

Causal-comparative studies attempt to determine the influence of a trait or behavior on some performance by comparing subjects who manifest the trait or display the behavior with comparable subjects who do not, or with comparable subjects who manifest or display it to a lesser extent. Causal-comparative research is often referred to as *ex post facto* (Latin for "from after the fact") research, since by the time the researcher seeks the cause of a behavior or trait, that behavior or trait has already evidenced itself through its influence on selected variables.

In causal-comparative studies the group which evidences the trait or behavior under study is known as the *defined group*. Researchers attempt to obtain a homogeneous defined group, for which they obtain careful measurements of relevant traits, attitudes, characteristics, and behaviors. They further identify subgroups of the larger defined group in an effort to ascertain any effect which their presence might have on findings and to permit later differential analysis (see p. 93). Often researchers will find appropriate subgroups for study discussed in published reports of similar studies. This is yet another benefit of reviewing the literature before selecting a research design. In identifying the defined group, the researcher must consider the measures to be used in the study and the level of significance which will be employed in analyzing differences between the defined group and the group of subjects to which it will be compared.

The group of individuals who evidence the trait or behavior to a lesser extent or not at all is known as the *comparison group*. The comparison group should differ from the defined group as little as possible, except in regard to the variable under study. Random selection of subjects from the defined population for the comparison group is among the most reliable methods, although the selection of matched subjects is possible. Such matching tends, however, to violate some of the statistical assumptions underlying later analyses. Researchers sometimes use multiple comparison groups, particularly when subgroup analysis and comparison is anticipated.

Causal-comparative studies generally employ either a parametric two-group experimental design (if the subjects are randomly selected for the defined and comparison groups) or a nonparametric two-group design (if nonrandom selection is employed). The most frequently employed parametric experimental designs are the control-group posttest-only design and the pretest-posttest control-group design. The most frequently employed nonparametric experimental design is the nonequivalent control-group design. Parametric and nonparametric analyses are discussed on p. 151.

Statistics Frequently Employed in Analyzing Data

Descriptive statistics. These include the means of groups, their standard deviations, rank scores, frequencies among categories, distributions, variances, group medians, modes, and ranges. Such descriptive statistics are described in Chapter 17.

Test for significance between group means. The researcher chooses the appropriate test on the basis of the number of groups compared and whether the sample was randomly selected. The most frequently employed significance tests are t-tests. If the researcher uses more than one comparison group, he or she usually employs analysis of variance. These tests are described in Chapter 17.

Correlations among the variables under study. The most frequently employed correlation statistics are the Pearson product-moment coefficient and the contingency coefficient. These correlational analysis are described in Chapter 17.

Difficulties in Interpreting the Results

The difficulty of causal attribution which is present in all relationship studies is also present in causal-comparative studies. Since you are not manipulating the exposure of subjects to variables but rather are examining the behavior of subjects in whom the variables are present in greater or lesser degree, you cannot say with certainty that the variable on which you find that the defined and comparison groups differ has *caused* the difference in behavior which you find. Although there is apparently a strong correlation between the defined variable and the performance measure variable, remember that, as mentioned in Chapter 10, correlation does not insure causality.

For this reason, the researcher in causal-comparative studies should examine the set of criteria necessary for attributing causality to a variable which was presented in Chapter 10 (see p. 89). You should be particularly sensitive to the possibility of *reverse causality*. That is, you should consider carefully the possibility that the performance-measure variable caused the defined variable.

Van Dalen (1979, pp. 299–307) has suggested that five types of variables other than the defined variables might influence findings:

1. *Extraneous variable (artifactual cause)*: A variable other than X or Y causes both and thereby insures that X and Y will correlate when no causality exists between them.

2. *Component variable (attribution to the part)*: Sometimes a variable which appears to cause a behavior or trait may encompass several component variables. Socioeconomic status is such an encompassing variable. A component

variable such as income, education, or the like may actually prove more causally influential.

3. *Intervening variable (occurrence in time between X and Y)*: One of the conditions for attributing causality to a variable is precedence in time. It is possible that a variable believed to be a cause came before another intervening variable which was actually the cause. In order to identify intervening variables, the researcher seeks to identify variables which might constitute a chain of cause and effect.

4. *Antecedent variable (past artifactual causality)*: It is possible that a variable that came before the variable believed to be a cause of the performance is the actual cause and that it is responsible for both the variable and the performance.

5. *Suppressor variable (obscured relationship)*: Sometimes when all conceptual and theoretical evidence points to a causal relationship, the researcher is unable to find such a relationship. It is possible that the influence of a suppressor variable is obscuring the influence. Sex, race, and age of the subject have often served as suppressor variables in studies.

Researchers state the possibility that the defined variable and the performance-measure variable will fail to satisfy the causality criteria, or that one or more of the five variables described above might produce the findings as *alternative hypotheses* which they seek to identify and control (see Chapter 3). In causal-comparative studies, alternative hypotheses are often referred to as *strong inferences*.

Researchers seek to identify the presence of the variables described by Van Dalen in a variety of ways. To identify extraneous and component variables, the researcher usually examines the conceptual foundations of the performance measured and purported to be caused by the defined variable. To reveal the presence of intervening and antecedent variables, the researcher examines carefully the time sequence of events. The researcher should have identified any suppressor variables when he or she gathered extensive demographic data on subjects in forming defined and comparison groups. One of the most effective ways to identify and control the influence of these five variables is through the use of stratified or subgroup (differential) analysis, which permits the researcher to analyze correlations among a variety of variables and the behavior or trait.

THIRTEEN

STUDIES DESIGNED TO EVALUATE PROGRAMS OR DEVELOP PRODUCTS

Chapter 13 discusses studies which evaluate educational programs or assist developers in preparing products for use in educational settings. It also examines procedures and problems inherent in each type of study.

Educational researchers are frequently asked to evaluate educational programs or to use research techniques to assist in the development of new educational products. Although in doing so they frequently employ research methodologies described in previous chapters, such evaluation and development studies differ in important ways from the studies previously discussed. They are influenced strongly by both political and financial factors, and their results are frequently used in different ways than those of other types of studies.

Politics play a major role in evaluation studies, which members of the educational hierarchy may attempt to use to discredit opponents or to strengthen their own positions. Researchers conducting evaluation studies frequently find themselves subjected to political pressures. Some of these pressures are discussed later in this chapter. There may also be political pressure exerted in development studies, since the development of the product is usually a result of group efforts, and one faction of developers or users may campaign to influence the end product.

Finances have a strong influence on both evaluation and development studies. Since many evaluation studies attempt to evaluate large-scale programs, they are expensive and time consuming. Administrators may wish to save resources for use elsewhere, and this can severely restrict researchers in conducting their evaluation studies. Similarly, in development studies the pressures of mounting development costs and expensive field trials often militate for reduced field testing, limited revisions, or even for premature release of the developed product.

While other types of studies also can be subject to political and financial pressures, few studies operate in the openly politically determined and politically controlled environment of evaluation studies nor under such financially determined parameters as development studies. The difference may well be one of degree and of researcher control. Additionally, while most research studies are designed with the intention that the results be generalized to other target populations, evaluation and development studies are generally intended for one-time assistance in making a decision.

EVALUATION STUDIES

Educational administrators are sometimes required by a source of funding to evaluate a funded program. Other times, administrators wish to evaluate an educational program either for political reasons or as a result of a sincere desire to determine if that program is effectively producing the desired results. Evaluation studies may consist of evaluations of two types: formative (or process) evaluations and summative (or product) evaluations.

Formative evaluation involves the collection of data while a program is in the developmental, implementational, or operational phase. The researcher seeks in the *developmental stage* to ascertain the program's general goals, the specific outcomes or behaviors which it is to produce, and the current performance level of the population to be exposed to the program. In the *implementational phase* the researcher seeks to determine if the program is being implemented appropriately and if the population to be served has been properly identified and exposed to the program. In the *operational phase* the researcher examines how well the program is running, whether the staff responsible for running it is capable of doing so, and if any unforeseen difficulties are beginning to evidence themselves. In this phase the researcher often gathers quantifiable data, subjecting them to statistical analysis to determine the effectiveness of the program to date. If administrators anticipate that they will wish to have evaluation during the operational phase, they should make certain that the researcher has gathered baseline data during the developmental stage. Statistical analyses of data concerning performance of subjects relative to their baseline performance (prior to implementation of the program) is often of the single-group pretest-posttest type without a control group (see p. 70) and as such is subject to many of the threats listed on page 70 and discussed in Chapter 15. Sometimes researchers identify comparable "sister institutions" with comparable baseline performance and use the performance of the subjects there as a control for evaluating the effectiveness of the program.

Summative evaluation involves the collection of data after a program has been in place for what administrators deem to be long enough to demonstrate its effectiveness in producing the desired outcomes. In actual practice, summative evaluations are often conducted annually, frequently at the end of the academic year. A summative evaluation generally supplies some of the data employed in determining if a program will be continued or terminated. Often it employs the statistical analysis approaches described in the previous paragraph.

One approach to summative evaluation is known as *cost-benefit* or *input-output* research. The researcher seeks to determine the relationship between the resources expended and the outcomes obtained. The resources required to implement and maintain a program are *costs* (or *inputs*). The measured outcomes of the program are the *benefits* (or *outputs*).

In setting up and running educational programs, administrators may use formative evaluation without later summative evaluation. They may do this to demonstrate a "scientific basis" for the original implementation while avoiding the later political hazards of summative evaluation. One "hazard" of summative evaluation is that very few programs, no matter how favorably they are viewed or how effective they seem, can produce dramatic and statistically significant changes in the performance of those with whom they are used, particularly if the program has been in place only a short time. The larger the population with which the program is used, the less likely the change is to be dramatic. Further, even significant results of an evaluation study may not have much meaning to the public.

Sometimes administrators call for summative evaluation without previous formative evaluation. The reason may be a lack of foresight or perhaps a political environment such that a summative evaluation may be used to serve the purposes of the current administration. Ideally, administrators should use both formative and summative evaluation, since this combination is more likely to produce reliable overall evaluation and it permits them to correct shortcomings as the program develops and to make periodic assessments of the program's progress.

Types of Evaluation Models

Researchers often use models of evaluation to assist them in evaluating programs. The cost-benefit (input-output) model mentioned above is an example. This section discusses three other evaluation models which researchers sometimes employ.

The CIPP Model.   This is a four-stage model.

STAGE I:	*Context evaluation*: identifying the elements of a specific educational setting and discrepancies between what exists now and what administrators desire to occur.
STAGE II:	*Input evaluation*: analyzing available resources and strategies in order to select the most appropriate course of action.
STAGE III:	*Process evaluation*: collecting data about the program and maintaining records of the program's progress.

STAGE IV: *Product evaluation*: determining the extent to which the program achieved its stated goals.

In each of these four stages the researcher determines what type of information an administrator will need to make a decision, obtains that information, and synthesizes it to present it in a fashion which will make it most useful in making the decision. In general, evaluator and administrator cooperate in identifying and synthesizing the necessary information.

Discrepancy evaluation.   The researcher examines the degree of agreement between program standards and program performance. *Program standards* are the criteria for utilization of resources, procedural operations, program management, and final outcomes which the program developers identified. *Program performance* is what occurred when the program was tested in actual operation in the educational setting. There are five steps in discrepancy evaluation:

1. The evaluator and program developer define standards in measurable terms. This usually entails formulation of *behavioral objectives*, which serve later as criteria against which to measure the success of the program.
2. Instruments to measure each standard are identified and selected, or appropriate instruments are developed. These measurement instruments must match the behavioral objectives formulated in the previous step.
3. Data on the actual performance of the program are collected.
4. The evaluator analyzes the data to determine the extent of discrepancy between standards and performance. This is a comparison between the behavioral objectives and the performance results gathered in the previous step.
5. The evaluator reports his or her findings to appropriate decision makers.

Adversarial evaluation.   This is a four-stage process.

STAGE I: The researcher and administrator formulate a list of probable issues to evaluate. Often the personnel involved in the program are surveyed in this first stage.

STAGE II: The researcher and administrator select those issues which they consider salient to the success of the program under evaluation. Sometimes survey respondents are asked to rank each issue according to their perception of its significance. Issues which receive the widest range of support and the greatest intensity of support (highest rankings) are then selected.

STAGE III: Selected interested staff form opposing evaluation teams (''adversaries''): one team supports the program and one team opposes it. Each team gathers evidence (through interviews, examination of documents, collection of new data, etc.) and prepares arguments.

STAGE IV: The agency holds sessions similar to formal debates, at which arguments and supporting evidence are presented before a jury (panel) of decision makers.

Adversarial evaluation tends to produce widespread involvement and to emphasize the importance of the opinions of program staff. Its political structure favors a highly political and competitive environment in which alternative opinions and suggestions for improvement often appear. It is, however, expensive and time consuming. The same political structure which favors a wide range of opinions and the proposal of alternative solutions also favors political intrigue and a tendency for a team's persuasive eloquence and political clout to produce a favorable decision, rather than either the soundness of their arguments or the superiority of their position.

Pressures on Evaluators

Evaluation studies may be conducted by inside or outside evaluators. An *inside evaluator* is regularly employed by the educational agency responsible for running the program. An *outside (third-party) evaluator* is not a regular employee but is someone with whom the agency contracts to have the program evaluated. Whether inside or outside, the evaluator often is subjected to pressures designed to influence his or her evaluation.

While many authors contend that evaluators for programs should ideally be both objective and neutral, Kean (1983) has suggested that frequently such is not the case. He argued that internal and external pressures often compromise neutrality, but argued further that lack of neutrality need not disqualify an evaluator. Kean suggested that evaluators (be they inside or outside) are subject to a variety of compromises due to these pressures. He proposed that evaluators frequently make such compromises in order to maintain sufficient objectivity to evaluate programs. Kean listed six compromises (pp. 369–370):

1. The Affective Compromise. The evaluator may well have feelings about the program he or she is to evaluate. Such feelings may compromise the evaluator's objectivity. Kean suggested that evaluators address this compromise by recognizing the influence of these feelings and adjusting expectations appropriately. That is, if the researcher has strong favorable feelings toward the program, he or she should consider establishing higher evaluation standards than usual to adjust for this bias. If his or her feelings toward the program are strongly unfavorable, the investigator should be careful to establish realistic expectations for the program.

2. The Association Compromise. Sometimes an evaluator becomes so involved with a project that he or she begins to feel a vested interest in its receiving a favorable evaluation. This is particularly true for inside evaluators who may have been instrumental in getting the program under evaluation started. Kean suggested that evaluators may address this compromise in a variety of ways. Among them he suggested the use of a panel of independent evaluators, each with different responsibilities, the use of stages of evaluation with reports filed at the end of each stage, and the use of an *evaluation auditor* to determine how well the evaluator did his or her job.

3. The Factual Compromise.   Since the evaluation process is not conducted in a political vacuum, evaluators sometimes find themselves asked to modify the results of their evaluations to suit political purposes of the staff or administration of the program under evaluation or of the agency which requested the evaluation. The only control for such a compromise is integrity; if evaluators succumb to such pressure, their evaluations lose all validity.

4. The Fiscal Compromise.   Sometimes an evaluator becomes bound to a favorable evaluation by "golden chains." That is, the evaluator's salary or employment is incorporated in the program under evaluation, and unfavorable evaluation of the program might result in loss of the evaluator's job. Kean suggested that evaluators might address this compromise through the use of creative budget allocations or of organizational arrangements which reduce the financial dependency of the evaluator. Kean's solution assumes, however, that the decision makers wish the evaluator they employ to have such "independence."

5. The Philosophical Compromise.   Sometimes evaluators are asked to evaluate programs which are based on philosophies with which they agree strongly. The evaluator may then feel strongly predisposed to evaluate the program favorably. Kean suggested that evaluators see their philosophical knowledgeability as a strength and use it to help them in making critical and detailed evaluations. He cautioned them against assuming that a match between their own philosophy and the program's indicates a quality program.

6. The Political Compromise.   Evaluators recognize that the results of their evaluations (and the evaluation process itself) have political implications. If a program receives an unfavorable evaluation, those who sponsored its creation or adoption may be discredited. Kean suggested that evaluators resist the political pressure to evaluate a program favorably in order to protect the originators (or "innovators"). He suggested that evaluators play up the integrity and objectivity of sponsors who encourage and support honest evaluations regardless of the favorability of the results.

Criteria for Judging the Adequacy of an Evaluation Study

Stufflebeam, Foley, Gephart, Guba, Hammond, Merriman, and Provus (1971, Chapter 1) suggested that researchers use eleven criteria in three categories to judge the adequacy of the design and execution of an evaluation study.

1. *Scientific criteria:*
   a. *Internal validity:* Does the evaluation design provide information it is designed to provide?
   b. *External validity:* Do the evaluation results apply only to the sample of individuals included in the evaluation, or can they be generalized to other groups (or the same group at other times)?
   c. *Reliability:* Are the results replicable? Would the same results occur if the study were done again?
   d. *Objectivity:* Are the results open to alternative interpretation, or would competent judges agree that the interpretation provided is adequate?
2. *Practical criteria:*
   a. *Relevance:* Are the evaluation data adequate to serve the purposes for which they were intended?
   b. *Importance:* Are the data collected necessary in order to answer the questions addressed, or should some measures be culled from the data as superfluous?
   c. *Scope:* Does the information gathered in the evaluation have sufficient scope and detail to provide an adequate judgment about the phenomena being evaluated?
   d. *Credibility:* Can the integrity of the evaluator be relied upon? Was the evaluation carried on openly, and does the evaluator have a history of integrity?
   e. *Timeliness:* Did the evaluator provide the evaluation information when it was useful, or was it supplied to decision makers too late to be of any real value?
   f. *Pervasiveness:* Do all the persons who should know about and use the evaluation information have it?
3. *Prudential criterion:* Did the evaluator make wise decisions about the use of time, funds, and personnel?

PRODUCT DEVELOPMENT STUDIES

Development studies are closely related to *evaluation studies*. Organizations attempting to produce products for sale or distribution to educational agencies frequently employ development studies to help assure that the product will meet the objectives of its developers and will find a ready market. Development studies are usually called *R & D (Research and Development) studies*.

Development is usually viewed as a reiterative process in which the new product is tested and revised until it is deemed ready to be marketed. The steps of this process are as follows:

1. Identifying the product to be developed. This is typically done by describing the nature of the proposed product, what it will include, and how it will be used. The developer prepares a specific statement of the objectives to be accomplished through use of the product. In identifying a potential product, developers consider the nature of the need for it, the technical skills required to produce it, the nature of the personnel that will be involved in developing it, and the time required to produce and test it.

2. Reviewing the literature.   The developer next examines the literature to determine what is known about similar or related products and how potential users (coaches, trainers, teachers, psychologists, administrators, etc.) seek to accomplish objectives which this product is intended to help them accomplish. Often interviews and observations in appropriate educational settings are employed to help developers gain a greater command of practical realities. Sometimes developers carry out predevelopment studies of the educational environment in which their products are to be used in order to help them understand that environment more fully.

3. Planning the development program.   This includes defining the *skills* to be developed through use of the product, stating *objectives* (preferably in behavioral terms) which the product is to help users attain, and determining the way in which the new product will fit into the *sequence of use* of other related products or processes. Personnel requirements, financial needs, and material requirements as well as the need to use schools as test sites must also be considered.

4. Developing a prototype of the product.   At this stage the product should be developed as fully as possible and the developer should prepare instructional materials, accompanying handbooks, and evaluation devices.

5. Conducting a preliminary field test.   Usually this involves half a dozen users who work in the type of environment in which the new product would be used. Emphasis is placed on qualitative appraisal of the product. Developers need to be aware that they may produce a Hawthorne effect (see p. 136) on these preliminary users which may distort their evaluation. The users may like being asked to evaluate the product. We all like to feel that our opinions are valued. Users may transfer this "liking" from the *process* of being asked to the *product* being evaluated.

6. Revising the product in keeping with findings of the preliminary field test.   Any shortcomings or omissions which were disclosed are corrected.

7. Conducting a main field test.   Such a field test normally employs a quasi-experimental or experimental design. Usually such field tests are conducted in half a dozen to a dozen appropriate settings, using samples of 30 to 100 subjects. The researcher evaluates pretest and posttest scores in light of course objectives and control-group data. The researcher gathers and examines additional information on product utilization and practical concerns as well as on the receptivity of students and users to the product.

8. Revising the product in keeping with the findings of the main field test. Once again, the product developers try to correct any omissions or shortcomings disclosed by the field study.

9. Conducting an operational field test. Operational field tests are usually carried out in ten to thirty appropriate settings, using larger samples where possible (40 to 200 subjects). The developer is not involved in this test. Its purpose is to determine the extent to which the product is ready to be used in the setting for which it was designed. Questionnaires, interviews, and surveys are used to evaluate the product's utility and completeness.

10. Revising the product in keeping with the findings of the operational field test. Shortcomings and omissions which can be corrected at reasonable expense are corrected. Developers generally try by this point to have corrected *all* shortcomings and omissions.

11. Disseminating information on the product and setting up a distribution apparatus for making it available to potential users.

Frequent Errors
in Development Studies

Excessive polish in early stages. If the product receives too much designing polish ("More chrome! More packaging! More class!") early on, the nature of the financial commitment may preclude later revision or rejection of the product in favor of others ("I know it doesn't work, but, dang it, we've got a fortune in this!" *or* "It looks good; who'll know anyway?").

Excessive dependence on field testing. It is both expensive and time consuming to run field tests. If developers become too dependent on field testing, the product may never come to market or, if it does, it may be prohibitively expensive owing to the cost of those field trials. In early stages of testing, developers may be able to draw conclusions about a product from simulations just as effectively as from actual use in educational settings and with substantially fewer headaches.

An unrealistic belief that things will run smoothly and nothing will go wrong. The *Titanic* was "unsinkable." The great blackout around New York happened despite elaborate backup devices which made it "virtually impossible." Before the Three Mile Island accident, proponents of nuclear power were speaking of such plants as "foolproof." Developers need to anticipate that problems will arise and setbacks will occur. Schedules and budgets should incorporate provision for such difficulties. Developers need to try to discover and make allowances for any difficulties which users might have with the products, especially if field tests do not reveal any difficulties. The need to seek out potential difficulties is increased when the product involves newer technologies, such as computers or synchronized electronic devices, since many of the difficulties which may be encountered may depend upon variations in the devices used or may not as yet have been discovered, owing to limited experience with the newer technology.

Failure to allow sufficient time or funds to complete the project.

Necessary Elements
of Development Studies

Time.   Development studies require long-range commitments. They frequently require several years to complete. The developer needs to insure that administrators, staff, and all others who are involved are aware of the study's goals, objectives, and requirements. They must be willing to commit the necessary time and money to the project.

Clearly stated goals and objectives.   Many people are involved in carrying out a development study. The developer therefore needs to establish clearly stated goals and objectives. *Clearly stated* means free of jargon and specialized terms, worded simply, and understandable to everyone involved. Such goals and objectives help to minimize misunderstandings.

An overall plan.   The developer should develop an overall plan for the study which outlines procedures, responsibilities, and approximate time requirements.

Clear and open lines of communication.   The developer needs to establish and maintain clear lines of communication. The people involved in the study should feel free to communicate with the developer about needs and problems. In keeping with these aims, the researcher should issue periodic reports to inform those persons involved of the progress of the study in satisfying its goals and objectives.

Periodic review, evaluation, and revision.   The developer should gather data on the progress of the study. Such data should include not only test scores, but also information on attitudes toward the product and problems encountered in carrying out the study. The developer should gather data not only from staff and users, but also from students, parents, or clients (if appropriate). An area of particular interest to the developer should be the cost of carrying out the study. Once data are gathered, the developer needs to consider whether revisions of the study's plan are warranted. If so, he or she needs to discuss revisions with the staff involved.

A final report.   The final report should not be a simple listing and description of successes. It should describe problems and solutions tried. It should give administrators and potential users in other educational settings a feel for the difficulties the developer encountered. It should help them decide whether the particular materials produced in the study are likely to succeed in their situations. The developer should also include suggestions and strategies for improving the ways in which the materials are tested or used.

FOURTEEN

MEASUREMENT INSTRUMENTS

This chapter discusses the two types of measurement instruments, examines instrument validity and reliability, and considers the selection of measurement instruments and the interpretation of the scores produced. It also presents some relevant calculations used in evaluating measurement instruments.

A *measurement instrument* is a device used to gather information concerning subjects. If a study involves observing subjects, then the observer and the form on which he or she records the observations are both measurement instruments. If a study involves a survey, then the interviewer (and interview form) or the questionnaire or attitude inventory are measurement instruments. In most cases, however, when researchers refer to measurement instruments they are referring to the test, form, or device on which the performance is recorded rather than to the individual doing the recording. If a study seeks to measure the achievement of the subjects in a given subject area, the measurement instrument is frequently referred to as a *test*. If administered at the beginning of a study, it is known as a *pretest*; if at the end, as a *posttest*.

TYPES OF INSTRUMENTS

There are two types of measurement instruments: norm-referenced and criterion-referenced.

A *norm-referenced instrument* compares the performance of the subject being measured with that of others. Standardized achievement tests which were normed using large test populations and which report scores in percentiles or age and grade equivalent scores are typical of norm-referenced instruments, as are evaluative observations (see Chapter 11).

A *criterion-referenced instrument* measures the performance of the subject and compares it to established standards or criteria. Mastery tests in which scores of subjects are reported as percentages of correct response are typical of criterion-referenced instruments.

Researchers use norm-referenced tests when their primary concern is to determine how the subjects under study compare with other comparable subjects. They use criterion-referenced tests when they wish to determine how the performance of subjects compares to some goal or standard.

INSTRUMENT VALIDITY

Validity refers to the extent to which something does what it claims to do. A measurement instrument is *valid* if it measures or represents what it claims to measure or represent. Researchers consider five types of validity in evaluating measurement instruments.

1. Face validity.   Face validity refers to whether the instrument appears to be all right. That is, does it *look* right? Many researchers do not consider face validity at all. Others contend that if a measurement instrument doesn't look quite right, that fact may have a subtle influence on the performance of the subjects being measured.

2. Content validity.   This is the extent to which an instrument covers content which is appropriate to the research study, to the samples and population to be studied, and, if appropriate, to the curriculum or therapy to which the subjects have been exposed or will have been exposed. Researchers determine the content validity of a measurement instrument by considering the content which might have been included, the use to which the instrument will be put, the ways in which items were selected to be included, and the ways in which the designer of the instrument confirmed that the included items cover the desired content adequately.

3. Predictive validity.   This is the extent to which the performance or behavior of a subject conforms to the performance or behavior predicted by the instrument. Usually it is determined by correlating the original score on the instrument with some measure of the later behavior called the *criterion measure*, which is often supplied by a standardized achievement test. Two concepts important to evaluating the predictive validity of a test are base rate and cross validation.

Base rate refers to the proportion of subjects in the population whose performance on a measure meets a required criterion. If the incidence is extremely high or extremely low (almost everyone succeeded or almost everyone failed), then chance plays too great a role in predicting success or failure and the predictive validity of the test is low. Instruments tend to have greatest predictive power when they seek to predict performance where the base rate is neither high nor low.

Cross validation addresses the possibility that some property of the sample may account for the predictive success or failure of an instrument. In order to control for this possibility, the researcher can use multiple sampling from the same population to confirm his or her original findings. You will recall from Chapters 7 and 8 that increased sampling leads to increased confidence in the reliability (representativeness) of the samples drawn.

4. Concurrent validity.   One of the most frequently employed measures of validity for instruments, concurrent validity is determined by calculating the correlation between the scores obtained when an instrument is administered to a group and the scores obtained when another instrument of known validity (a *criterion measure*) is administered to the same group at or near the same time. Usually the researcher allows at least a brief interval between administration of the two instruments in order to control for sensitization to similarity between them and for fatigue. Researchers disagree on how long this interval should be. Its length depends in large measure on the complexity of the instrument. A good way to determine how long an interval to allow is to examine studies which have employed concurrent validity to validate instruments similar to yours. Concurrent validity is often used to identify related or alternative test measures.

5. Construct validity.   This refers to the extent to which an instrument actually measures a theoretical construct which it purports to measure and not something else. Theoretical constructs are used to explain the causes of certain behaviors. These constructs cannot be observed directly, but rather must be inferred from observing those behaviors for which they are suspected to be the causes. Intelligence, anxiety, and creativity are examples of hypothetical constructs. One might say that construct validity is a measure of how well a measurement instrument conforms to the theory and the methods of applying theory which exist in a given area.

INSTRUMENT RELIABILITY

Reliability refers to the consistency with which an instrument produces equivalent scores. Such equivalence is determined in relation to repeated administrations as well as administrations to a variety of subjects. A highly reliable instrument can be depended upon to produce the same or nearly same score when administered twice to the same subject or when administered to two subjects of equivalent talent and experience.

The reliability of an instrument is usually expressed as a *correlation coefficient* (see Chapter 10). The higher the coefficient (*r*) of the instrument, the more reliable it is in measuring the performance of subjects. When samples are small or the differences among subjects measured with the instrument are likely to be small, researchers generally try to employ measurement instruments of high reliability (*r* > .85). When samples are large or the differences among subjects are likely to be large, researchers can use instruments of lower reliability (*r* > .6). Researchers always attempt to employ the instrument with the highest reliability that they can both obtain and afford and that satisfies the needs of the study.

Methods of Calculating
the Reliability of an Instrument

Researchers generally use one or more of four coefficient calculations to determine the reliability of an instrument: the coefficient of internal consistency, the coefficient of rational equivalence, the coefficient of equivalence, and the coefficient of stability. They can use such formulas only if the information gathered by the instrument can be quantifiable. For this reason, these calculations are most frequently performed to determine the reliability of tests. The difficulty in analyzing the reliability of instruments designed to measure characteristics and opinions of subjects lies in trying to quantify certain types of responses.

1. Coefficient of internal consistency (also known as the split-half reliability coefficient).   This coefficient calculation is frequently used in determining the reliability of a test. In order to use it, you must have an instrument which contains approximately the same number of items of basically the same nature. Once you have used the instrument to measure the sample, you divide the instrument into two subinstruments (usually one subtest made up of odd-numbered items and one of even-numbered items). Using the Pearson product-moment correlation formula (see pp. 171–174), you correlate these two subinstruments. Once that is done, you use the Spearman-Brown prophecy formula (Thorndike and Hagen, 1961, p. 80) presented below to calculate the coefficient:

$$r_w = \frac{2r_h}{1 + r_h}$$

where r_w = the predicted reliability of the whole instrument

r_h = the correlation between the two halves of the test.

2. Coefficient of rational equivalence (also known as the Kuder-Richardson coefficient). In order for the researcher to use this coefficient to determine the reliability of an instrument, the responses of subjects whose performance the instrument is measuring must be classifiable as either "correct" or "incorrect." This approach analyzes individual items on the instrument and produces a rather conservative estimate of its reliability. Once all subjects have been measured using the instrument, you determine what percentage of the total number responded correctly to each item and what percentage did not; then you use this information to complete Kuder-Richardson formula twenty (Richardson & Kuder, 1939), which is presented below:

$$r = \frac{n}{n-1} \times \frac{s^2 - \Sigma\, pq}{s^2}$$

where
r = the estimated reliability of the instrument

n = the number of items on the instrument

s^2 = the variance of the instrument (the squared standard deviation of the scores—see pp. xx)

$\Sigma\, pq$ = the sum of pq for all items together

pq = the percentage of correct responses to an item multiplied by the percentage of incorrect responses to that item.

3. Coefficient of equivalence (also known as alternate-form reliability). Alternate forms of the same instrument administered to the same group at the same time or separated by a short interval to minimize the effects of test sensitization and test fatigue. Once again, researchers disagree on the length of this rest interval. A search of the literature should help you decide. It is usually from a few minutes to a couple of hours long, depending on the complexity of the instrument involved. The scores of the group of subjects on the forms of the instrument are then correlated using the Pearson product-moment correlation or multiple correlation. This is perhaps the most commonly used estimate of reliability for standardized tests. This approach does not require that the items be of the same type, merely that the responses be quantifiable. A version of this approach is used to determine *interrater reliability*. The observers are the "alternate forms" of observation and the uniform observation (usually a videotape or audiotape recording) is the "group" against which they are measured.

4. Coefficient of stability (also known as test-retest reliability). The instrument is used to measure the sample. After a short delay, the same instrument is administered to the same sample. Determining the length of the delay here is difficult and will require considerable reading and thought about the probable areas of sensitization resulting from taking the test a second time. You then correlate the scores of the sample on the instrument using the Pearson product-moment correlation or multiple correlation. As with the coefficient of equivalence, the only requirement here is that the responses to the instrument be quantifiable.

SELECTING A
STANDARDIZED INSTRUMENT

Researchers usually do not choose to design original instruments because of the rigors involved in developing, testing, revising, and verifying them. The process of instrument development usually parallels the process employed in a product-development (R & D) study. Developing valid and reliable instruments is both difficult and time consuming. Most researchers therefore choose to select an appropriate instrument from the many which are available commercially.

One of the most productive ways of identifying appropriate measurement instruments is by searching the literature. In reading about similar studies, researchers often come across information about instruments which might prove useful in their studies. Researchers also consult a variety of reference works on tests and measurements. Among those frequently consulted are:

Buros Mental Measurement Yearbook

Personality Tests and Reviews

Scales for the Measurement of Attitudes

Tests and Measurements in Child Development: Handbooks I and II (vols. 1 and 2)

Tests in Print

The types of information which researchers wish to obtain about a potential instrument include:

1. Information about why and how the instrument was developed, by whom, and when.
2. Information about how the validity of the instrument was determined.
3. Information regarding how the instrument has been used and with what types of samples and populations.
4. Information concerning the reliability of the instrument and how that reliability was calculated.

5. Information about any limitations or shortcomings of the instrument.

Once you have identified a potentially useful instrument and have gathered the information described above, you must consider whether that instrument is suited to the sample and population involved in the study and whether the way in which the instrument is designed to be used is appropriate to your research situation.

INTERPRETING
NORM-REFERENCED SCORES

Researchers often employ standardized tests to measure the performance of subjects in their studies. While researchers usually do not have much difficulty interpreting the scores of subjects on standardized *criterion-referenced* tests (since these are almost always expressed in terms of the percentage of correct response), they sometimes have difficulty interpreting the scores of subjects on standardized *norm-referenced* tests, where scores may be reported as raw scores, age-equivalent scores, grade-equivalent scores, percentile scores, or stanine scores.

A *raw score* merely tells the researcher how many items the subject answered correctly. This number will vary from test to test and is the basis for deriving norm-referenced scores. You cannot use raw scores for comparing subjects unless all subjects took the very same form of the same standardized test.

An *age-equivalent score* expresses the performance of the subject in relation to the typical performance of others of similar age. Age-equivalent scores are expressed in terms of the years and months represented. Thus, an age-equivalent score of 5.4 stands for *five years and four months*. An age-equivalent score of 5.4 does not suggest that the subject performs as well as someone five years and four months old would in *any* situation. It merely suggests that the subject did as well on *that* specific standardized test as a subject would have who was five and one-third years old.

A *grade-equivalent score* is similarly expressed. If a second-grader received a grade-equivalent score of 6.2 on a standardized test, it would *not* mean that he was capable of doing sixth-grade work as presented in the second month of sixth grade. It would mean instead that the subject performed as well on *that* test as one would expect of a sixth grader in the second month.

Percentile scores also are sometimes misunderstood by beginning researchers. A percentile score expresses the percentage of the total number of subjects who took the test who did worse than the subject who received the score. Thus, a percentile score of eighty-five means that the subject did *better than eighty-five percent of the subjects* who took the test. It does not tell what percentage of the items the subject answered correctly. Percentile scores range from 1 to ninety-nine. It is impossible to score in the 100 percentile, since that would mean one scored higher than *everyone* who took the test (including oneself!), an impossible accomplishment. By convention, there is no 0 percentile.

Stanine scores range from one to nine. Stanine is an abbreviation for *standard nine*-point scale. Stanine scores are based on the normal curve. A stanine score of five is the mean for subjects taking the test. Working out from there, each number above or below five divides the group of subjects into categories which differ from one another by one-half standard deviation (sd): four includes scores which are equal to or more than ½ sd *below* the mean but less than one sd below it. A stanine score of six includes scores which are equal to or more than ½ sd *above* the mean but less than one sd above it. Each number represents a movement of ½ sd further from the mean. Thus a stanine score of one is equal to or greater than two sd *below* the mean and a score of nine is equal to or greater than two sd *above* the mean. Figure 14-1 illustrates these relationships.

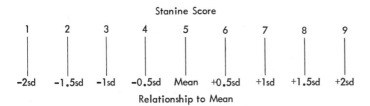

Fig. 14-1

Researchers sometimes question the accuracy of the scores reported. A researcher can never be certain that the score a subject receives is an accurate measure of the score he or she should have received. In order to determine the range within which the researcher can predict a subject's correct score with stated probability values, researchers use the *standard error of measurement*. The standard error of measurement helps you determine how near the score the subject received is to the score he or she actually should have received. Researchers use the following formula to calculate the standard error of measurement of an instrument:

$$s_m = sd \times \sqrt{1 - r}$$

$$\text{where } s_m = \text{the standard error of measurement}$$
$$sd = \text{the standard deviation of the test}$$
$$r = \text{the reliability coefficient of the test as calculated by whichever formula.}$$

Since the standard error of measurement is normally distributed, you use your knowledge of the normal curve to describe your level of certainty in stating the score which would have been most accurate for that subject. Thus, the researcher states that there is a 68 percent chance that the subject's "true" score falls within plus or minus one standard error of measurement of the score he or she received, and there is a 95 percent chance that the subject's "true" score falls within plus or minus two standard errors of measurement of the score received.

FIFTEEN

THREATS TO THE VALIDITY OF A STUDY

Researchers may make errors in designing studies and interpreting the results. Chapter 15 discusses factors which influence the extent to which interpretations of research findings may be considered valid.

The scientific method requires that researchers who conduct difference studies make every effort to assure that any comparisons made and any conclusions based on those comparisons be *valid*. That is, if comparing the performance of groups, a researcher needs to have assured in all ways possible that the groups compared are equivalent, so that he or she can assert at the conclusion of the study that any differences among or between groups are due to the differential influences of the treatments and not to the influence of extraneous variables.

Chapter 3, you will recall, discussed hypotheses—not only null and research hypotheses, but also alternative hypotheses. An *alternative hypothesis* identifies an extraneous variable and contends that it, and not the compared treatments, determined the findings of the study. Perhaps the easiest way to identify alternative hypotheses is to consider the threats to validity which are discussed in this chapter.

Chapter 14 defined *validity* as the measurement or representation of what something claims to measure or represent. Thus, if a study's methodology is valid and, in turn, its findings are valid, then that study is valid. Researchers seek to identify threats to validity and to phrase them as alternative hypotheses prior to beginning a study. They then seek to formulate ways to control for each threat in order to assure the validity of the study's methodology. Obviously, if researchers wait until a study is underway or completed to identify such threats, it is unlikely that they will be able to control for them. Additionally, when reading research reports you will wish to consider the threats to a study's validity in order to determine if the study was conducted properly, if the findings can be trusted, and if the findings are applicable to other settings and populations.

There are two types of threats to the validity of a study: threats to internal validity and threats to external validity.

THREATS TO INTERNAL VALIDITY

The degree to which a study is *internally valid* is determined by the confidence with which the researcher can state that the study's findings are due to the influence of the treatment administered and not to the influence of extraneous variables. Such confidence is born of consideration and control of a variety of threats to validity due to the operation of extraneous variables. The authoritative source for discussions of internal validity is Campbell and Stanley (1963), who identified and discussed eight major threats to internal validity.

1. History (effects of time).   Experimental treatments occur over a period of time, and this makes it possible for other factors to come into play and influence the dependent variable. This is generally not a problem in short studies but should be considered seriously in studies which cover a semester, a year, or longer. History is considered to be a threat *only in studies which involve a single group without a control group*. The reason: one would assume that if history had an effect, all groups under study would be affected equally.

2. Maturation (effects of changes within subjects).   If a study lasts long enough, the subjects will mature physically and psychologically. Particularly when the researcher is working with younger subjects, this maturation may account for the change in the dependent variable. Maturation is considered to be a threat *only in studies involving a single group without a control or in studies using a static-group comparison*. In multiple-group studies where random selection is employed, one would expect maturational effects to be equal among groups. In single-group studies, the researcher has no comparison group to help him or her assure that what is measured by changes in the dependent variable isn't just maturation of subjects. This may also be the case with static-group comparisons where the quality of comparisons between groups may be questionable, and the absence of a pretest makes the resultant findings less easily attributed to treatments.

3. Testing (learning to take tests).   In studies where a pretest is administered, taking the pretest may influence the subject's later performance on the posttest. The subjects may become better test takers. This contamination of the scores on the posttest usually diminishes as the interval of time between pretest and posttest increases. This is viewed as a threat to *studies in which a single group is involved*, since in a control-group study one would expect any increase in test-taking ability resulting from taking a pretest to be evenly distributed among all groups in the study.

4. Instrumentation (changes in measurement devices).   A gain or loss in the dependent variable may be a result of a change in the measuring instrument rather than a result of the treatment. What the change in the dependent variable would be measuring in this case would be the difference between the measuring instruments. This can be a problem when observers are used, since different observers or changed attitudes in observers can lead to changed observations (in this case, the observer is the measurement device). Another form of instrumentation threat occurs when subjective scoring or low reliability among measures or observers may account for differences in scores on the dependent variable. Instrumentation is a threat *only in studies where multiple observations or measurement devices are employed.*

5. Statistical regression (selection from the extreme).   When the scores of subjects who are selected to participate in a study deviate significantly from the mean score or norm of the population from which they were selected, their scores can be expected to move toward that mean score or norm with repeated measures. The reason is that measures tend to be most accurate in assessing performance at or near the mean and increasingly less accurate as the deviation of the performance from the mean increases. Statistical regression is usually a threat to *studies in which subjects are selected because they differ from the population norm* (for example, studies of the gifted, studies of the emotionally disturbed, studies of remedial instruction). Statistical regression is also a threat in *studies where means are used to replace numerous missing scores* (10 percent or more).

6. Differential selection (error of selection).   If the standards by which subjects are chosen for the experimental and control groups are different, any differences in posttreatment scores on the dependent variable may well reflect original differences between the groups on the dependent variable or on a variable related to the dependent variable. Differential selection is a threat *only to studies in which comparison groups are employed.* The threat of differential selection may be controlled through the use of random selection and assignment. It may be a serious threat to studies in which intact groups are used. Researchers generally use statistical procedures to attempt to establish equivalence between intact groups.

7. Experimental mortality (attrition or loss of subjects).   Often one loses subjects who drop out of a study before it is completed. If there is any pattern or bias to the type of student who drops out, this may account for the change in the dependent variable. This is particularly a threat when more subjects drop out of one group than another. Experimental mortality is considered a serious threat when subjects drop out of small samples. As the size of the sample increases, loss of a few subjects becomes less of a threat, provided that there is not a consistent pattern to the type of subject lost from the study.

8. Selection interactions (differential influences among groups which are not related to treatment differences).   The threats of history, maturation, and testing all address studies involving single groups. It is also possible for events to occur which influence subjects in one group and not another (*history-selection interaction*), for one group to gain more testing experience and test-taking ability than another (*testing-selection interaction*), or for one group to mature more quickly than another (*maturation-selection interaction*). Such interactions may account for differences in performance between treatments when more than one group is involved, and they may influence posttreatment findings even when subjects in groups in the treatments were equivalent on the dependent variable at the time they were selected. The researcher should consider whether any difference in the dependent variable at the conclusion of the study might be a result of differences in *extraneous events* occurring in one treatment but not in the other, of differences in *maturational rates* between treatments, or of differences in the extent to which one treatment gains *experience in testing* as compared with another treatment. Researchers normally control for selection interaction threats by using random selection and assignment of subjects. Selection interaction threats are therefore most serious when working with intact groups.

The author proposes the following as another possible selection-testing interaction threat to internal validity:

9. Interaction of previous testing and selection (past test experience as a cause for differential effects).   All the selection interaction threats discussed above related to occurrences after the sample for the study was selected. It is also possible that experiences of subjects in one group with tests prior to their selection might account for differences in posttreatment performance between treatments. Such previous experience with testing would seem most likely to occur in schools which have a record of participating in educational research studies. The researcher might well expect subjects in such schools to have more experience with a variety of standardized test instruments used in research than subjects in schools in which few research studies have been conducted. Previous testing-selection interaction seems most likely to prove a threat to studies which do not involve pretesting or multiple comparative measures, since in studies using multiple measures greater test-taking ability should evidence itself in baseline data gathered on such measures. Random selection should control for this threat.

It seems most probable that previous testing-selection interaction would be a threat to studies involving intact groups in a posttest-only design, particularly if the intact groups were from different schools. Similarly, if pretest scores are used to *match* subjects in groups, previous testing-selection interaction may also prove a threat. In such matching, the pretest scores of subjects with greater previous testing experience should be higher than those of subjects who have had less experience in taking tests. This could produce inaccurate matches which, in turn, might produce markedly nonequivalent groups. The researcher should inquire about the existence and nature of previous studies which were conducted using all or part of the proposed sample for the study.

THREATS TO EXTERNAL VALIDITY

The degree to which a study is *externally valid* is determined by the extent to which the researcher can state that its findings are applicable to samples and populations other than the sample used in the study. This is often referred to as the *generalizability* of the findings. The authoritative source for discussions of external validity is Bracht and Glass (1968), who identified two major classes of external validity: population validity and ecological validity.

Population validity.   Is the sample similar to other populations to which the findings of the study would be generalized? If not, generalizations are invalid.

Sample typicality. Is the sample typical of the population from which it was drawn?

Experimentally accessible population versus target population. Does the population from which the sample was drawn typify or represent other populations to which the findings would be generalized?

Interaction of sample and treatment. Were the results influenced by unmeasured and uncontrolled subject variables (for example, psychological predispositions, aptitudes, or attitudes) which are peculiar to this sample or population?

Ecological validity.   Is the treatment or testing environment in some way unique to this study and therefore ungeneralizable to other situations? To evaluate the ecological validity of a study, the researcher looks for:

A complete description of the experimental conditions and treatment. Replicability is a powerful form of confirmation that findings do indeed generalize. In order to replicate a study, researchers need to have a complete description of procedures, treatments, and analyses.

Multiple treatments which might interfere with attributing the findings to a single treatment cause. This is often a problem in studies in settings in which subjects are offered electives or where other persons working with the subjects are presenting treatments in addition to those applied in the study, and both types of treatments might be expected to influence results.

The Hawthorne effect. Receiving special attention or perceiving how they are expected to perform may lead subjects to perform differently than they normally would. This is generally a short-term influence, since most behaviors return to their usual patterns once the subject becomes accustomed to the treatment. That is, any gain due to the influence of the Hawthorne effect usually disappears with the passage of time, and the researcher who has allowed time for this effect to fade need not be overly concerned about it. Since many studies in educational settings compare counseling, coaching, administrative, or instructional techniques over several weeks, a semester, or a year, the Hawthorne effect is usually not an influence unless the counselor, coach, administrator, teacher, or other experimenter plays up the value of one technique over another. The Hawthorne effect is a plausible threat, however, in studies of short duration, or in studies where only the subjects in the experimental treatment are volunteers.

Novelty or disruption effects. Just being different or disrupting the routine may account for the treatment's effect. Such an influence is most likely to occur in an environment in which change is unusual.

Experimenter effect. Some trait, attitude, or behavior of the experimenter may account for the findings. The label *experimenter* includes both the individual who designed the study and the administrator, counselor, teacher, coach, or staff member who is involved in administering the treatment. The influence of either or both of these types of individuals, as it affects the findings, is referred to as an *experimenter effect*. This threat refers not to the treatment, but rather to the influence of the *specific* experimenter involved, which might not occur if a different experimenter were carrying out the study. When the experimenter is responsible for subjective evaluations of subjects, the experimenter effect may be evidenced in biased evaluations.

Pretest sensitization. The pretest may have alerted the subjects to begin thinking about the behavior or attitude to be studied and may have influenced the findings (usually a threat only in attitude research). If a pretest were not given, the findings might be different.

Posttest sensitization. Ideas presented first in the treatment and later in the posttest may "sound familiar" or "seem to fit," so they are chosen, thus influencing the findings. This threat suggests that if a posttest were not administered, subject learning might not "come together"; that is, it might remain latent. In effect, learning on the posttest itself has occurred—perhaps because of the phrasing of the test, because of the examples used on the test, or because of the intensive thought involved in completing the posttest.

Interaction of history and treatment effects. Were the findings a result of the time frame in which the study was conducted? Were extraneous events occurring at the time of the study which influenced the findings? If the study were carried out today, would the results differ? This threat is particularly a concern when examining research findings which are dated or which were produced during a time frame in which strongly influential variables were present which are present no longer. Consider, for example, the probable difference between the findings of studies of attitudes toward given groups of foreigners and authority figures during times of war and times of peace.

Measurement of the dependent variable. Was the dependent (treatment) variable clearly defined? Did the researcher measure the dependent variable that *should have been measured* in light of the nature and purpose of the study and in relation to the conclusions drawn? Did the instrument employed measure the dependent variable that it was *supposed to measure*? Are the findings dependent upon the type of measurement used? Would another method of measuring the dependent variable change the direction and nature of the findings?

Interaction of time of measurement and treatment effects. Would administration of more than one posttest over a period of time change the findings? This seems most likely to be a threat in studies where the effect being measured is *relatively unstable*, such as changes in attitude behavior which are based on exposure to a short-term treatment.

THREATS TO VALIDITY
IN NONDIFFERENCE STUDIES

We have discussed threats to validity in terms of studies which compare groups or seek to identify differential effects of treatments (difference studies). These threats apply as stated to most educational research studies because most such studies do indeed make comparisons. Some studies (and pre-studies), however, do not make comparisons. Chapter 12, for example, discussed how researchers determined if a historical research study's conclusions were valid. Similarly, Chapter 14 discussed criteria for assessing the validity of evaluation studies which could be used in addition to the threats discussed in this chapter, and Chapter 9 discussed validity in single-subject designs.

Three of the threats to internal validity presented earlier in this chapter are also relevant to evaluating the validity of the findings and conclusions of studies which do not involve comparisons. These three are:

1. *Differential selection* (correct sampling): Did the researcher select an appropriate sample to participate in the study? Was an appropriate sampling technique used?

2. *Experimental mortality* (adequate response or participation rate): Did a sufficiently large number of subjects participate? Was there a pattern to who

participated? If it was an observation study, how many of the subjects being observed dropped out of the study? Was there any pattern to the attrition?

3. *Instrumentation* (reliable and valid instrument): Did the form used elicit or record the types of responses or performances it was supposed to? Was it reliable and uniformly interpretable? If the researcher recorded the responses, was he or she capable of using the instrument uniformly?

The threats to external validity discussed earlier pertain equally well to non-comparison studies' conclusions, since the same problems occur in generalizing the results of studies to other populations and samples.

HANDLING AND INTERPRETING THREATS TO VALIDITY

Researchers seek to identify and control as many threats as possible. They then discuss in detail in the research report the various threats identified and how each was controlled. Sometimes, however, researchers are unable to minimize the influence of one or more of the threats to internal or external validity. When you encounter this situation, you do not attempt to cover up such threats, but rather discuss in detail the nature of each threat and what you believe its influence on the findings of the study was.

In interpreting the research reports of others, you need to consider carefully each of the threats described above. As mentioned in Chapter 6, you need not reject the findings of a study merely because the published report does not contain a complete description. You note the threat and write to the researcher for further information to resolve whether there is cause for concern. If you are unable to resolve the issue, there is cause for concern, and you may wish to replicate the study using your population to confirm that the treatment described in the report is effective in your setting with your population. In all cases, replication is the surest way to confirm the generalizability (external validity) of a study's findings.

SIXTEEN

RESPONSIBILITIES OF THE RESEARCHER

This chapter discusses some of the legal and ethical responsibilities of the researcher. It attempts to help researchers avoid errors and omissions which could cause harm to subjects, ruin researchers' reputations, and prevent researchers from conducting future studies. The discussion is divided into two major sections: responsibilities related to ethical treatment of subjects and responsibilities related to carrying out the study and reporting its findings.

RESPONSIBILITIES RELATED TO ETHICAL TREATMENT OF SUBJECTS

Some General Guidelines on Ethical Practices in Research

1. When there is some question as to whether a procedure or study is ethical, the researcher needs to ask advice and to identify methods of insuring proper procedures.

2. The researcher is responsible for informing subjects of any facts about the study which might reasonably be expected to influence their willingness to participate.

3. The researcher should explain any aspects of the study about which the subject inquires.

4. The researcher should be open and honest at all times. If the study requires mild deception or the concealing of facts, you need to inform the subjects of the nature of the deception or concealment as soon as possible after the conclusion of the study and to explain why it was necessary.

5.   The researcher must honor the subject's refusal to participate or request to drop out of a study. This is particularly important when you are in a position of authority and may have formal or informal methods of coercing participation. Ethics require that subjects have the freeedom to choose whether to participate.

6.   The researcher cannot ethically change later any of the "ground rules" established at the beginning of the study which may have influenced the subject's decision to participate. Once you and the subject agree to a condition, it should be changed only by mutual, free consent.

7.   The researcher is responsible for protecting subjects from harm or danger. If a possible hazard exists in a study, you must inform the subject before he or she agrees to participate, and you must take all possible precautions to minimize the hazard. If a research procedure presents any danger of serious or lasting harm to a subject, you must refuse to use it.

8.   Once the researcher has obtained all data, he or she needs to provide subjects with information about the nature and purposes of the study and to resolve any misunderstandings. If this informing (*debriefing*) of the subjects is to be delayed, you should have sufficient reason to justify such a delay, and it should not bring harm to subjects.

9.   "Harm to subjects" is not just physical or mental anguish. Harm could take the form of increased feelings of insecurity, loss of respect, or inability to obtain a job because reported findings influence the decision of a potential employer. Harm could also include receiving a low grade or not being chosen for a team as a result of the reported findings. Subjects should not suffer in any way as a result of their participation. If, as a result of participating, a subject does suffer some harm, you are responsible for seeing that the consequences are corrected. In practical terms, this may mean counseling or remediation of any deficiencies which can be attributed to the subject's participation in the study.

10.   The researcher is responsible for protecting the subjects' privacy. Data should be confidential. Where data are to be shared, they should be identified by coded numbers to which only you have access. Subjects' names or initials should not be used on data sheets or in reports. You should take great care to maintain confidentiality of data. The procedures to be used to protect data should be explained to subjects as part of obtaining informed consent.

11.   If animals are being used in research, the researcher should examine the *Rules Regarding Animals* drawn up by the Committee on Precautions and Standards in Animal Experimentation of the American Psychological Association.

12.   Research involving drugs should be conducted only in clinics, hospitals, or research facilities designed to safeguard the welfare of subjects—and then only by qualified and certified physicians.

13.   The researcher is responsible for seeing that everyone who works with or under him or her treats all subjects in the study ethically and with respect. Although there is enough legal blame for all to share if staff in the study violate the subjects' rights or treat them improperly, the ultimate responsibility is your own. You should make all staff aware of proper treatment of subjects. Regardless of the issue of legal blame, you have the moral responsibility to see that things are done properly. A breach of ethics in a single study may follow a researcher for the rest of his or her career.

Some Considerations of Ethics in Classroom Research

Their contracts with taxpayers and employers charge teachers to make all reasonable efforts to insure that students receive the highest-quality, most effective instruction possible. In keeping with that charge, teachers are expected to identify the instructional techniques which will prove most effective with each child. This may well entail the practical testing of such techniques in the classroom. Provided that it is not done carelessly or without consideration for its impact on students, such experimentation is normal and expected and therefore is not unethical. This assumes that a teacher maintains the concern for the welfare of the students required by the ethics of the teaching profession.

A teacher may elect to supply some students with extra help, provided that it is above and beyond the normal instruction supplied to all students and that it is being supplied in order to determine if its benefits warrant supplying it to all students. A teacher cannot, however, ethically deprive one group of students of a treatment which will be supplied to another group of students if the teacher knows for a fact that the treatment enhances learning. Teachers need to be aware of local, state, and federal regulations governing instruction. If the law states that a student is to receive a certain type of instruction or is to be included in a class, the teacher cannot exclude that subject from that instruction or class even for the period of a brief study. If a teacher is conducting in-class research to determine which is the more effective instructional technique of several, he or she need not permit students to drop out of the study, since such a study may be considered part of the normal program of instruction.

Attitudinal and survey research in the classroom present special problems. Teachers need to take care in choosing questions. It is questionable whether a teacher could defend using students to obtain extensive, personal information about family life, parental habits, or financial status. The teacher-researcher is probably wisest to address only student attitudes toward instructional techniques, materials, or evaluation, since this form of attitudinal research does not violate the privacy of the family. Teachers must be willing to accept student requests not to participate in such research and should inform them that they have the right to make such requests without penalty.

If concerned that a proposed study may infringe on the educational rights of students, the teacher may wish to seek the informed written consent of the parents of each child. This entails informing parents of the nature and purpose of the study and agreeing to report individual findings to them if they so desire. Observational research does not generally require written consent, provided that the findings are not reported using names. The exception here is if videotape or audiotape recordings are used. If such recordings are made and will be kept for permanent record or will be viewed by anyone other than the teacher, written consent of the parents of the children is required.

Teachers must take care to protect the identity of students in studies. One particular area of ethical concern is the use of student-written papers or tests. Teachers cannot ethically share such materials when the student can be identified by a name, nickname, or distinguishing trademark on the paper (for example, use of an odd colored pen, unusual letter formation, or distinctive handwriting). If two or more teachers wish to participate in a study to test the effectiveness of a set of instructional techniques, they are governed by the same set of concerns as a single teacher. Additionally, they are responsible for maintaining the confidentiality of data. The teacher's lounge is not the appropriate place to discuss achievement and names in the same breath.

If a teacher-researcher is concerned that parents might claim that the teacher consciously chose to exclude their children, it may be wise to assign students randomly to a treatment. This approach may be used even when working with intact classes: the teacher may assign students in classes randomly to one treatment or the other. Teachers may also consider asking students to volunteer to participate in the study. Teachers may involve parents by describing the nature and purpose of the study and suggesting that they encourage their children to participate. Calling for volunteers is a strategy sometimes used to obtain students for studies requiring participation in extra instruction.

The Requirements of the Buckley Amendment and the National Research Act

The Family Educational Rights and Privacy Act of 1974 (usually known as the *Buckley Amendment*) also makes certain demands of educational researchers. This act seeks to protect the privacy of students' school records. It forbids researchers to make available data from student records in such a way that a student and his or her correlated personal or performance data could be identified. The exception here is when the researcher can obtain the written permission of the student (if he or she is 18 years of age or older) or of the student's parents (if the student is under 18 years of age). Such written consent must state the specific data to be used, the purpose for which they will be used, and to whom they will be shown, and it must be signed and dated.

The Buckley Amendment, however, excludes school personnel who are working on legitimate educational projects. They may consult records without written permission, provided that they do not disclose personally identifiable data. Since few researchers wish to identify individuals by name and since interest in group data is more prevalent, the Buckley Amendment does little to restrict school research.

Official representatives of organizations conducting research studies for local and state educational agencies are also exempted from the written-consent provision of the Buckley Amendment if they are researching test measures, are involved in the administration of aid-to-student programs, or are working to improve instruction. Each school system has to consider and approve requests to utilize its files. In general, therefore, as long as the researcher is seeking to help school systems improve instruction, is working in cooperation with or with the approval of the school administration, and is careful to protect the privacy of subjects whose records are examined, there should be no need to obtain written consent.

The National Research Act of 1974 requires that an institutional board review research projects involving human subjects in that organization. This board is charged with determining if a proposed study conforms to ethical standards. The review board may consist of school administrators or may be composed of representatives from staff, faculty, and administration. Provided that the researcher has conformed to the guidelines presented above, he or she should have no difficulty obtaining approval from such a board.

Researchers who are classroom teachers confirming the effectiveness of instructional techniques and who conform to the guidelines presented in the previous section need not submit a proposal to such a review board unless the school system states a specific requirement for such a proposal. A wise teacher-researcher, however, informs his or her building or departmental administrator and, if there is any question, submits a proposal to an institutional review board for approval.

RESPONSIBILITIES RELATED TO CARRYING OUT THE STUDY AND REPORTING ITS FINDINGS

Researchers need also to pay attention to the ways in which they conduct their studies and report their findings. One of a researcher's major concerns should be to maintain good relations with cooperating schools and agencies involved in the study. A single inconsiderate and selfish researcher can make it difficult or impossible for future researchers to work with those schools or agencies. Some of the requirements for maintaining good relations are discussed below.

A researcher going into an educational system should supply administrators with appropriate information on the nature, purpose, and possible implications of the study. You should demonstrate how the results might benefit the system or its students. You should also detail any special needs related to the study and describe how they will be addressed. The quantity of materials and teacher time required should also be discussed. The responsibilities of the researcher and of the system should be agreed upon before the study begins. A caution is warranted here: It is not uncommon for administrators to ask the researcher to modify a study to suit their needs or desires. If such modification does not pose a serious threat to the study's design, you should acquiesce; otherwise you should begin to search for another system for the study.

Some researchers fail to honor the established lines of authority in a system and thereby fail to fulfill their responsibilities to maintain good relations. Experienced researchers coming from outside the system generally start at the top of the hierarchy by conferring with the highest concerned administrator (usually the superintendent or school board in a public school system). Next, they usually confer with appropriate lower-level administrators. Conference with teachers, if appropriate, follows. Discussions with students, parents, and others may also help the researcher.

Few administrators or teachers welcome a "know-it-all." If you come to the system with the idea that you know best in all things, the study will most likely never be completed. Personnel in the system like to be consulted, to be asked for advice, and to contribute to the study. If you are perceptive, you may gain much of value from such input.

Many researchers begin with everyone involved feeling good about their projects. Some researchers then fail to monitor the study properly, misunderstandings occur, and the study becomes a burden to all concerned. Careful and continuous monitoring of the study and periodic visits to the system (if you aren't an employee) will help.

No educational system wants unfavorable publicity. The researcher needs to take care not to use an instrument or treatment which is in conflict with local standards and is therefore likely to cause unfavorable publicity. Likewise, you need to be cautious in conducting attitudinal research. While there is no protection against unwarranted attacks from people who work in the educational system, live in the community, or work for the local press, a researcher who has examined the social system in which the educational system is located, has consulted with personnel who work in the system, has obtained written consent forms, and has provided for the confidentiality of data is less likely to be the object of such attacks or to have them damage the study.

The researcher also has responsibilities in setting up the study and reporting how he or she investigated the topic prior to beginning the study. In researching a topic, you are responsible for conducting a complete and thorough review of relevant materials. If major errors in the search of the literature are made, if important sources of information are overlooked, or if the review is not current and up-to-date, you are at fault. The excuse that the materials were not readily available is inadequate. Research techniques call for searching out materials, not just taking ones near to hand. The availability of interlibrary loans, computer searches, microform copies, and access to resources by telephone all serve to invalidate the excuse that some materials were "inaccessible." The research report should demonstrate that a thorough and comprehensive search of the literature was performed prior to and during the study and that it helped the researcher gain a clearer understanding of the topic under study.

Research studies are founded on the work of others. You use their works to give meaning and direction to your own. In so doing, you often cite individual works and thoughts. The use of the work of others entails certain responsibilities.

In writing the research report, you must take care not to distort the ideas of others or to quote their writings out of context and thus change the original meanings. You are responsible for citing the original source whenever using a quotation or when a paraphrasing resembles the original. You should take great care to avoid the appearance of stealing the work of others. If secondary references are used and the author of a reference cites another's work, you are responsible for going to the original to confirm the accuracy of the secondary reference.

In citing references, the researcher is responsible not only for the accuracy of the content but also for using the correct form. Researchers who fail to attend to the accurate reporting of references (perhaps because they consider it too menial a task) do a disservice to later researchers who might wish to use their work as a basis for future work.

The findings of a study depend upon thorough and careful gathering and analysis of data. Researchers are responsible for checking to insure that all data are accurately collected and recorded. Inaccurate data may be misconstrued by people reading the report as a researcher's attempt to cheat in the study. Incompetence or carelessness may be used to explain such errors, but no sane researcher would consider choosing between being known as a fraud or being known as an incompetent.

Researchers are also responsible for insuring that all calculations are properly performed and that all statistical analyses are appropriate. If you are uncertain which statistical analyses to use, consult a statistician for advice.

A researcher also needs to be aware of the difference between *statistical significance* and *practical significance* (see p. 3). A study may produce statistically significant findings which have no practical significance. When you work with large samples, you may discover that even small differences which are of little or no practical significance may prove statistically significant. You always need to consider whether the findings of a study are practically significant and to address the question of practical versus statistical significance in the final report. Practical significance is *always* more important than statistical significance.

SEVENTEEN

STATISTICAL PROCEDURES FOR ANALYZING DATA

Chapter 17 discusses the three major types of statistics employed in analyzing research studies. Instructions for calculating a variety of parametric and nonparametric analyses of significance are included as well as sample analysis problems demonstrating their use.

This chapter is not intended to replace the many and varied texts on statistical analysis which are available. Rather, it is a ready source and reminder of how to perform and use some of the analyses most frequently employed in research studies in education.

TYPES OF SCORES AND STATISTICS

In quantifying the results of a study, researchers use four types of scores. They also use two types of statistical analyses to analyze the scores. These four types of scores and the two types of statistical analyses are discussed below.

Types of Scores

Researchers use a variety of instruments to obtain data about the characteristics and performance of subjects. Those data may take the form of continuous scores, rank scores, dichotomy scores, or category scores.

1. A *continuous score* (also known as an *interval score*) may occur anywhere along a continuum of scores. There is an equal interval between any score and the score immediately above it and between any score and the score immediately below it. Most scores used in educational research are continuous scores. All intervals are equal for continuous scores. Continuous scores may be either raw scores or derived scores.

As mentioned in Chapter 14, a *raw score* expresses the number of items which the subject answered correctly or the percentage of correct responses which the subject gave. A raw score does not compare the performance of the subjects who took the test. A *derived score* expresses the subject's performance in relation to some comparison group (usually the group of all subjects who were measured using the instrument). Examples of derived scores are *age-equivalent scores*, *grade-equivalent scores*, *percentile scores*, *stanine scores*, and *standard scores* (which are based on the standard deviation of scores).

2. A *rank score* states the subject's ordinal position in relation to the scores of other subjects who were measured using the instrument. Rank scores are usually expressed using words like "first," "second," "thirtieth," and the like.

3. A *dichotomy score* is an assigned score which divides a group of subjects into two distinct subgroups which differ in respect to some variable. Another frequently used name for a dichotomy score is a *nominal score*. Researchers use two types of dichotomy scores: true and artificial.

A *true dichotomy score* divides the subjects into two subgroups on the basis of a difference which actually exists and which observers could easily agree exists. Researchers use variables such as sex and race to make such "true" divisions. A true dichotomy score for the variable *sex* would indicate either that the subject was female or was male.

An *artificial dichotomy score* divides the subjects into two subgroups on the basis of performance on some variable. The division is arbitrary; that is, the researcher chooses the point at which to make it. Researchers often use IQ or reading scores or socioeconomic status (arbitrarily divided into "high" or "low") to create an artificial dichotomy between subjects.

4. A *category score* is an assigned score which divides the group of subjects into more than two subgroups which differ in respect to some variable. This division may be "artificial" or "true." For example, researchers may divide subjects into high-income, middle-income, and low-income groups, into high-, middle-, and low-socioeconomic-status groups, or into above-average, average, and below-average readers. Similarly, subjects could be divided into four age categories, seven height categories, or 22 nationality categories. Whenever you divide the subjects into more than two subgroups, you express this division using a category score.

Types of Statistics

Researchers use two types of statistics in analyzing subjects' performance and characteristics: descriptive statistics and inferential statistics.

Descriptive statistics.   These describe the characteristics and performance of subjects in relation to a set of variables of interest. Descriptive statistics usually describe the "average" performance or characteristics of subjects in the group and describe how much they vary from this average. This "average" for the subjects is usually determined using a *measure of central tendency*. The extent to which the subjects vary from this average is determined using *measures of variability*. Additionally, researchers sometimes use *measures of relationship* to describe relationships among the variables which describe the performance or characteristics of subjects. These three types of descriptive statistics are discussed below.

1. MEASURES OF CENTRAL TENDENCY.

These are scores taken to represent the researcher's best guess about the performance and characteristics of the "average" subject in a sample. The three measures of central tendency are the mean, the mode, and the median.

The *mean* is the most frequently used measure of central tendency. It is the arithmetic average of all the scores. It is obtained by adding up all the scores and dividing by the number of scores.

The *mode* is the score which occurred most frequently. That is, it was received by the largest number of subjects. If the same number of subjects received two different scores, the sample is said to be *bimodal*. If more than two scores occurred with equal frequency, the sample is said to be *multimodal*. If no two subjects received the same score, the sample is *nonmodal*. The mode is sometimes used by researchers to represent the "average" of the sample if there seem to be almost equal numbers of subjects receiving each score and the researcher is looking for a way to indicate that one or more score is a better indicator of the "average" because more subjects received that score.

The *median* is the score which has the same number of scores above it and below it. It is the score in the middle. To determine the median, researchers arrange the scores from smallest to largest, divide the number of scores by two, and count this number of scores from the top or bottom. If there is an odd number of scores (for example, 13), this division produces a number which is not a whole number (in our example, 6.5). If you count the whole-number portion of the result of the division (6 in our example) from the top and from the bottom, you will find that all but one number has been counted. That number is the number in the middle, the median. If the number of scores is even (for example, 14), division by two yields a whole number (in our example, 7). If you count this number from the top, you will identify one number. If you count from the bottom, the next lowest number in the list will be identified. Added together and divided by two, these two scores yield, in the middle of the set of scores, the median.

The median is usually used as a measure of central tendency when the scores to be represented by the "average" are distributed about the mean abnormally. That is, when there are many scores which are quite a bit higher or lower than the mean, they distort the mean, making it unrepresentative of the "average" subject. If there are a few very low scores in a set of otherwise similar scores, the mean could be quite a bit lower than the median. Similarly, a few very high scores could produce a higher-than-representative mean. In these instances, the median would be more representative of the sample.

Let's examine two sample lists of scores:

ODD NUMBER OF SCORES	EVEN NUMBER OF SCORES
61	75
60	75
59	74
58	72
55	71
<u>53</u>	70
52 = median	<u>65</u> ⎫ 64.5*
<u>50</u>	<u>64</u> ⎭
49	63
47	63
45	62
40	60
32	59
	58

number of scores = 13   number of scores = 14

$$\frac{13}{2} = 6.5 \qquad\qquad \frac{14}{2} = 7$$

$$*\text{Median} = 65 + 64 = \frac{129}{2} = \textbf{64.5}$$

Note: The scores identified by counting from the top and bottom are underlined. The median is printed in boldface.

When the mean is a reliable indicator of the "average" for the sample, the median and mode are usually very nearly the same as the mean.

2. MEASURES OF VARIABILITY.

These are statistics which indicate how homogeneous the group of subjects is in relation to a variable. That is, measures of variability tell how good an "average" the measure of central tendency is by examining how much each subject's score varies from that average. Four measures of variability are used to evaluate the homogeneity of the group. They are the range, the standard deviation, the variance, and the normal curve (or distribution of scores).

The *range* tells how great was the spread of the scores. It may be expressed as a single number or as a pair of numbers. If the range is expressed as a single number, it is determined by subtracting the lowest score from the highest score and adding 1. Thus, if the highest score were 75 and the lowest 52, the range would be 24 (75 − 52 = 23; 23 + 1 = 24). Other researchers express the range in a statement giving a pair of numbers: the low and high scores. Thus, they might say, "The scores ranged from 52 to 75."

The *standard deviation* (*sd* or *s*) tells how much on the average the scores the subjects received deviated from their mean. This is one of the most frequently used statistics in all research and it serves as the basis for many statistical analyses. The standard deviation is calculated by getting the mean for the subjects' scores, determining how much each subject's score differs (deviates) from the mean, and then multiplying that number by itself (''squaring it''). You add up these squared deviations from the mean and divide by the number of scores. This produces the *variance*, a statistic which is also used frequently in statistical analyses. To get the standard deviation from the variance, you take the square root of the variance. The resultant number is the standard deviation.

Let's examine how to calculate the variance and standard deviation from a typical set of scores. The formulas are as follows:

$$\text{variance:} \quad s^2 = \frac{\Sigma \, d^2}{N}$$

where
$s^2 =$ the variance
$\Sigma =$ the sum of
$d^2 =$ the difference between each score and the mean multiplied by itself (the deviation squared)
$N =$ the number of scores.

$$\text{standard deviation:} \quad sd = \sqrt{s^2}$$

where $sd =$ the standard deviation
$s^2 =$ the variance.

A sample set of scores:

SCORE (x)	(SCORE − MEAN) = DEVIATION		DEVIATION SQUARED
75	75 − 69 =	6	36
73	73 − 69 =	4	16
71	71 − 69 =	2	4
67	67 − 69 =	−2	4
65	65 − 69 =	−4	16
63	63 − 69 =	−6	36
$\Sigma x = 414$			$\Sigma \, d^2 = 112$

$$\bar{x} = \frac{414}{6} = 69, \quad N = 6$$

($\Sigma x =$ sum of the scores, $\bar{x} =$ the mean of the scores)

$$s^2 = \frac{\Sigma \, d^2}{N} = \frac{112}{6} = 18.67$$

$$sd = \sqrt{s^2} = \sqrt{18.67} = 4.32$$

You will recall from Chapter 7 that the *normal curve* is a distribution of scores which approximates the laws of chance (probability) in its arrangement. The normal curve serves as the theoretical basis for many forms of prediction and statistical analysis, enabling the researcher to draw inferences about the probability that some factor other than chance produced the results. Researchers compare the variability of the scores of their subjects to the theoretical variability displayed by the normal curve to determine if the scores' distributions differ significantly from what the normal curve would lead us to expect.

3. MEASURES OF CORRELATION.

These describe the relationship between or among the variables in a study. In attempting to determine the relationship between two variables, a researcher will use *bivariate* (two-variable) methods. This usually means using the Pearson product-moment calculation (see pp. 171–174) if the scores are continuous or the Spearman rank-order calculation (see pp. 174–177) if they are rank scores. If you are attempting to determine the relationship among more than two variables, you will use *multivariate* (many variable) methods. This usually means using multiple-correlation or multiple-regression calculations.

Inferential statistics.   Researchers use these to draw inferences from the statistics of a sample to an entire population. They use knowledge of the normal curve and significance or probability levels to help them in attributing the findings of a study either to chance or to the influence of some variable. Researchers often refer to the statistical analyses which they use in this way as *tests of significance.* Tests of significance may be of two types: parametric or nonparametric.

A *parametric test* is used to determine if there is a significant difference between or among the performance of groups whose subjects were randomly selected and whose scores are, therefore, normally distributed. Among the most frequently used parametric tests of significance are the *t*-tests and analysis of variance. The calculations for these tests are described in this chapter.

A *nonparametric test* is used to determine if there is a significant difference between or among the performance of groups whose subjects were not randomly selected or whose scores are not normally distributed. Such nonrandom selection is common in educational research where researchers work with intact classes, teams, staffs, or client groups. Among the most frequently used nonparametric tests of significance are the Mann-Whitney *U*-test, the Wilcoxon signed-pairs test, and the chi-square tests. These tests and their calculations are described in the next section.

TESTS FOR A SIGNIFICANT DIFFERENCE
BETWEEN TWO GROUPS

As mentioned above, tests of significance may be either parametric or nonparametric. The parametric tests of significance between two groups are the *t*-test for independent samples and the t-test for correlated samples. The nonparametric tests for significance between two groups are the Mann-Whitney U-test and the Wilcoxon signed-pairs test. These tests and the procedures by which they are calculated are presented below.

There is one additional test of significance which can be used to determine whether there is a significant difference between two groups: *analysis of covariance*. Analysis of covariance will be discussed, but its formula is quite involved and most researchers employ a computer to perform it. Those who are interested in examining the formula and how it is calculated should consult Bruning and Kintz (1968) for an excellent step-by-step presentation.

t-Test for Independent Samples

A *t-test for independent samples* is a parametric test which is used to determine if there is a statistically significant difference between the performance of the randomly selected subjects in two independent groups. By *independent* we mean that the subjects in the groups have not been matched and that the comparison is not between the performance of one group of subjects before a treatment and the same group after the treatment. Researchers often refer to the t-test for independent samples as a *t-test for independent means*, since a comparison of the means and of their respective accuracy as measures of central tendency is inherent in completing the test's calculations.

The procedure for calculating a t-test for independent samples is described below:

1.   Calculate the variance:

$$s^2 = \frac{\Sigma \, d_1{}^2 \; + \; \Sigma \, d_2{}^2}{n_1 \; + \; n_2 \; - \; 2}$$

where

Σ = the sum of
d = the deviation of scores from the mean ($X - \bar{X}$, where X = the score and $\bar{X}$ = the mean of scores for that group)
n = the number of subjects in a group

and the subscripts (1 and 2) indicate the group for which that number is being calculated. Thus, n_1 equals the number of subjects in group 1.

2.   Calculate standard error:

$$\text{st. error} = \sqrt{\frac{s^2}{n_1} + \frac{s^2}{n_2}}$$

3. Calculate t-value:

$$t = \frac{|\bar{X}_1 - \bar{X}_2|}{\text{st. error}}$$

The two vertical lines indicate that the difference between the means should always be expressed as a positive number.

4. Calculate the degrees of freedom (df):

$$df = n_1 + n_2 - 2$$

5. Consult the t-tables for significance level.

The t-tables are tables of numbers based on the probability curve. They correspond to various significance levels for different-sized samples. You look under the degrees-of-freedom (df) column at the level of significance you wish to obtain (usually .05 or .01). If the t-value which you obtained in the calculations is equal to or larger than the tabled value you found, you can say that there is a significant difference between the performances of the two groups. If it is not, you conclude that the difference might have been caused by chance. If there is a significant difference between groups in a test of significance, you determine which group did significantly better by comparing their means. If higher scores are desirable (as in achievement tests), then the group with the higher mean did better. If lower scores are desirable (as with times for running distances and for levels of anxiety), then the group with the lower mean did better.

One additional factor in determining the significance of any difference between group performances is whether the results should be interpreted using a one-tailed or a two-tailed test for probability. The "tails" referred to here are the ends of the normal curve. Chapter 18 will discuss these two types of interpretation, so for the time being we will not discuss them. For now, assume that you will be using two-tailed tests.

Let's look at an analysis of a sample study whose results might be analyzed using a t-test for independent samples.

You are studying two treatments designed to reduce test anxiety in high school students. Twenty students were randomly selected from a sophomore class of sixty. Ten of these twenty students were randomly selected to be assigned to one treatment to reduce anxiety (relaxation therapy) and the other ten were assigned to another treatment (desensitization). At the conclusion of the study all subjects were given a posttest designed to measure their anxiety levels. Possible scores on the posttest ranged from one (extremely low anxiety) to twenty (extremely high anxiety). The scores for the two groups were as follows:

Relaxation group:

SCORE (x_1)	DEVIATION (d_1)	$d_1{}^2$
1	$1 - 7 = -6$	36
2	$2 - 7 = -5$	25
4	$4 - 7 = -3$	9
5	$5 - 7 = -2$	4
6	$6 - 7 = -1$	1
8	$8 - 7 = 1$	1
8	$8 - 7 = 1$	1
10	$10 - 7 = 3$	9
12	$12 - 7 = 5$	25
14	$14 - 7 = 7$	49
$\Sigma x_1 = 70$		$\Sigma d_1{}^2 = 160$

$\bar{x}_1 = 7, \quad n_1 = 10$

Desensitization group:

SCORE (x_2)	DEVIATION (d_2)	$d_2{}^2$
3	$3 - 11 = -8$	64
6	$6 - 11 = -5$	25
6	$6 - 11 = -5$	25
6	$6 - 11 = -5$	25
9	$9 - 11 = -2$	4
13	$13 - 11 = 2$	4
14	$14 - 11 = 3$	9
17	$17 - 11 = 6$	36
17	$17 - 11 = 6$	36
19	$19 - 11 = 8$	64
$\Sigma x_2 = 110$		$\Sigma d_2{}^2 = 292$

$\bar{x}_2 = 11, \quad n_2 = 10$

Calculating variance:

$$s^2 = \frac{\Sigma d_1{}^2 + \Sigma d_2{}^2}{n_1 + n_2 - 2} = \frac{160 + 292}{10 + 10 - 2} = \frac{452}{18} = 25.11$$

Calculating standard error:

$$\text{st. error} = \sqrt{\frac{s^2}{n_1} + \frac{s^2}{n_2}} = \sqrt{\frac{25.11}{10} + \frac{25.11}{10}}$$

$$= \sqrt{2.511 + 2.511} = \sqrt{5.022}$$

$$= 2.241$$

Calculating *t*-value:

$$t = \frac{|\bar{x}_1 - \bar{x}_2|}{\text{st. error}} = \frac{|7 - 11|}{2.241} = \frac{|-4|}{2.241} = \frac{4}{2.241} = 1.785$$

Calculating degrees of freedom (*df*):

$$df = n_1 + n_2 - 2 = 10 + 10 - 2 = 18$$

Assuming that this is a two-tailed test (most tests are—see Chapter 18), you would now consult a *t*-table at the row beside 18 degrees of freedom. You would find that the value under the .05 probability level was 2.101. You will find a copy of the *t*-tables in the Appendix. Since your *t*-value is not equal to or greater than this value, you can say that there is *not* a significant difference between the performances of these two groups. Chance might have produced the distributions of scores in groups that we saw in more than five cases in a hundred. Thus, even though the difference in means seems large, it is not a *statistically significant* difference.

t-Test for Correlated Samples

A *t-test for correlated samples* is a parametric test which is used to determine if there is a statistically significant difference between the performance of randomly selected subjects in two groups which are related in one of two ways. The most common form of relationship is for these two groups to be composed of the very same subjects measured on their performance on two separate occasions (such as pretest-posttest measures). The other, less common relationship occurs when subjects were matched on some variable or variables and assigned to the groups on the basis of this matching (see Chapter 9, pp. 78–80). If either of these types of relationships exists for random samples, the researcher uses a *t*-test for correlated samples—also sometimes referred to as a *t-test for correlated means* or as a *t-test for related means*.

The procedure for calculating a *t*-test for correlated samples is as follows:

1. Calculate the difference (*D*) between pairs of scores. There should be equal numbers of subjects in each group. If there are not, you can use the mean of the group to match the score of a subject who does not have a corresponding subject in that group. Be aware of the threat of statistical regression if too many scores are matched using this method (see p. 133).
2. Square this difference (D^2).
3. Calculate a sum of the differences ($\Sigma\, D$).

4. Calculate a *t*-value:

$$t = \frac{|\Sigma D|}{\sqrt{\dfrac{N \cdot (\Sigma D^2) - (\Sigma D)^2}{N - 1}}}$$

where N = the number or pairs of observations
    Σ = the sum of.

The vertical lines indicate that the sum of the differences should be expressed as a positive number even if it is negative.

5. Calculate the degrees of freedom:

N − 1 where N = the number of pairs of observations

6. Consult the *t*-tables for significance level as described for the *t*-test for independent samples.

Let's examine an analysis of a sample study whose results might be analyzed using a *t*-test for correlated samples.

You are studying a method of inducing weight loss in severely obese individuals whose weights have been relatively stable for the past twelve months. You weigh the subjects at the start of the study. You then administer the treatment, which involves residence at a clinic and includes seminars on changing attitudes, nutritional and physical evaluation, counseling, and a program of physical exercise. At the end of the eight-week program you weigh each individual. You then use a *t*-test for correlated samples to compare their posttreatment weights to their pretreatment weights in order to see if there is a significant difference. The weights were as follows:

Pretreatment Weight (x_1)	Posttreatment Weight (x_2)	Difference (D)	Difference Squared (D^2)
325	312	13	169
315	285	30	900
296	286	10	100
282	261	21	441
275	249	26	676
246	226	20	400
231	215	16	256
230	203	27	729
225	204	21	441
197	167	30	900
$\bar{x}_1 = 262.2$	$\bar{x}_2 = 240.8$	$\Sigma D = 214$	$\Sigma D^2 = 5012$

Calculating a t-value:

$$t = \frac{|\Sigma D|}{\sqrt{\dfrac{N \cdot (\Sigma D^2) - (\Sigma D)^2}{N - 1}}}$$

$$= \frac{|214|}{\sqrt{\dfrac{10 \cdot (5012) - (214)^2}{10 - 1}}}$$

$$= \frac{214}{\sqrt{\dfrac{50,120 - 45,796}{9}}} = \frac{214}{\sqrt{\dfrac{4324}{9}}}$$

$$= \frac{214}{\sqrt{480.444}} = \frac{214}{21.92} = 9.763$$

Calculating degrees of freedom:

$$df = N - 1 = 10 - 1 = 9$$

Once again assuming that this is a two-tailed test, you would now consult a t-table at the row beside 9 degrees of freedom. You would find that the value listed under .05 probability was 2.262. The value under the .01 level was 3.250. Since your t-value of 9.763 is larger than both of these values, the difference between pretreatment weight and posttreatment weight for this group of subjects is statistically significant beyond the .01 level ($p < .01$). This result suggests that the treatment was effective at producing significant weight losses during the period of the study.

Mann-Whitney U-Test

The *Mann-Whitney U-Test* is the nonparametric equivalent of the t-test for independent samples. You use the Mann-Whitney U-test when you are trying to determine if there is a statistically significant difference between the performance of the *nonrandomly* selected subjects in two independent groups. The nonrandom subjects might be individuals who volunteered for the projects, or the two groups might be intact groups.

The procedure for calculating a Mann-Whitney U-test is as follows:

1. Look at all the scores in both groups. Put them in rank order (from low to high). In cases of ties, split the ranks to accommodate.

2. Add up all the rank numbers assigned to the first group (ΣR_1).
3. Add up all the rank numbers for the second group (ΣR_2).
4. Calculate the U-values for each:

$$U_1 = (N_1 \cdot N_2) + \frac{N_2 \cdot (N_2 + 1)}{2} - \Sigma R_2$$

$$U_2 = (N_1 \cdot N_2) + \frac{N_1 \cdot (N_1 + 1)}{2} - \Sigma R_1$$

where N is the number of subjects, and subscripts 1 and 2 indicate the group number.

5. Compare U_1 and U_2. Select the *smaller* of the two values. This is the U-value.
6. Compare this U-value to the values in the table. To find the appropriate value in the table, you will need to use the number of subjects in one group to find the correct column and the number of subjects in the other group to find the correct row. Once you have found the appropriate value in the table, compare it to the U-value you got.
7. If your U-table is *smaller* than the value in the table, then there is a significant difference between the performances of the two groups.

Let's examine an analysis of a sample study whose results might be analyzed using a Mann-Whitney U-test.

You are working with two intact classrooms of fourth-grade students. One class contains nine students and the other contains eleven. The class of nine is being taught spelling by the usual method employed in the school. The class of eleven, however, is being taught spelling by a new experimental technique. At the end of the first semester you wish to see if there is a statistically significant difference between the two groups' spelling performance on a 100-word spelling test. The lowest possible score, therefore, is zero and the highest is 100. The scores produced are as follows:

TRADITIONAL GROUP (x_1)	EXPERIMENTAL GROUP (x_2)	ORDERED SCORES	RANK	FROM GROUP
95	85	40	1	2
92	80	51	2	2
90	73	52	3.5	2
88	71	52	3.5	2
87	65	61	5	2
84	63	63	6	2
83	61	65	7	2
80	52	66	8	1
66	52	71	9	2
$\Sigma x_1 = 765$	51	73	10	2
$\bar{x} = 85$	40	80	11.5	2
	$\Sigma x_2 = 693$	80	11.5	1
	$\bar{x}_2 = 63$	83	13	1

Table continued . . .

TRADITIONAL GROUP (x_1)	EXPERIMENTAL GROUP (x_2)	ORDERED SCORES	RANK	FROM GROUP
		84	14	1
		85	15	2
		87	16	1
		88	17	1
		90	18	1
		92	19	1
		95	20	1

Sum of ranks for the two groups:

RANKS FOR GROUP 1	RANKS FOR GROUP 2
8	1
11.5	2
13	3.5
14	3.5
16	5
17	6
18	7
19	9
20	10
$\Sigma R_1 = \overline{136.5}$	11.5
	15
	$\Sigma R_2 = \overline{73.5}$

Calculations for U-values:

$$U_1 = (N_1) \cdot (N_2) + \frac{N_2 \cdot (N_2 + 1)}{2} - \Sigma R_2$$

$$= (9) \cdot (11) + \frac{11 \cdot (11 + 1)}{2} - 73.5$$

$$= 99 + 66 - 73.5 = 165 - 73.5 = 91.5$$

$$U_2 = (N_1) \cdot (N_2) + \frac{N_1 \cdot (N_1 + 1)}{2} - \Sigma R_1$$

$$= (9) \cdot (11) + \frac{9 \cdot (9 + 1)}{2} - 136.5$$

$$= 99 + \frac{90}{2} - 136.5 = 99 + 45 - 136.5$$

$$= 144 - 136.5 = 7.5$$

$U_1 = 91.5$, $U_2 = 7.5$; the smaller U-value is $U_2 = 7.5$.

Assume that you are once again using a two-tailed test. If you consult the U-tables at the intersection of row 9 and column 11 (or vice versa), you find that the .05-level value is 23. The .01-level value is 16. Your U-value of 7.5 is smaller than either of these, so you can conclude that there is a significant difference between the performances of these two classes with $p < .01$. Since the mean score on the spelling test for the group taught by the traditional method was 85, higher than the 63 mean for the experimental group, and since higher spelling achievement is the desired end result of spelling instruction, these results suggest that the traditional spelling technique is superior to the experimental method. Of course, since the two groups were not randomly selected, you would need to examine differential selection threats (see Chapter 15) to determine if these findings were valid.

Wilcoxon Signed-Pairs Test

A *Wilcoxon signed-pairs test* is the nonparametric equivalent of the *t* test for correlated samples. It is used when the researcher wishes to determine if there is a statistically significant difference between the performance of *nonrandomly* selected subjects who are in some way related. As mentioned earlier, that relationship may be based on matching or on the two "groups" actually being the same group of subjects measured at different times. The nonrandom subjects could be intact groups or volunteers.

The procedure for calculating a Wilcoxon signed-pairs test is as follows:

1. Calculate the difference between matched pairs of scores.

2. If the difference between a pair of scores is 0, drop that pair from analysis.

3. Put these differences in order without regard to whether they are positive or negative. (Order the low score first.) In cases of ties, split the ranks.

4. Add up all the rank numbers for differences with negative values (minus signs). Call this value $T -$.

5. Add up all the rank numbers for differences with positive values (plus signs). Call this value $T +$.

6. Compare $T -$ and $T +$. Select the smaller of the two values.

7. Compare the smaller value to the values in a Wilcoxon table beside the row label which corresponds to the number of pairs of scores which differed from one another and at the intersection of the appropriate level of probability columns (usually .05 and .01).

8. If your Wilcoxon value is *smaller* than the value in the table, you can conclude that there is a significant difference between the two groups of scores.

Let's examine an analysis of a sample study whose results might be analyzed using a Wilcoxon signed-pairs test:

You are studying the effectiveness of a counseling program which is intended to help problem students in junior high improve their classroom behavior. Problem students were identified as those who received on the average more than six demerits from their teachers each week for misbehavior in the classroom. As part of the study, these students will attend a one-hour group counseling session each week, and each student will also spend forty-five minutes with the school counselor each week in an individual counseling session. At the end of the one-year study you compare the average number of demerits received each week by students in the study for the next four weeks to the average number they received prior to the study. You find:

Pairs of Scores Rank-Ordered by Difference Between Pairs

RANK	PRETREATMENT AVERAGE (x_1)	POSTTREATMENT AVERAGE (x_2)	DIFFERENCE	POS. OR NEG.
Drop	6.75	— 6.75	= 0	Drop
Drop	9.9	— 9.9	= 0	Drop
1	6.15	— 6.18	= −.03	Negative
2	9.1	— 9.0	= .1	Positive
3	8.2	— 8.4	= −.2	Negative
4	10.2	— 9.8	= .4	Positive
5	6.15	— 6.9	= −.75	Negative
6	6.33	— 4.5	= 1.83	Positive
8.5	8.0	— 6.0	= 2.0	Positive
8.5	7.32	— 5.32	= 2.0	Positive
9	6.2	— 3.4	= 2.8	Positive
10	7.3	— 3.3	= 4.0	Positive
11	7.0	— 2.1	= 4.9	Positive
12	6.21	— 1.1	= 5.0	Positive

$$N = 12, \quad \bar{x}_1 = 7.486, \quad \bar{x}_2 = 5.904$$

$$T- = 1 + 3 + 5 = 9$$
$$T+ = 2 + 4 + 6 + 8.5 + 8.5 + 9 + 10 + 12 = 71$$

The smaller of these two Wilcoxon values is 9.

When you consult the Wilcoxon table at row 12 (14 − 2 pairs with no difference = 12 pairs of scores which differ), you find that the tabled value in the .05 column is 13 and the tabled value in the .01 column is 9. Your Wilcoxon value of 9 is smaller than 13, so you can conclude that there is a significant difference between the two averages at the .05 level ($p < .05$). Since your Wilcoxon value of 9 is the same as (and not smaller than) the tabled value at the .01 level, you cannot say that $p < .01$.

Once again, in interpreting these statistical results the researcher needs to consider the threats to validity discussed in Chapter 15. Statistical analyses merely tell if a significant difference exists, a difference which is unlikely to have occurred by chance. Statistical analyses do not tell what caused that difference.

Analysis of Covariance

Analysis of covariance may be used with parametric or nonparametric samples. Analysis of covariance is a test which uses some earlier-measured variable, one which is correlated with the scores to be compared between groups, to adjust those scores to minimize any difference between groups which are not due to the treatment. This earlier-measured variable is known as the *covariate*. Often this is an IQ score, a pretest score, or some standardized test score which is available for all the subjects in each group. Analysis of covariance is one of the more frequently used statistical analyses employed in quasi-experimental studies, since it enables researchers to minimize the differential selection threat to validity in such nonparametric studies.

Sometimes you will see studies which use a *t-test for change scores* (also known as a *t-test for gains*) instead of an analysis of covariance to adjust for initial difference among groups. This test was used quite frequently before computer analyses became commonly available. A *t*-test for change scores subtracts a pretreatment measure of a variable (a pretest score) from a posttreatment measure of that variable (a posttest). For each subject in each group this produces a *change score*. The researcher then uses a *t*-test for independent samples (if the sample is parametric) or a Mann-Whitney *U*-test (if the sample is nonparametric) to compare the performances of the two groups.

There are several problems with using change scores:

1. There may be a *ceiling effect* which restricts the size of gains likely to be achieved by subjects who earn high scores on the pretest. The nearer a subject's score comes to a perfect score, the smaller the likelihood of improving that score and the smaller the potential gain.

2. Change-score analysis assumes that it is equally easy for students with different scores to make equal gains. Ceiling effects restrict this, but, more importantly, it is usually more difficult for students receiving higher scores to improve as dramatically as subjects who receive lower pretest scores because of the way in which tests are designed. Lower-achieving students need only learn material of average or below-average difficulty in order to raise their scores, since the lower end of most tests is designed to measure knowledge of this material. In contrast, students who received higher pretest scores have already demonstrated knowledge of this material and must learn more difficult material in order to raise their scores, since the upper end of most tests is designed to measure knowledge of this more difficult material.

3. *Regression to the mean* (see *statistical regression*, p. 133) may occur naturally and influence the size and direction of changes. Pretest and posttest scores may be viewed as repeated samplings. Repeated sampling normally tends to produce scores which are nearer the mean. Thus, subjects scoring at the extremes (high or low) can be expected to receive posttest scores which are nearer the mean than were their pretest scores, making it appear that lower achieving-students made greater gains than perhaps they did while higher-achieving students may appear not to have made much progress.

More complicated tests like analysis of covariance involve fairly complex mathematical calculations. Researchers in the past may have used change scores because they were easy to calculate by hand. With the advent of computerized analyses and greater accessibility to them, this reason should no longer prove valid. Given the choice, researchers should employ analysis of covariance.

It is possible to use more than one variable (covariate) in analysis of covariance to adjust the later score to control for initial differences between groups. Researchers sometimes use a combination of IQ, achievement, and pretest scores to adjust subjects' later scores. Analysis of covariance may also be used to compare the performance of more than two groups. It is related to analysis of variance, a form of the *t*-test extended to analyze more than two groups, which is discussed next.

ANALYSIS OF VARIANCE: A TEST OF SIGNIFICANCE AMONG MORE THAN TWO GROUPS

Analysis of variance is used to compare the performance of randomly selected subjects in more than two groups. Like analysis of covariance, it involves rather complex calculations which few researchers would perform by hand. A computer can perform such calculations quickly and accurately. It is possible, however, to perform an analysis of variance by hand, so long as the researcher takes it in stages and shows patience, courage, and care.

An analysis of variance is calculated in four stages: (I) calculating the total sum of squares; (II) calculating the within-groups sum of squares; (III) calculating the between-groups sum of squares; and (IV) putting it all together to get an *F*-value. You then go to an *F*-table and compare your *F*-value with the values listed. If this *F*-value proves significant, you perform a comparison of individual means using one of several tests. The most frequently used post-analysis-of-variance test of this type is probably Scheffé's test, which is presented below. Scheffé's test, like the Duncan's multiple-range test and other similar tests, is interpreted in the same fashion as a *t*-test.

The stages and steps for calculating an analysis of variance are described below:

STAGE I: Calculating the Total Sum of Squares (*SS*)

1. List the scores for each subject in each group.
2. Calculate a *grand mean* for the total sample:

$$\frac{\Sigma X}{N} = \bar{X}_G$$

where X = score of each subject
N = number of subjects in all groups combined
$\bar{X}_G$ = grand mean for the total sample.

3. Calculate the deviation of each score from this grand mean (d_G).

4. Square each of these deviations ($d_G{}^2$).

5. Add up all squared deviations for the sample:

$$\Sigma \, d_G{}^2 \; = \; Total \; Sum \; of \; Squares \; (SS_T)$$

STAGE II: Calculating the Within-Groups Sum of Squares

1. List scores for each subject in each group.

2. Calculate a group mean for each group:

$$(\bar{X}_1, \bar{X}_2, \bar{X}_3, \ldots, \bar{X}_n)$$

where $\bar{X}$ = the mean

n = the number of groups

and the subscript (1 through n) identifies the group for whom the score is the mean.

3. Calculate the deviation of each score from its group mean (d_w):

$$(X_1 - \bar{X}_1), (X_2 \, a - \bar{X}_2), \ldots (X_n - \bar{X}n)$$

4. Square these deviations ($d_w{}^2$).

5. Total the squared deviations for each group:

$$(\Sigma \, d_1{}^2, \Sigma \, d_2{}^2, \ldots, \Sigma \, d_n{}^2)$$

6. Add the summed squared deviations for the groups together:

$$\Sigma \, d_1{}^2 + \Sigma \, d_2{}^2 + \Sigma \, d_3{}^2 + \cdots + \Sigma \, d_n{}^2 = \Sigma \, d_w{}^2$$

This is the *Sum of Squares Within groups (SS$_W$)*.

STAGE III: Calculating the Sum of Squares Between Groups

1. List the mean for each group:

$$\bar{X}_1, \bar{X}_2, \bar{X}_3, \ldots, \bar{X}_n$$

2. Calculate the deviation of each group mean from the grand mean:

$$(\bar{X}_G - \bar{X}1); (\bar{X}_G - \bar{X}_2); \ldots; (\bar{X}_G - \bar{X}_n) = d_B \text{ for each group.}$$

3. Square these deviations:

    $$d_{B1}{}^2; d_{B2}{}^2; d_{B3}{}^2; \ldots; d_{Bn}{}^2$$

4. Multiply the squared deviation between groups ($d_B{}^2$) for each group by the number of subjects in that group:

    $$(n_1 \cdot d_{B1}{}^2); (n_2 \cdot d_{B2}{}^2); (n_3 \cdot d_{B3}{}^2); \ldots; (n_n \cdot d_{Bn}{}^2)$$

5. Add the resultant figures together:

    $$n_1 \cdot d_{B1}{}^2 + n_2 \cdot d_{B2}{}^2 + n_3 \cdot d_{B3}{}^2 + \ldots + n_n \cdot d_{Bn}{}^2 = \Sigma \, nd_B{}^2$$

    This is the Sum of Squares Between groups (SS_B).

STAGE IV: Putting It All Together

1. Draw up a summary table like the one below:

SOURCE	SS	df	MS	F
Between				
Within				
Total				

Fig. 17-A

2. Fill in the between SS (SS_B) and within SS (SS_W). Added together, they should give you the same total SS (SS_T) that you figured in Stage I. If they don't, you have a math error.

3. To figure the degrees of freedom (*df*) *between* groups, subtract one from the number of groups:

    $$(N - 1) = df \text{ between}$$

    Fill in this number in the table.

4. To figure the degrees of freedom (*df*) *within* groups, figure the degrees of freedom for each group and then add them up:

    $$(N_1 - 1) + (N_2 - 1) + (N_3 - 1) + \cdots + (N_n - 1) = df \text{ within}$$

    Fill in this number in the table.

5. To figure the mean square (MS) *between* groups (MS_B), divide the SS *between* (SS_B) by the df *between* (df_B):

$$MS_B = \frac{SS_B}{df_B}$$

Write this figure in the table.

6. To figure the mean square *within* groups (MS_W), divide the sum of squares within (SS_W) by the degrees of freedom *within* (df_W):

$$MS_W = \frac{SS_W}{df_W}$$

Fill in this number in the summary table.

7. Now you are ready to calculate the F-value:

$$F = \frac{MS_B}{MS_W}$$

8. Do the math, and then consult the F-tables to see if your F-value is significant.

The tables require that you know the degrees of freedom in the numerator and in the denominator. *Don't panic!* You have these. The degrees of freedom in the numerator are the df_B; the degrees of freedom in the denominator are the df_W.

You want your F-value to be equal to or larger than the value in the tables. If your value is larger than the tabled value in "the upper 5 percent points" when you use the correct degrees of freedom, then $p < .05$ and there is a significant difference at the .05 level. Why not see now if your F-value is equal to or larger than the tabled value in the "upper 1 percent point" with the appropriate degrees of freedom? If it is equal to or larger than the tabled value, you can say that $p < .01$, and you have a significant difference among the scores for these groups at the .01 level.

If you do find a significant difference among groups, you will want to use a Scheffé's test to compare group performances to one another to determine which groups differ significantly from one another.

A *Scheffé's test* is calculated as follows:

1. Calculate an F-value for each pair of means using the formula:

$$F = \frac{(\bar{X}_F - \bar{X}_S)^2}{\left(\dfrac{MS_W}{n_F}\right) + \left(\dfrac{MS_W}{n_S}\right)}$$

where F and S are subscripts representing the first and second groups being compared to each other

$n =$ the number of subjects in the group

$MS_W =$ the mean-squares-within figure from step 6 of Stage IV above.

2. Consult an F-table at the .10 level using df_B (from Stage IV) to identify the appropriate column and df_W (from Stage IV) to identify the appropriate row of the table. Write down the value at the intersection of this column and row.

3. Multiply this value by the df_B to get an F-prime (F') value:

$$F' = F\text{-table value} \cdot df_B$$

4. Compare the F-values for each pair of means that you calculated in step 1 to the F' value that you got in step 3. Any F-value which is equal to or larger than the F' value indicates that a significant difference exists between the performance of the two groups which produced those means.

Sample Analysis-of-Variance Problem

At this point it might be wise to examine how one might analyze the results of a study using an analysis of variance.

You are interested in determining which of three approaches to teaching cursive handwriting is most effective with third-graders. You have a class of fifteen students. At the beginning of the school year you use simple random sampling (see pp. 56–57) to divide the class into three groups of five subjects each. Each group is taught cursive handwriting by the method selected for that group for thirty minutes each day. The groups are all instructed in the hour and a half between 9:00 and 10:30 each morning with the order in which they are taught rotating, so that each group has approximately the same number of opportunities to be instructed at 9:00 as at 9:30 and 10:00. At the end of the school year you evaluate all your students' handwriting using a handwriting evaluation scale. Possible scores on this scale range from zero (very poor handwriting) to twenty (excellent handwriting). In order to assure that your evaluations are reliable, you ask two fellow teachers to score the fifteen subjects on the scale. Interrater reliability among the three of you is high ($+ .965$).

The scores received by the subjects are as follows:

METHOD 1 (x_1)	METHOD 2 (x_2)	METHOD 3 (x_3)
8	10	13
10	12	15
10	13	17
11	14	17
11	16	18
$\Sigma\, x_1 = 50$	$\Sigma\, x_2 = 65$	$\Sigma\, x_3 = 80$
$n_1 = 5$	$n_2 = 5$	$n_3 = 5$
$\bar{x}_1 = 10$	$\bar{x}_2 = 13$	$\bar{x}_3 = 16$

STAGE I: Calculating the Total Sum of Squares (SS$_T$):

1. and 2. All scores added together $= 195\ (50 + 65 + 80)$. Number of subjects in sample $= 15$.

$$\bar{X}_G = \frac{195}{15} = 13$$

3.

X_1	$(X_1 - \bar{X}_G) = d_G$	$d_G{}^2$		X_2	$(X_2 - \bar{X}_G) = d_G$	$d_G{}^2$
Group 1:				**Group 2:**		
8	-5	25		10	-3	9
10	-3	9		12	-1	1
10	-3	9		13	0	0
11	-2	4		14	$+1$	1
11	-2	4		16	$+3$	9
		$\Sigma\, d_{G1}{}^2 = 51$				$\Sigma\, d_{G2}{}^2 = 20$

X_3	$(X_3 - \bar{X}_G) = d_G$	$d_G{}^2$
Group 3:		
13	0	0
15	$+2$	4
17	$+4$	16
17	$+4$	16
18	$+5$	25
		$\Sigma\, d_{G3}{}^2 = 61$

Total *SS* (SS_T) $= 51 + 20 + 61 = 132$

STAGE II: Calculating Within-Groups SS$_W$

X_1	$(X_1 - \bar{X}_1) = d$	d^2		X_2	$(X_2 - \bar{X}_2) = d$	d^2
Group 1:				**Group 2:**		
8	-2	4		10	-3	9
10	0	0		12	-1	1
10	0	0		13	0	0
11	$+1$	1		14	$+1$	1
11	$+1$	1		16	$+3$	9
$\Sigma\, X_1 = 50$		$\Sigma\, d_1{}^2 = 6$		$\Sigma\, X_2 = 65$		$\Sigma\, d_2{}^2 = 20$
$\bar{X}_1 = 10$				$\bar{X}_2 = 13$		

X_3	$(X_3 - \bar{X}_3) = d$	d^2
Group 3:		
13	-3	9
15	-1	1
17	$+1$	1
17	$+1$	1
18	$+2$	4
$\Sigma\, X_3 = 80$		$\Sigma\, d_3{}^2 = 16$
$\bar{X}_3 = 16$		

Within-groups *SS* (SS_W) $= 6 + 20 + 16 = 42$

STAGE III: Calculating the SS Between:

Mean/Group	$(\bar{X} - \bar{X}_G) = d_B$	d_B^2	n	$n \cdot d_B^2$
$\bar{X}_1 = 10$	-3	9	5	45
$\bar{X}_2 = 13$	0	0	5	0
$\bar{X}_3 = 16$	$+3$	9	5	45
$\bar{X}_G = 13$		SS_B (Sum of Squares Between groups)		= 90

STAGE IV: Putting It All Together:

Summary Table:

SOURCE	SS	df	MS	F
Between	90	2	45	12.857
Within	42	12	3.5	
Total	132			

Fig. 17-B

$$df_B \text{ (numerator)} = (N - 1) = 3 - 1 = 2$$
$$df_W \text{ (denominator)} = (N_1 - 1) + (N_2 - 1) + (N_3 - 1)$$
$$= (5 - 1) + (5 - 1) + (5 - 1)$$
$$= 4 + 4 + 4 = 12$$

$$MS_B = \frac{SS_B}{df_B} = \frac{90}{2} = 45$$

$$MS_W = \frac{SS_W}{df_W} = \frac{42}{12} = 3.5$$

$$F = \frac{MS_B}{MS_W} = \frac{45}{3.5} = 12.857$$

df in numerator: 2 df in denominator: 12
F-value required for significance at the .05 level: 3.89
F-value required for significance at the .01 level: 6.93

(A copy of the F-tables is available in the Appendix.)

Since your F-value was greater than the tabled values at both the .05 level and the .01 level, you now know that there is a significant difference among the performances of these groups. You will want to do a Scheffé's test, therefore. The calculations are as follows:

1. Calculate F-values for each pair of means using the formula:

$$F = \frac{(\bar{X}_F - \bar{X}_S)^2}{(\frac{MS_W}{n_F}) + (\frac{MS_W}{n_S})}$$

Group 1 and Group 2:

$$F = \frac{(10 - 13)^2}{(\frac{3.5}{5}) + (\frac{3.5}{5})} = \frac{(-3)^2}{(.7) + (.7)} = \frac{9}{1.4} = 6.43$$

Group 1 and Group 3:

$$F = \frac{(10 - 16)^2}{(\frac{3.5}{5}) + (\frac{3.5}{5})} = \frac{(-6)^2}{(.7) + (.7)} = \frac{36}{1.4} = 28.57$$

Group 2 and Group 3:

$$F = \frac{(13 - 16)^2}{(\frac{3.5}{5}) + (\frac{3.5}{5})} = \frac{(-3)^2}{(.7) + (.7)} = \frac{9}{1.4} = 6.43$$

2. Find the tabled F-value at the .10 level at the intersection of the df_B column ($df_B = 2$) and the df_W row ($df_W = 12$). The tabled value is 2.81.
3. Multiply this value by the degrees of freedom between ($df_B = 2$) to get an F' value:

F-prime $= F$-table value $\cdot df_B$
$F' = 2.81 \cdot 2 = 5.62$

4. Compare F-values for each pair of means to this F-prime value:

> Group 1 and Group 2: $F = 6.43 > F' = 5.62$
> Group 1 and Group 3: $F = 28.57 > F' = 5.62$
> Group 2 and Group 3: $F = 6.43 > F' = 5.62$

Based on Scheffé's test, every group's performance differs significantly from every other's. You will note that this test uses the .10 probability level instead of the .05 level. This is one of those few times when researchers use a level greater than .05. This is fine and creates no problems. Scheffé's test is rigorous, and using this probability level does not compromise its results.

Since higher scores on the evaluation scale indicate better handwriting, a higher group mean will indicate better group performance. Since Group 1's mean of 10 is lower than either Group 2's mean (13) or Group 3's mean (16) and those differences are statistically significant, you can conclude that Group 1's treatment appears to have been the *least* effective. Since there is also a statistically significant difference between Group 2 (mean = 13) and Group 3 (mean = 16) and Group 3's mean was higher, you can conclude that Group 3's instruction appears to have been the more effective. As always, you need to consider threats to the study's validity in deciding if the statistical findings reflect sound reasoning and methodology.

CORRELATION COEFFICIENTS

A correlation coefficient compares the variation in one variable to the variation in another variable. This section presents the calculations for the two most frequently used correlation coefficients: the Pearson product-moment correlation coefficient and the Spearman rank-order correlation coefficient.

Pearson Product-Moment Correlation Coefficient

This is the most frequently used correlation coefficient in educational research. Researchers use the Pearson product-moment coefficient when the variables (scores) to be correlated can be expressed as continuous scores (see p. 146). The calculations for this coefficient are as follows:

1. For each subject in the sample, list the subject's score on the first variable (variable X) and his or her score on the second variable (variable Y).
2. Calculate a mean for scores of all subjects on variable X ($\bar{X}$).
3. Calculate a mean for scores of all subjects on variable Y ($\bar{Y}$).
4. Using the mean for variable X, calculate the deviation for each score on variable X received by each subject:

$$d_X = X - (\bar{X})$$

5. Using the mean for variable Y, calculate the deviation for each score on variable Y received by each subject:

$$d_Y = Y - (\bar{Y})$$

6. For each subject, multiply the deviation of the score received on variable X by the deviation of the score received on variable Y:

$(d_X \cdot d_Y)$ for each subject

7. Add these cross-multiplied deviations together to get a sum:

$\Sigma \, (d_X \cdot d_Y)$

8. Square the deviation of each subject's score on X:

(d_X^2)

9. Add these squared deviations on X together to get a sum:

$(\Sigma \, d_X^2)$

10. Square the deviation of each subject's score on Y:

(d_Y^2)

11. Add these squared deviations on Y together to get a sum:

$(\Sigma \, d_Y^2)$

12. Now you have all the numbers to plug into the formula for the *Pearson product-moment correlation coefficient*:

$$r_{xy} = \frac{\Sigma \, (d_x \cdot d_y)}{\sqrt{\Sigma \, d_x^2 \cdot \Sigma \, d_y^2}}$$

where

r_{xy} = the correlation coefficient
Σ = the sum of
d_x = deviations on X
d_y = deviations on Y.

13. Once you have obtained the correlation coefficient (r_{XY}), you will want to test whether it is significantly different from zero. That is, how likely is it that sampling error accounts for this correlation? In effect, you are trying to discover if the relationship you have identified is a result of the influence of

chance selection or the result of an actual correlation. The test to determine this is a type of t-test. Its formula is:

$$t = \frac{r \cdot \sqrt{n - 2}}{\sqrt{1 - r^2}}$$

where

$r =$ the correlation coefficient
$n =$ the number of subjects in sample.

14. The degrees of freedom (df) for this t-test equal:

$$n - 2$$

15. Once you have calculated a t-value, you consult the t-tables under $n - 2$ degrees of freedom. If the t-value that you calculated was equal to or larger than the tabled value at the selected level of probability (usually .05; sometimes .01), then the correlation coefficient is significantly different from zero. You may then say that one would expect such a difference to occur by chance only five times out of a hundred if the obtained t-value equaled or exceeded the tabled value at the .05 level and only one time out of a hundred if the obtained t value equaled or exceeded the tabled value at the .01 level of significance.

Let's look now at a sample calculation of a Pearson product-moment correlation coefficient.

You wish to determine the correlation between a score on a physical dexterity test and a score on a mental maturity test. For each of ten subjects, you have both a score on the dexterity test (expressed as a number from zero to ten) and a score on the mental maturity test (expressed as a number from 0 to 20)

The figures look like this:

(Dexterity) X	(Maturity) Y	$(X - \bar{X})$ d_x	$(Y - \bar{Y})$ d_y	$d_x \cdot d_y$	d_x^2	d_y^2
9	19	+1	+2	2	1	4
8	17	0	0	0	0	0
8	15	0	-2	0	0	4
6	14	-2	-3	6	4	9
8	16	0	-1	0	0	1
8	18	0	+1	0	0	1
7	15	-1	-2	2	1	4
9	19	+1	+2	2	1	4
9	19	+1	+2	2	1	4
8	18	0	+1	0	0	1
$\Sigma x = 80$	$\Sigma y = 170$			$\Sigma (d_x \cdot d_y) = 14$	$\Sigma d_x^2 = 8$	$\Sigma d_y^2 = 32$
$N = 10$	$\bar{X} = 8$ $\bar{Y} = 17$					

Using the figures supplied above to calculate the correlation coefficients, you find:

$$r_{xy} = \frac{\Sigma\,(d_x \cdot d_y)}{\sqrt{\Sigma\,d_x^2 \cdot \Sigma\,d_y^2}} = \frac{14}{\sqrt{8 \cdot 32}}$$

$$= \frac{14}{\sqrt{256}} = \frac{14}{16} = +.975$$

You calculate a t-value to see if the correlation coefficient that you obtained above is significantly different from zero:

$$t = \frac{r \cdot \sqrt{n-2}}{\sqrt{1-r^2}} = \frac{(.875) \cdot \sqrt{10-2}}{\sqrt{1-(.875)^2}}$$

$$= \frac{(.875 \cdot (2.83)}{\sqrt{1-(.766)}} = \frac{2.476}{\sqrt{(.234)}}$$

$$= \frac{2.476}{.482} = 5.139$$

where the $df = n - 2 = 10 - 2 = 8$.

When you consult the t-tables to compare your t-value with theirs, you find that with 8 degrees of freedom the tabled value at the .05 level is 2.306 for a two-tailed test. For a two-tailed test the tabled value at the .01 level is 3.355. Since your t-value of 5.139 is larger than the tabled value at the .01 level, you conclude that this correlation coefficient is significantly different from no correlation at the .01 level ($p < .01$).

Spearman's Rank-Order Correlation Coefficient

When the scores to be compared are rank scores (see p. 147), researchers use the Spearman rank-order correlation coefficient. It is calculated as follows:

1. List the rank score on the first variable (X_R) and the rank score on the second variable (Y_R) for each subject.
2. Subtract the rank score on the second variable from the rank score on the first variable to obtain a difference ($D = X_R - Y_R$) for each subject.
3. Square this difference for each subject (D_2).
4. All up all the squared differences for the subjects to get a sum ($\Sigma\,D^2$).

5. Use the results of the above calculations in the following formula to get a Spearman's rho coefficient:

$$r_{XY} = 1 - \frac{6 \cdot (\Sigma \, D^2)}{N \cdot (N^2 - 1)}$$

6. Once you have obtained the correlation coefficient (r_{XY}), you will want to test whether it is significantly different from zero. That is, how likely is it that sampling error accounts for this correlation? In effect, you are trying to discover if the relationship you have identified is a result of the influence of chance selection or the result of an actual correlation. The test to determine this is a type of t-test. Its formula is:

$$t = R_{XY} \cdot \sqrt{\frac{N - 2}{1 - (r_{XY})^2}}$$

7. The degrees of freedom (df) for this t-test equal:

$$n - 2$$

8. Once you have calculated a t-value, you consult the t-tables under $n - 2$ degrees of freedom. If the t-value that you calculated is equal to or larger than the tabled value at the selected level of probability (usually .05; sometimes .01), then the correlation coefficient is significantly different from zero. You may then say that one would expect such a difference to occur by chance only five times out of a hundred if the obtained t-value equaled or exceeded the tabled value at the .05 level and only one time out of a hundred if the obtained t-value equaled or exceeded the tabled value at the .01 level of significance.

Let's examine a sample calculation of a Spearman's rank-order correlation coefficient.

Your annual budget for next year has been reduced by your funding source. You have asked your staff for input regarding where to make financial cuts. As part of your request to the staff, you asked them to list the twelve services you provide in order of priority with the lowest-priority service receiving a 12 and the highest-priority service a one. You told your staff that you would probably eliminate lower priority services until your projected next year's budget could support the remaining services. When all members of your staff had returned their priority listings, you calculated a mean priority rating for each service and rank-ordered the services as rated by the entire staff. As you looked over this mean rank listing, you remembered that at the start of this year, before you had any financial problems, you asked your staff to do a similar ranking. In that earlier priority listing your staff was asked to list in priority order the twelve services on the basis of which services were of most importance to your clientele. You wonder what relationship exists between a priority listing based on perceived *importance* and one based on *financial constraints*. To find out, you decide to figure a Spearman's rank-order correlation coefficient:

Service Number	Mean Importance Rank (X_r)	Mean Financial (Y_r)	Difference $(D = X_r - Y_r)$	Difference Squared (D^2)
1	1	1	0	0
2	6	8	-2	4
3	2	3	-1	1
4	8	9	-1	1
5	3	2	1	1
6	4	4	0	0
7	5	5	0	0
8	7	6	-1	1
9	11	10	1	1
10	10	11	-1	1
11	12	12	0	0
12	9	7	2	4
$N = 12$				$\Sigma D^2 = 14$

Plugging these numbers into the formula for the Spearman rank-order coefficient, you find:

$$r_{xy} = 1 - \frac{6 \cdot (\Sigma D^2)}{N \cdot (N^2 - 1)} = 1 - \frac{6 \cdot (14)}{12 \cdot ((12)^2 - 1)}$$

$$= 1 - \frac{6 \cdot 14}{12 \cdot (144 - 1)} = 1 - \frac{84}{12 \cdot (143)}$$

$$= 1 - \frac{84}{1716} = 1 - .049 = +.951$$

Although this correlation is quite high, you calculate a *t*-value to confirm whether it is statistically significant:

$$t = r_{xy} \cdot \sqrt{\frac{N - 2}{1 - (r_{xy})^2}} \qquad = .951 \cdot \sqrt{\frac{12 - 2}{1 - (.951)^2}}$$

$$= .951 \cdot \sqrt{\frac{10}{1 - .904}} \qquad = .951 \cdot \sqrt{\frac{10}{.096}}$$

$$= .951 \cdot \sqrt{104.167} \qquad = .951 \cdot 10.206$$

$$= 9.706 \qquad\qquad df = N - 2 = 12 - 2 = 10$$

When you consult a *t*-table with 10 degrees of freedom, you find that for a two-tailed test at the .05 level the tabled value is 2.228. Your *t*-value of 9.706 is larger than this. At the .01 level, the tabled value is 3.169. Since your *t*-value is larger than this value, you conclude that the correlation that you found differs significantly from no correlation and is unlikely to have occurred by chance.

CHI-SQUARE ANALYSES

Chi-square is a nonparametric analysis which is used when data are assigned to separate and clearly defined categories. Chi-square is used to determine whether there is a statistically significant discrepancy between the actual (or *observed*) distribution of responses or ratings among categories and the theoretical (or *expected*) distribution which chance might produce.

In a chi-square analysis, all analyzed data must be in the form of frequency counts, whether they are produced by responses of subjects or by recorded observations of subject behavior. Chi-square analyses are frequently used in analyzing the findings of characteristic studies which employ surveys or observation, since they can help the researcher determine if the distribution of response or observed behavior differs significantly from what chance would lead us to expect. There are two types of chi-square analyses: a *one-sample chi-square* and a *multiple chi-square*.

ONE-SAMPLE CHI-SQUARE (DIFFERENCES AMONG CATEGORIES)

In a one-sample chi-square, the researcher compares the observed frequency distribution of behavior or response of a single group in relation to a set of categories with the expected frequency distribution. The steps for calculating a one-sample chi-square are described below:

1. Calculate the *expected* frequency distribution among categories by the following formula:

    where

    $$E = \frac{N}{C}$$

    E = expected frequency
    N = the number of subjects
         in the sample
    C = the number of
         categories.

2. Determine the *observed* frequency distribution among the categories by distributing responses or behaviors among categories.

3. Create a one sample chi-square table which lists categories and both expected and observed frequencies.

Category

	1	2	3	4	5
Observed Frequency	*	*	*	*	*
Expected Frequency	**	**	**	**	**

Fig. 17–C

*These cells are filled with the actual frequencies of responses or behavior in each category as established in step 2.

**These cells are filled with the expected frequencies of response or behavior as calculated in step 1. Each Category will receive the same expected frequency number.

4. Calculate a *chi-square* (x^2) *value* using the formula:

$$x^2 = \Sigma \frac{(O - E)^2}{E}$$

where

Σ = the sum of
O = observed frequency in
    each category
E = expected frequency in
    each category.

5. Calculate the degrees of freedom (*df*) for the sample:

$df = C - 1$ where C = the number of categories.

6. Consult the chi-square tables using the appropriate degrees of freedom and the level of significance you have chosen (usually .05; sometimes .01). Compare the chi-square value you obtained in step 4 with the tabled value. If your chi-square value is equal to or larger than the tabled value, you can say that there is a significant difference between the expected distribution and the observed distribution among categories (significant at the .05 or .01 level, depending upon which level you chose and whether your *chi-square value* was equal to or larger than the tabled value at that level of significance). A chi-square table is supplied in Appendix X. If your *chi-square value* is smaller than the tabled value, you can say that there is no significant difference between the expected and observed frequency distributions and chance could account for what difference existed.

7. If your x^2 value is equal to or larger than the tabled value, you may wish to examine the category chi-square value which composed the total x^2 value to determine in which category (or categories) the frequency of response deviated from the expected frequency:

$$\text{Category } x^2 \text{ value} = \frac{(O - E)^2}{E}$$

To determine which category frequency deviations are significant, compare the category chi-square value with the tabled value(s) you identified in step 6. Knowing which category frequencies deviated significantly may suggest avenues of study to determine causality.

Let's examine a sample chi-square analysis of differences for one sample among categories:

You have surveyed the first 100 people you met. You asked each only one question: "Would you please express your opinion of the job public schools are doing in educating children by selecting one of the following three responses: a poor job, an average job, or a good job?"

After you tallied all responses, you found that twenty-five people chose poor job, ten people chose average job, and sixty-five people chose good job.

The calculations are as follows:

1. You calculate the expected frequency distribution by the formula:

$$E = \frac{N}{C} = \frac{100}{3} = 33.33$$

    where

    $N = 100$ because you used 100 subjects
    $C = 3$ because you used three categories
        (poor, average, good).

2. You have your observed frequencies: 25, 10, and 65
3. You create your table:

Evaluation of Performance

		POOR	AVE.	GOOD
Frequency	OBSERVED	25	10	65
	EXPECTED	33.33	33.33	33.33

Fig. 17-D

4. You calculate your chi-square value using the formula:

$$x^2 = \Sigma \frac{(O - E)^2}{E}$$

where

$E = 33.33$ for each category
$O = 25$ for poor, 10 for average, and
    65 for good.

$$x^2 = \frac{(25 - 33.33)^2}{33.33} + \frac{(10 - 33.33)^2}{33.33} + \frac{(65 - 33.33)^2}{33.33}$$

$$= \frac{(-8.33)^2}{33.33} + \frac{(-23.33)^2}{33.33} + \frac{(31.67)^2}{33.33}$$

$$= \frac{69.39}{33.33} + \frac{544.29}{33.33} + \frac{1002.99}{33.33}$$

$$= 2.08 + 16.33 + 30.09 = 48.50$$

5. You calculate the degrees of freedom:

$$df = C - 1 = 3 - 1 = 2$$

6. You consult the chi-square tables using 2 degrees of freedom. You find that at the .05 level, the tabled value is 5.99. You find that at the .01 level, the tabled value is 9.21. At the .001 level, the tabled value is 13.82. Since your chi-square value of 48.50 is much larger, you may say that the distribution of responses to your survey differs significantly from a chance distribution ($p <$ .001). This suggests that forces other than chance are at work.

7. You examine the category chi-square values you obtained. They are *poor*: 2.08; *average*: 16.33; and *good*: 30.09. Of these, the values for *average* and *good* are both significantly different from the expected values (their chi-square values are greater than 13.82). You observe that the frequency of respondents choosing *average* was 10, less than the expected 33.33; and that the frequency of choosing the response *good* was 65, more than the expected 33.33. You can say that significantly fewer respondents chose *average* and

significantly more respondents chose *good* than were expected. You cannot say that there was any significant difference between the number of respondents choosing *poor* and the expected number, since its chi-square value was less than the tabled value at even the .05 level of significance.

8. You might wish also to use proportional statistics to describe your findings, since most lay persons find percentage figures easy to understand. Thus, 65 percent of the respondents chose *good*, 10 percent chose *average*, and 25 percent chose *poor*.

Multiple Chi-Square (Differences Among Samples or Subsamples)

In a multiple chi-square, the researcher compares the observed frequency distributions of behaviors or responses of two or more groups in relation to a set of categories with the expected frequency distribution among those categories if all groups were combined to constitute a single homogeneous sample. The steps for calculating a multiple chi-square are as follows:

1. Create a contingency table like the one below:

Category of Response (as many as needed)

Group (as many as needed)	1	2	3	TOTALS
1				
2				
3				
TOTALS				

Fig. 17-E

2. In each of the three categories, fill in the number of individuals in the group who gave that category of response or behavior (observed frequencies).

3. Fill in the categories for each group as above.

4. Total the frequencies in each row (horizontal) and write the number in the totals box at the right of each row.

5. Total the frequencies in each column (vertical) and write that number in the totals box at the bottom of each column.

6. To calculate the expected frequency for each *cell* (the name for each of the boxes in the table), multiply the total at the end of its row by the total at the bottom of its column and divide the resultant number by the total number of subjects in all groups (the figure presented in the right-hand lower totals cell):

$$\frac{R \cdot C}{N}$$

where

R = row or group total
C = column or category total
N = total number of subjects.

As you calculate each of these expected frequencies, write them in parentheses beside their corresponding observed frequencies.

7. Once you have expected frequencies (in parentheses) and observed frequencies for all cells, you are ready to calculate your x^2 using the formula:

$$x^2 = \Sigma \frac{(O - E)^2}{E}$$

8. Calculate your degrees of freedom (df) using the formula:

$$df = (C - 1) \cdot (G - 1)$$

where

C = the number of categories
G = the number of groups.

9. Consult x^2 tables as described in the one-sample chi-square analysis.

Let's look at a sample multiple chi-square analysis.

You want to compare three sections of a history course to determine if one section appears to be more popular with college students at different class levels. It is a required course and all three sections are offered at the same time on the same days of the week, although each has its own instructor. The instructors are Mr. Boring, Ms. Dull, and Dr. Snooze. The class levels of students enrolled in these sections of this course are sophomore, junior, and senior.

1. You prepare your contingency table using enrollment figures for each section and a class-level subdivision for students supplied by the registrar's office. Your observed-behavior (enrollment) contingency table looks like this:

		Section (Instructor)		
	BORING	DULL	SNOOZE	TOTALS
Soph.	5	10	10	25
Junior	10	15	10	35
Senior	15	10	15	40
Totals	30	35	35	100

Class Level

Fig. 17-F

2. You calculate the expected frequencies for each cell using the formula:

$$\frac{R \cdot C}{N}$$

$$\text{Soph. / Boring} = \frac{25 \cdot 30}{100} = \frac{750}{100} = 7.5$$

$$\text{Soph. / Dull} = \frac{25 \cdot 35}{100} = \frac{875}{100} = 8.75$$

$$\text{Soph. / Snooze} = \frac{25 \cdot 35}{100} = \frac{875}{100} = 8.75$$

$$\text{Junior / Boring} = \frac{35 \cdot 30}{100} = \frac{1050}{100} = 10.5$$

$$\text{Junior / Dull} = \frac{35 \cdot 35}{100} = \frac{1225}{100} = 12.25$$

$$\text{Junior / Snooze} = \frac{35 \cdot 35}{100} = \frac{1225}{100} = 12.25$$

$$\text{Senior / Boring} = \frac{40 \cdot 30}{100} = \frac{1200}{100} = 12$$

$$\text{Senior / Dull} = \frac{40 \cdot 35}{100} = \frac{1400}{100} = 14$$

$$\text{Senior / Snooze} = \frac{40 \cdot 35}{100} = \frac{1400}{100} = 14$$

3. You now write the expected frequency in parentheses in each cell. Your new contingency table looks like:

		Section (Instructor)			
		BORING	DULL	SNOOZE	TOTALS
	Soph.	5 (7.5)	10 (8.75)	10 (8.75)	25
Class Level	Junior	10 (10.5)	15 (12.25)	10 (12.25)	35
	Senior	15 (12)	10 (14)	15 (14)	40
	Totals	30	35	35	100

Fig. 17-G

4. You now calculate your chi-square values using the formula:

$$x^2 = \Sigma \frac{(O - E)^2}{E}$$

$$\text{Soph. / Boring} = \frac{(5 - 7.5)^2}{7.5} = \frac{(-2.5)^2}{7.5} = \frac{6.25}{7.5} = .83$$

$$\text{Soph. / Dull} = \frac{(10 - 8.75)^2}{8.75} = \frac{(1.25)^2}{8.75} = \frac{1.56}{8.75} = .18$$

$$\text{Soph. / Snooze} = \frac{(10 - 8.75)^2}{8.75} = \frac{(1.25)^2}{8.75} = \frac{1.56}{8.75} = .18$$

$$\text{Junior. / Boring} = \frac{(10 - 10.5)^2}{10.5} = \frac{(-.5)^2}{10.5} = \frac{.25}{10.5} = .02$$

$$\text{Junior / Dull} = \frac{(15 - 12.25)^2}{12.25} = \frac{(2.75)^2}{12.25} = \frac{7.56}{12.25} = .62$$

$$\text{Junior / Snooze} = \frac{(10 - 12.25)^2}{12.25} = \frac{(-2.25)^2}{12.25} = \frac{5.06}{12.25} = .41$$

$$\text{Senior / Boring} = \frac{(15 - 12)^2}{12} = \frac{(3)^2}{12} = \frac{9}{12} = .75$$

$$\text{Senior / Boring} = \frac{(10 - 14)^2}{14} = \frac{(-4)^2}{14} = \frac{16}{14} = 1.14$$

$$\text{Senior / Boring} = \frac{(15 - 14)^2}{14} = \frac{(1)^2}{14} = \frac{1}{14} = .07$$

The total chi-square value is therefore the sum of these individual values.

$x^2 = (.83) + (.18) + (.18) + (.02) + (.62) + (.41) + (.75) + (1.14) + (.07)$
$\quad = 4.20$

5.   You calculate your degrees of freedom:

$$df = (C - 1) \cdot (G - 1) = (3 - 1) \cdot (3 - 1) = (2) \cdot (2) = 4$$

where

$C = 3$ for the number of instructors
$G = 3$ for the three class levels (sophomore, junior, and senior).

6.   You consult the chi-square tables. With 4 degrees of freedom, the tabled value at the .05 level is 7.81. Since your chi-square value of 4.20 is smaller than this value, you may say that there is no significant difference between students' choices of instructors for this course even when the class level of the students is considered. A chance distribution might have produced the same enrollment figures.

VIOLATING STATISTICAL ASSUMPTIONS

There are certain assumptions upon which statistical analyses are based. Frequently the conditions under which studies must be conducted result in lesser or greater violations of these assumptions. This section will list several of these assumptions, will describe the ways in which researchers violate them, will discuss some "cures" which researchers use to ameliorate the violations, and will identify, where appropriate, any concerns which researchers should consider in applying such "cures."

Assumption: Once samples are selected, all subjects participate.

Violations: In research in the schools, students transfer in and out of school systems frequently. Students are also absent on test dates. In psychological research, the subject is guaranteed the right to withdraw at any point.

Some frequently applied "cures":

1. If a subject leaves before random selection occurs, that subject is ignored.

2. If a subject fails to take the pretest but is present for the treatment, use the grand mean (mean of all subjects in all groups) of the pretest to represent his or her pretest score.

3. If a subject is present for the pretest but drops out or transfers out either before or during the treatment and thus does not take the posttest, use the mean of his or her treatment group on the posttest.

A concern: If a large number of subjects either fails to take the pretest or fails to take the posttest, using means to replace their scores can induce regression to the mean (see *statistical regression*, p. 133). Such regression can distort the findings of the study. Regression seems most likely to be a problem in studies which use small samples or when more than 5 percent of the sample is lost.

Assumption: The variables under study are normally distributed among groups.

Violation: Researchers often use parametric tests even when absence of random selection or presence of observed deviations suggest or confirm that variables are not normally distributed.

Some frequently applied "cures":

1. The researcher can use nonparametric tests (chi-square, Mann-Whitney U, Wilcoxon matched-pairs, Kruskal-Wallis, etc.) instead.

2. The researcher can ignore nonnormality in distribution of the variables and use parametric tests anyway. "It has been found empirically that even if the assumptions underlying the *t*-test are violated, the *t*-test will still provide in most instances an accurate estimate of the significance level for differences between sample means" (Borg & Gall, 1979, p. 455). "The empirical evidence suggests that even for quite small samples, say, of the order of 5 to 10, reasonably large departures from normality will not seriously affect the estimation of probabilities for a two-tailed *t*-test. A one-tailed *t*-test is, however, apparently more seriously affected by nonnormality" (Ferguson, 1976, p. 170). Such flexibility in relation to the assumption of normality is true for most other parametric tests as well.

A concern: Gross departures from normality should not be ignored. Such departures can result in misleading findings.

Assumption: The groups' individual scores vary equally from their group means. "The *t*-test [or any other parametric test] . . . assumes that the distributions of the variables in the populations from which the samples are drawn are normal. It assumes also that these populations have equal variances. This latter condition is referred to as homogeneity of variance. The *t*-test should be used only when there is reason to believe that the population distributions do not depart too grossly from the normal form and the population variances do not differ markedly from equality" (Ferguson, 1976, p. 166).

Violation: Researchers often *assume* that the variables are normally distributed and do not confirm the fact. "With most sets of real data the assumptions underlying the analysis of variance are, at best, only roughly satisfied. The raw data of experiments frequently do not exhibit the characteristics which the mathematical models require" (Ferguson, 1976, p. 235). "The effect of a departure from normality is to make the results appear somewhat more significant than they are" (Ferguson, 1976, p. 234).

Some frequently applied "cures":

1. The researcher can use a test of homogeneity of variance to confirm the equality of variance. These tests are not very sensitive for samples of less than 30 subjects, however.

2. The researcher can ignore the variances. "Moderate departures from homogeneity [of variance] should not seriously affect the inferences drawn from the data" (Ferguson, 1976, p. 234).

3. Where a fairly gross departure from normality exists, the researcher can use a more rigorous confidence level (for example, look for significance at .01 instead of .05).

4. The researcher can use nonparametric tests (e.g., Mann-Whitney U, chi-square, Wilcoxon matched-pairs, Kruskal-Wallis, etc.) to analyze the data.

Assumption: The measures which are used to compare subjects produce comparable scores.

Violations: Some researchers attempt to use grade-equivalent or age-equivalent scores which are not continuous and are not amenable to statistical comparisons. Others use raw scores on different tests. Two tests very seldom have comparable raw scores since one test may be longer or more difficult. Still other researchers use percentile scores or stanine scores, which may vary from test to test depending upon the group used to norm the test.

Some frequently applied "cures":

1. The researcher can convert the scores received on each test to standard scores or normal scores, thus permitting easy comparison. For information on converting to standard or normal scores, see Ferguson (1976, pp. 435–452).

2. The researcher can administer the very same form of the test. While this entails the threat of pretest sensitization, if researchers can allow a fairly long time interval between the two tests to allow for some fading of this sensitization, they sometimes use this "cure."

3. The researcher can use tests of known comparability (as expressed by reliability coefficients, comparable lengths, and comparable difficulties). In practice, alternate forms of some tests meet these requirements, although as tests become more powerful, such "perfect" comparability becomes less likely.

A concern: Standardized tests give the most accurate meausres at or near the mean. As the score received moves out beyond the $\pm$ 1 standard deviation, it becomes less reliable as an accurate measure. Extreme scores (greater than $\pm$ 2 standard deviations) tend to be unreliable because they exceed the range of measurement for which the test was designed. When one attempts to compare extreme scores on one test with later scores on another test, regression to the mean becomes a problem. It is probably wiser to administer another test on the *appropriate* level to students who receive extreme scores on a first measurement instrument.

STATISTICAL ANALYSES
AND THE COMPUTER

For many years researchers had to be extremely competent in higher-level math in order to analyze the results of their studies. This led many researchers to use less sophisticated (but easier to calculate) analyses and precluded other researchers from conducting and analyzing research studies at all. Most universities now either have their own large computers (called ''mainframes'') or subscribe to services which permit their staffs and students to use on-campus terminals to gain access to computers located somewhere off campus. These computers are capable of performing the most complex statistical analyses, provided that the researcher uses the appropriate computer program.

A mainframe computer usually consists of a large processing unit hidden behind locked doors in a dust-free environment, card readers and entry terminals available in a user area, and a very fast line printer located behind a counter or window. After your program has run, you go to the counter or window where you originally handed in your program or obtained your password and get your program's *printout* (printed pages) of results. You then go off to read and interpret this printout or to correct errors in your program, bring it back, and rerun it.

There are a number of packages of computer programs designed to perform statistical analyses on these mainframe computers. Two of the better known of these are Statistical Packages for the Social Sciences (SPSS) and Statistical Analyses System (SAS). Both are capable of performing all the statistical analyses most frequently used by researchers (*t*-tests, analyses of variance, correlations, chi-square, and other nonparametric tests) as well as many of the more rarefied analyses required by sophisticated research designs (such as discriminant function analysis, cluster analysis, and other complex multivariate tests). Both packages are fairly easy to use, although you will need some help from an experienced user in order to get started. The instruction manuals for these packages (referred to usually as "documentation") assume a high level of technical and mathematical competence and may intimidate beginning researchers. Don't despair. University computing centers are usually filled with people who can help you. Your advisor may also be able to help you, as may one of the resident statisticians on campus.

Time on a mainframe computer is very expensive; hundreds of dollars an hour is not unusual. The good news is that you pay only for the actual time that your program runs, and a *very* long program of typical analyses might run only 2 minutes on such a computer. It may, however, take you several hours to prepare computer cards (called "keypunching," since the machine *punches* little holes in cards which help the computer find *key* information) or to enter the information by typing on a computer terminal (called "keying the information in").

Another approach to computer analysis of data from research studies is to use one of the many available packages of programs for microcomputers. Microcomputers (such as the Radio Shack Models III and IV, the Apple II and III, and the IBM Personal Computer) are often available in schools, universities, and many businesses.

A microcomputer usually consists of a system unit with one or two disk drives (to read and record data from diskettes—see discussion below), a keyboard, a monitor (a special type of television set without a channel knob), and a printer. You put the appropriate diskette in the left-hand disk drive and enter information which starts the program. You usually select the analysis you wish to perform from a list on the screen (called a "menu"). You then enter your data and await your printout on the printer.

While microcomputers are not as fast as mainframes and usually cannot handle extremely complex analyses or analyses involving thousands of subjects, they are readily available and often their statistical analysis programs are easier to learn to use and easier to use.

Programs for microcomputers usually come on *diskettes*. A diskette is a square black envelope which contains a thin, round disk covered with an extremely thin layer of the material that is used on audio cassette recording tapes. There is a slot at the bottom, a label in the top left-hand corner, and a 1¼" hole in the center. Diskettes require care in handling; a few tips are in order:

1. Do not touch the disk itself (through the bottom slot); always handle by the black envelope.

2. Never expose a diskette to heat (such as might be present in a closed car on a hot day, on a radiator, or on top of a monitor).

3. Do not bend or fold diskettes or use paper clips or staples to attach them to anything.

4. Do not write on diskettes (either on the label or on the black envelope). Prepare labels before you put them on diskettes. If you *must* write on a diskette's label after it is on the diskette, use a felt-tipped pen and press *very* lightly.

5. Keep liquids and dust away from diskettes.
6. Do not smoke around diskettes.

In selecting a package of statistical analysis programs for a microcomputer, you should look for several features:

1. The package should produce random samples and it should use a different seed number each time (see p. 57).

2. The package should permit you to enter and store files on diskette for later analysis or reanalysis.

3. The package should come with an easily understood instruction manual (documentation) and should give some explanation of the use of each analysis.

4. The package should offer both parametric and nonparametric analyses (see p. 151).

5. The package should provide for registering ownership and obtaining updated versions of the program.

The increased technological sophistication of microcomputers and their increased capabilities have enabled researchers to perform analyses which were beyond their abilities on even the most powerful mainframe computers years ago. It has been the author's experience that many beginning researchers feel more at ease with the microcomputer and find it easier to perform their statistical analyses on a microcomputer. The reason may be that many people feel more in control when working with a microcomputer than with the mainframe. This may be a function of the ability to see all the equipment in one place, to handle the program diskettes and the diskettes which store the data, and to watch the computer "think." Another reason may be the fact that making mistakes on a mainframe is expensive while it merely consumes time when working with a microcomputer. Lastly, good microcomputer programs tend to be "friendlier." That is, when you make a mistake or enter an illogical response, they display easily understood messages on the screen to point out the error and to help you correct it. In the near future, mainframe computer programs may well adopt similar messages.

EIGHTEEN

INTERPRETATION OF RESULTS

This chapter discusses ways of presenting the results of research studies and how to interpret the material presented. It also examines the two types of errors in interpreting results and one- and two-tailed tests of significance.

Chapter 3 defined a *hypothesis* as "a statement of what the researcher believes will be the relationship between two or more variables in a study." A *research* (or *directional*) *hypothesis* was defined as one in which the researcher states which group of subjects he or she expects to perform significantly better, and a *null* (or *nondirectional*) *hypothesis* as one in which the researcher states an expectation that there will be no significant difference between or among the performances of the groups in the study. Chapter 3 recommended that researchers use null (nondirectional) hypotheses because it is usually easier to demonstrate that groups differ significantly than to predict which group will perform significantly better. Chapter 3 pointed out also that the statistical analyses for a null hypothesis are more powerful and rigorous. An added benefit of using null hypotheses is *face validity*: their nondirectionality seems to give readers of the research report a stronger feeling that the researcher was unbiased and objective in conducting the study.

ONE-TAILED (DIRECTIONAL) AND TWO-TAILED (NONDIRECTIONAL) TESTS OF SIGNIFICANCE

As mentioned earlier, which type of hypothesis you employ can affect the way in which the results of the statistical analysis are used to determine the significance of any differences. If you use a directional (research) hypothesis in a difference study between two groups, you will interpret your test of significance as a one-tailed test of significance. If you use a nondirectional (null) hypothesis in such a study, you will interpret your test as a two-tailed test of significance. In studies involving more than two groups, the type of hypothesis you use does not influence how you interpret the statistical analyses.

The "tails" referred to here are the ends of the normal curve. A one-tailed test compares the distribution of scores for your study to one half of the normal curve. A two-tailed test compares your study's distribution of scores to the entire normal curve. The *t*-value (or *U*-value or Wilcoxon value) that is required to declare a difference significant in a one-tailed test is substantially less than the value required for significance in a two-tailed test. This means that it is easier to obtain significant results in a study using a one-tailed test. As you will learn later in this chapter, this reduced level of difficulty in attaining significance invites a *Type I error*: It may cause a researcher to accept a difference as significant when, in fact, it is not.

Most researchers use nondirectional hypotheses and two-tailed tests of significance. They do this to increase the likelihood that a difference that they accept as significant will, in fact, be significant and not merely a chance occurrence. Researchers sometimes choose to use a directional hypothesis and a one-tailed test of significance, however, when they have a strong belief that one group will do significantly better than another. This strong belief should be founded on examination of previous research findings and on trends in the results of previous studies. It should also be based on sound theoretical reasoning.

Let's consider for a moment an example of a study in which you might have reason to use a one-tailed test of significance. Suppose that you are studying the influence of exercise on aerobic capacity. You pretest the aerobic capacity of a group of subjects who have had no formal program of exercise in the past two years and who do not earn their livings performing manual labor. You randomly select one-half of the subjects to participate in an aerobics exercise program three times a week for a year. At the end of the year you compare the aerobic capacity of the group who exercised to their own pretest capacity and to the aerobic capacity of the subjects who took no exercise. It is both logical and demonstrable that frequent exercise should increase aerobic capacity. Therefore, you might well wish to use a *one-tailed, t-test for correlated samples* to compare the exercise group's poststudy capacity to its pretest capacity. You might well wish also to use a *one-tailed t-test for independent samples* to compare the poststudy capacity of the exercise group to that of the nonexercise group.

Let's consider a second study which would employ a directional hypothesis. Suppose you are studying the amount of painkiller that a subject can tolerate before he or she is unable to perceive some stimulus to the affected location. You administer gradually larger doses of the anesthetic and test the extent to which the subject is able to detect a pinprick in the site of the injection. Logically, you can deduce that the larger the dose, the less likely the subject is to be able to detect the pinprick. This is yet another time when a one-tailed *t*-test for correlated samples could be used.

The key to deciding whether to use a one-tailed or two-tailed test of significance is to determine if there is a *strong* reason to believe that one group will perform better than another. If there is any doubt in your mind, use a two-tailed test.

SIGNIFICANCE LEVELS

Once you have determined whether to use a one-tailed or two-tailed test, you need to select a significance (or probability) level against which to measure the significance of the results of your statistical analysis. As mentioned in earlier chapters, researchers generally use the .05 probability level as the point at which they determine the results to be significant. The use of the .05 level means that when the results of the significance test are compared to the values in the appropriate table, if the difference is judged to be significant, there are only 5 chances in 100 that the difference which was rated as significant could have occurred by chance. Researchers seldom use probability levels greater than .05 (for example, .10 or .20) since most researchers consider that such probability levels introduce too great a probability of accepting as significant a difference which occurred by chance. While researchers may note in the report of their studies' analyses that the results were significant at the .01 or .001 level, this does not indicate that the results are "more" significant than results significant at the .05 level. Statistical significance is somewhat like pregnancy or death: A woman is either pregnant or she isn't; you are either dead or you aren't; your results are either significant or they aren't. One cannot be "more pregnant" or "more dead" than someone else. Researchers who report significance *beyond* the .05 level are usually trying to indicate the magnitude of the statistical results, not to indicate "greater" significance. It is almost a certainty that such researchers would feel equally confident if their results achieved significance at the .05 level.

You should be suspicious of researchers who report a significant difference at levels greater than .05. Some researchers speak of results as "approaching statistical significance," "near significant," or "marginally significant." Consider for a minute what you would think if a friend told you she was "almost pregnant." Either the results reached the significance level set by the researcher at the beginning of the study or they did not. If a researcher reports that the results approached significance, he or she should do so only in discussion, and such discussion should accompany a statement that the difference was found to be nonsignificant by the standards set at the beginning of the study. If the research presents arguments related to the power of the test (discussed later in this chapter) which are persuasive, you may wish to reconsider the significance of findings if they "approach significance", but do so with care.

TERMS AND ABBREVIATIONS

This section will discuss a few of the more common terms and abbreviations which researchers use in reporting the results of their studies.

Results of a study and reports of statistical analyses are generally tied to the study's hypotheses. If the study uses a null hypothesis (or several null hypotheses), the results will be stated in terms of "accepting" or "rejecting" the null hypothesis. If the results of the statistical analyses indicate that the difference between or among groups is not significant (often indicated in tables by NS), the researcher usually states that the null hypothesis being tested was "accepted." Since the null hypothesis stated that there would be no significant difference between or among groups, accepting it as true is logical. If the results of the statistical analyses indicate a significant difference (often indicted in tables by $p < .05$, $p < .01$, or $p < .001$), the researcher usually states that the null hypothesis being tested was "rejected" in favor of the research hypothesis, which he or she then states.

Rescarchers generally use p to indicate the probability level for statistical results. Sometimes researchers refer to the probability or significance level as the *alpha level*. $p < .05$ means that the difference that was found should occur by chance fewer than 5 in 100 times that the study was conducted. $p < .01$ indicates a less than 1-in-100 probability of the result being a product of chance. Sometimes researchers report probability ranges (for example, $.01 < p < .05$). Although this is a perfectly acceptable way to report results, when you see a probability range reported, you should examine carefully the numbers used. A few researchers use this technique to "disguise" results which are "almost significant" (for example, $.05 < p < .10$). When examining a report of the relationship of the test of significance to probability, be aware also of the *symbol* used to compare p to the probability level. $p > .05$ is the exact opposite of $p < .05$.

Researchers can make two types of errors in accepting or rejecting hypotheses: Type I and Type II. A *Type I error* occurs when the researcher rejects the null hypothesis in favor of a research hypothesis when, in fact, any difference between or among the groups occurred by chance. Researchers generally use the .05 level of significance to minimize the likelihood of making a Type I error, since such a level sets a rigorous standard for results to attain significance (fewer than 5 chances in 100 of a Type I error). A *Type II error* occurs when the researcher accepts a null hypothesis when actually it should be rejected in favor of a research hypothesis which accounts for the findings. The lower the probability (alpha) level that a researcher uses to judge significance, the greater is the chance of making a Type II error. If you choose too rigorous a standard against which to compare results to attain significance, the results of many studies which *should* attain significance will not do so. This is why most researchers do not set a lower required level for significance than .05, even if their results attain lower levels (for instance, .01 or .001). Researchers are generally more willing to make a Type II than a Type I error. You can think of the .05 level as the one that most researchers have chosen as the happy medium between Type I and Type II errors. Researchers set the probability level *before* they begin the study and if they plan to use a level other than .05, they state the reason.

In recent years, many researchers have begun to calculate the *power* of a statistical test. The more power a test has, the less likely it is to produce a Type II error. While the formula for calculating the power of a test is beyond the scope of this book, it is possible to state two ways in which you can increase the power of the significance test that you use in your study. The first way is to use as large a sample as you can get within the constraints of your resources and which fits the needs of your study. The power of a statistical test is closely related to sample size. The second way is to use instruments which are reliable and which tend to produce a broad range of scores and large differences in the performances of the groups compared. The larger the difference between the performances of the groups compared, the greater the power of the significance test.

In reporting the results of statistical analyses, researchers sometimes state the t-value, U-value, F-value, x^2 value, or Wilcoxon value as well as the degrees of freedom (df) and probability level attained. For example, in reporting the results of a t-test, a researcher might write: $t(12) = 3.482, p < .01$. The number in parentheses (12) indicates the degrees of freedom. The 3.482 indicates the value which was produced by the analysis (in this case, the t-value). A report of the results of an analysis of variance or of an analysis of covariance might contain $F(6, 9) = 4.131$, $p < .05$. The 6 indicates the degrees of freedom in the numerator (the column heading in the F-table) and the 9 indicates the degrees of freedom in the denominator (the row label in the F-table).

Researchers sometimes abbreviate analysis of variance as ANOVA and analysis of covariance as ANACOVA or ANCOVA, possibly as a result of their use as labels on some of the more popular computer programs. Researchers sometimes abbreviate other tests by using the name of the designer(s) of the test (for example, Wilcoxon, Mann-Whitney, Spearman).

IDENTIFYING AND DISCUSSING
THE RESULTS

Attainment of statistical significance is not "proof" of anything except that the results were unlikely to have occurred by chance. No study's results ever "prove" anything. Results give the researcher evidence. It is up to the researcher to *interpret* what those results mean and to attempt to explain what forces (variables) in the study produced the results. The researcher usually does this in the *Discussion* section of the research report. In that section, he or she relates the findings to the theoretical and historical foundation which preceded the study (and which should have been discussed in the introductory section of the report). You need to relate the results of each statistical analysis to the appropriate hypothesis and to explain why you believe that the results support either acceptance or rejection of that hypothesis. This usually entails a discussion of why alternative hypotheses are not valid and, if the null hypothesis is rejected in favor of a research hypothesis, why that research hypothesis and not some other is the correct one.

In interpreting the results, the researcher needs also to address the question of practical significance a well as statistical significance. You should discuss what contribution the findings of the study make to everyday practice and their implications for possible specific changes. You should also discuss any shortcomings of the study and ways in which future studies might be planned in light of your experience with this one. Finally, researchers frequently suggest new areas for study which their results suggest might contribute either to greater general knowledge of the topic of the present study or to the later interpretation or confirmation of its results.

NINETEEN

PREPARATION OF RESEARCH AND REPORTS

This chapter gives some general guidelines on organizing arguments and presenting material in research proposals and reports. Also it presents a complete research proposal and the introductory sections of several proposals with marginal comments. This chapter does not offer a sample research report since one was presented earlier (see pp. 43–49) and since the introductory sections of a research proposal are identical to those of a research report.

SOME GENERAL GUIDELINES FOR ORGANIZING WRITTEN MATERIAL

1. In your review of the literature you may find that opinions or research findings vary. If so, you may find that they cluster around certain opposing "schools of thought." In such cases you may use the differences between these schools as the bases around which to organize and compare writings and findings. If you find one major study which others have supported and which few studies have opposed, you may wish to use a discussion of the foundations and findings of that study as the framework around which to organize other findings. You may then *compare* studies (discuss how they are similar) or *contrast* them (discuss how they are different).

2. In reporting the findings of studies pertinent to your study, do not simply list them. Show that you understand them and can incorporate them into a conceptual base (as disclosed by your review of the literature and as clarified by your hypotheses).

3. Avoid "mechanical" discussions of research studies which dissect and present each study in the same fashion. Incorporate such material into your discussions; do not use assembly-line procedures. Few things are more boring than assembly-line presentations of literature.

4. Use quotations wisely and sparingly. They are like grains of salt: a few add a lot; too many overwhelm that which they were supposed to enhance. Use a quotation when it contributes substantially to clarity. Avoid stringing quotations from different writers together. Such strings of quotes usually read poorly because of style differences.

SOME GUIDELINES ON PREPARING
AND PRESENTING WRITTEN MATERIAL

1. Always write an outline of the major points in your piece of writing before actually writing it (see pp. 203–204). This should help you see how your thoughts fit together.

2. Don't hesitate to use the "cut and paste" technique on your drafts. Often you will discover after writing a section that the paragraphs somehow seem out of order. If so, use scissors and tape to rearrange them.

3. When presenting or discussing the written work or speeches of an individual, always use the past tense ["Smith (1962) wrote . . ." not "Smith (1962) writes . . ."]. Authors may change opinions over a period of time. By using the past tense, you are being more exact and allowing for changes in authors' beliefs, opinions, or attitudes.

4. In referring to yourself, do not write "I." Refer to yourself using an expression such as *the* (or *this*) *author*, *the* (or *this*) *writer*, *the* (or *this*) *researcher*, or *the* (or *this*) *investigator*. Once you use one expression to refer to yourself, use that same expression every time you refer to yourself. Don't call yourself "the writer" one time and "this researcher" another. Also be careful not to use "the" in front of your title ("the writer") one time and "this" the next time. In a paragraph, you may also refer to yourself as "he" or "she" once you have referred to yourself as "the writer" (or whatever).

5. When you make a statement and then follow it with a footnote or a reference in parentheses, the reader is led to believe that *you* are making the statement and that you find support for the statement in the reference.

6. When you write that an author made a statement ["Smith (1962) wrote . . ."], the reader assumes that you are not saying whether you agree or not, but are rather *presenting* evidence or opinion.

7. In general, it is wiser to let your writers and researchers argue for you. Let them *suggest, propose, contend, argue, posit, hypothesize, conjecture, postulate*, and the like. In so doing, you maintain the appearance of objectivity.

8. The statement above suggests that you let your references present their own cases. This does not mean that you try to remain invisible. One of the most effective methods of formulating an argument using references is to present a train of evidence, opinion, and writings and then add your "caboose" which draws it all together. For example, after you have presented a train of conflicting findings from studies and conflicting opinions, you write, "In the light of the disagreement among writers and researchers, this author [or whatever you call yourself] suggests that the major point of disagreement is . . ." *or* "The findings of the studies presented above further suggest to him [her] that . . . ." These are merely examples, not models; the point is that you interpret, relate, summarize, or synthesize the train of thoughts through your own writing.

9. Do not use "obvious" or "obviously." In research nothing is obvious. Use "apparent" sparingly.

10. When you are presenting the works of others, you want to relate them to one another. When there is agreement among the references, you can assist your reader in seeing this agreement by using phrases like:

"In agreement with Jones (1981), Smith (1982) wrote . . ."

"Smith (1982) concurred . . ."

"Similarly, Smith (1982) suggested . . ."

"Smith's findings (1982) were comparable . . ."

"Smith (1982) supported Jones' work (1981) . . ."

"This writer found support for Jones' work in the writings of Smith (1982) . . ."

When there is disagreement among the references, you can help your reader by using phrases like:

"In contrast . . ."

"In disagreement with . . ."

"Smith's findings (1982) disagreed . . ."

"Not all researchers agreed with Jones, however; Smith (1982) found . . ."

"Conflicting studies (Smith, 1982; Wesson, 1984) suggested that . . ."

"The review of the literature revealed conflicting findings: Smith (1982) argued . . ."

11. Avoid statements such as "Authors (or writers or studies) support (or agree or disagree or argue) . . . ." The reader will ask, "Do *all* authors (writers, studies) support it?" Beginning researchers sometimes use sweeping statements about agreement or disagreement among researchers, writers, and studies without considering their implications. You would probably be wiser to use phrases like "Some researchers . . .," "Many writers . . .," and "Several studies . . . ."

12. Be careful about saying "and others" in referring to studies, authors, and researchers. In speech and in everyday writing it is acceptable to make reference to unnamed "others." In scientific writing, however, you need to be more specific. It is acceptable to use "and others" at the end of an introductory sentence which leads into a paragraph or section which then enumerates the specific studies, authors, and researchers which were referred to by the global "and others."

13. Avoid writing in the passive voice ("findings were discovered," "tests were administered," "students were asked"). Use the active voice instead and say who performed the action ("This writer discovered findings," "the teacher administered the tests," "the experimenter asked students"). If you use the passive voice more than just a very few times, the reader begins to believe that you are trying to hide. The reader begins to doubt your competence and confidence.

14. Avoid beginning sentences with "There is (was)," "There are (were)," and "It is (was)." Such beginnings often result is unsupported statements or in failure to achieve agreement between nouns and verbs. (For example, "It is the works that led to the findings.")

15. "Teacher" or "student" goes with "his" or "her," not with "their." A singular noun goes with a singular pronoun: "Each student received his or her test," not "Each student received their test."

16. "Themself" and "ourself" are not words.

17. Writers sometimes get into trouble because they try to squeeze too much into one sentence. If a sentence is getting very long, try to rewrite it as two or three shorter sentences.

18. Avoid jargon. Explain specialized terms. In general, write in a clear and simple style. Trying to sound "sophisticated" or "intelligent" usually results in sounding phoney. Try never to use a "fifty cent" word when a "ten cent" word will do.

19. Don't ever hand in a first draft. Let it sit for at least a few hours—a day or two is better—and then approach it again. You should be able to view it with "fresh eyes" and then improve it.

20. If your advisor is receptive to reading drafts, try to let him or her see your second or third draft. Don't hand your advisor really rough drafts. Drafts should be clearly typed and should not contain errors described in this section.

21. If you plan to send your research report to a journal, examine recent copies of that publication. If it prescribes that you use a given manual of style, do so. Use the organizational format of the journal's articles in preparing your report. Send only final drafts to a journal.

22. You may wish to consult a work like Strunk and White (1959), Walsh and Walsh (1972), Watkins and Dillingham (1979), or Warriner and Griffith (1973) for some guidance in writing.

A COMPLETE SAMPLE PROPOSAL

This section presents a complete sample research proposal. The author includes it to assist readers in designing proposals of their own. Included is a set of questions, statements, and hypotheses related to the problem under study. Also included is an outline of the concepts and facts the proposal discusses.

All references in this sample proposal are fictitious and are included to illustrate the use of documentation and the preparation of a reference list. The author has chosen to use the American Psychological Association (APA) format for references because he finds it easy to use, because it eliminates the cumbersome and often repetitive footnotes which are employed by some other reference formats, and because it is rapidly becoming the accepted standard for research journals.

QUESTIONS, STATEMENTS, AND HYPOTHESES RELATED TO THE STUDY OF THE RELATIVE EFFECTIVENESS OF TEACHER-PRODUCED SPELLING MATERIALS AND COMMERCIALLY PRODUCED, NATIONALLY AVAILABLE SPELLING PROGRAMS

INTEREST QUESTIONS

1. How should spelling be taught?
2. Can teachers improve their students' spelling skills?
3. How is spelling learned?
4. Should spelling be taught using drill?
5. Can all students learn to spell?
6. What are the steps in learning to spell?
7. Which should come first, spelling or vocabulary?
8. Should spelling and vocabulary be taught together?

COMPARATIVE QUESTIONS

1. What types of spelling programs benefit students most?
2. What types of students do better in spelling?
3. What types of spelling exercises lead to the greatest retention of spelling skills?

RESEARCH QUESTION

In terms of improved ability to spell, do fourth-grade students benefit more from working with a variety of teacher-produced spelling exercises or from working with a nationally published spelling program?

PURPOSE STATEMENT

It is the purpose of this study to examine the extent to which teacher-produced spelling materials help fourth-grade students improve their spelling abilities. This examination seeks to explore the effectiveness of such spelling materials when compared with commercially produced spelling materials.

PROCEDURAL STATEMENTS

(See the appropriate section in the research proposal.)

RESEARCH HYPOTHESIS

Fourth-grade students who receive spelling instruction using teacher-produced materials will demonstrate significantly greater increase in spelling ability (as measured by a pretest-posttest comparison of performance on spelling tests on words commonly misspelled by fourth-graders) than will comparable fourth-graders who work with a commercially available, nationally produced spelling program.

NULL HYPOTHESIS

There will be no significant difference in spelling achievement (as measured by a pretest-posttest comparison of scores on tests of words commonly misspelled by fourth-graders) between fourth-grade students who receive spelling instruction using teacher-produced materials and comparable fourth-grade students who work with a commercially available, nationally produced spelling program.

ALTERNATIVE HYPOTHESES

1. Any differences in achievement between the two groups will be due to differences in the teachers' approaches to instruction.

2. Any differences in achievement between the two groups will be due to the spelling words included on the tests.

3. Any differences in achievement between the two groups will be due to differences in the composition of the two groups.

4. Any differences in achievement between the two groups will be due to the extent to which the two teachers feel motivated by the training sessions.

OUTLINE OF MAJOR THOUGHTS PRESENTED
IN RESEARCH PROPOSAL ON RELATIVE
EFFECTIVENESS OF TEACHER-PRODUCED
SPELLING MATERIALS AS COMPARED WITH
COMMERCIALLY PRODUCED SPELLING
MATERIALS

INTRODUCTION TO THE PROBLEM AND NEED FOR THE STUDY

1. There is a move toward the "basics."
2. Concern for the 3 R's is high.
3. Scores on standardized tests have fallen.

4. Traditionally, spelling has been considered part of writing.
5. Research shows that spelling scores are going down along with writing scores.

6. Curricula usually include spelling instruction.
7. This writer checked curriculum guides.

8. Commercial firms also demonstrate an interest in spelling.
9. Some spelling workbooks.
10. Some spelling kits.
11. Idea books and activity books.

12. Problem for elementary teacher: Which type of material?
13. With commercially produced: learning to use.
14. With teacher produced: time to design, produce, test, revise.
15. Literature review showed teachers feel pressed for time.

16. To save time, which material warrants time invested?
17. Steel article on suiting local needs with teacher-produced.
18. Wool article on teaching style match.
19. Tin and Iron: benefits of experts and field tests of commercial materials.
20. This writer says: wiser to use research findings to decide.

21. This writer sought studies.
22. Only found three.
23. None on spelling.

24. Not much research available.

STATEMENT OF PURPOSE

25. Purpose statement.

26. Procedural statements:
   a. Confer with administrators.
   b. Identify population.
   c. Strategy one for sample:
       (1) random 4.
       (2) ask teachers.
       (3) random assignment to treatment.
   d. Strategy two for sample:
       (1) volunteer total sample.
       (2) random 4 from volunteers.
       (3) random assignment to treatment.
   e. Training sessions (experimental):
       (1) to identify techniques.
       (2) to produce and compare.
   f. Training sessions (control):
       (1) Lizard and Swan kit.
       (2) how use.
   g. Synthesize word list.
   h. Taped tests.
   i. Random 5 for pretest.
   j. Random 5 for posttest.
   k. Meeting on how to use tests.
   l. Eight-week study.
   m. Check on teachers every two weeks.
   n. Midpoint preparation questionnaire.
   o. Comparison of scores.

Hypothesis Statement

References

A RESEARCH PROPOSAL FOR A STUDY OF THE RELATIVE
EFFECTIVENESS WITH FOURTH-GRADERS OF TEACHER-PRODUCED
SPELLING MATERIALS AND COMMERCIALLY PRODUCED, NATIONALLY
AVAILABLE SPELLING PROGRAMS

(including a procedural outline and a statistics sheet)

submitted by
Arthur F. Mitchell

July, 1984

INTRODUCTION TO THE PROBLEM AND NEED
FOR THE STUDY

In recent years, there has been a great deal of attention directed toward the teaching of the "basics." Parents, teachers, and administrators have expressed a concern for the teaching of the three "R's"—reading, writing, and arithmetic (Allspice, 1972; Ginger, 1976; Oak, 1979; Oregano, 1984; Pine, 1974; Red, 1978; Thyme, 1976; Yellow, 1980). This concern is most probably a result of public reaction to the eight-year trend in standardized achievement test scores. Nationwide, standardized achievement test scores have fallen an average of six percentage points each of the past eight years, suggesting that student competence in reading, writing, and arithmetic skills has fallen comparably (Bayleaf, 1980).

Traditionally, spelling skills have been considered as part of the body of writing skills (Blue, 1954, p. 86; Caraway, 1980, pp. 102–103; Dill, 1961, p. 14; Maple, 1963; Majoram, 1932, p. 412; Sage, 1975, pp. 106–108). In her study of spelling achievement among elementary students, Green (1979) found that there was a high correlation between scores on the writing skills section of standardized tests and scores on separately administered spelling achievement tests. Magnolia (1977) conducted a seven-year longitudinal study of spelling skills among elementary students in six schools in a large city in Georgia and found that student scores on standardized tests of spelling had declined an average of five and one-half percent over the years 1969–1976. The findings of these two studies and others (Apple, 1961; Black, 1958; Curry, 1983; Poplar, 1978) suggest that scores on tests of spelling skills have declined comparably when compared with scores on tests of general writing skills.

The curricula in most schools have long addressed the teaching of spelling skills. The teaching of spelling skills is included in many curriculum guides developed by school systems. This writer examined two dozen language arts curriculum guides from different school districts in four states which he found on the shelves of the Curriculum Laboratory of a local university. He found that all the guides examined contained references to the teaching of spelling in grades one through six. While these guides may not represent a random sample, the fact that they all addressed spelling skills, some in great detail, suggests that the teaching of spelling is an area of concern for school personnel.

This same concern is demonstrated by commercial firms which produce instructional materials for schools. Several of the larger firms market spelling workbooks (Alligator, 1979; Coyote, 1980; Insect and Kangaroo, 1978; Lion, 1982). Additionally, some firms are now marketing spelling programs, most of which are self-contained, use individual levels of instruction, and are expensively packaged (*Complete Program in Spelling*, 1979; *Lizard & Swan Spelling*, 1980; *Mucmallin Spelling Program*, 1980; *Self-instructive Spelling*, 1980). Still other approaches to the teaching of spelling skills are offered by the numerous "idea and activity" books on the market (e.g., Cotton & Denim, 1969; Doubleknit, 1976; Flannel, 1976; Linen, 1978; Nylon & Gingham, 1972; Polyester, 1980; Silk, 1964).

Elementary teachers are thus faced with an active concern for the teaching of spelling skills and a wide variety of commercially produced spelling materials. Some teachers choose to use the spelling workbooks, some choose to use the marketed spelling programs, and still others use "idea and activity" books to help them produce their own spelling materials. Teachers who use commercially produced spelling materials are faced with learning how the producers intended these materials to be used and with the possible need to modify the materials to suit the needs and limitations of their students. Teachers who choose to produce their own spelling materials are faced with the time-consuming task of preparing, testing, and revising these materials. The literature in education reflects the time restraints and pressures of accomplishing all necessary tasks which many teachers already feel (Magenta, 1980; Paprika, 1979; Pear, 1974; Tan & Orange, 1977; White & Willow, 1979).

In light of the desire to use available time as wisely as possible, teachers need to be able to determine which methods of teaching are most efficacious. Should they use commercially produced materials, or should they produce their own? Steel (1965) argued that materials produced by the teacher are more likely to be effective with students than commercially produced materials, since teacher-produced materials are more likely to suit the needs and abilities of those students. Wool (1973) argued that teacher-produced materials are more likely to suit the teaching style of the teacher and are therefore more likely to be effectively used in the classroom than are commercially produced materials. In contrast, Tin and Iron (1977) contended that most commercially produced materials are thoroughly tested in a variety of school settings and thus reflect the advice and suggestions of a variety of experts and teachers, and are therefore more likely to be effective than teacher-produced materials. It appears to this writer that deciding whether to use commercially produced materials or to develop and produce one's own should be based upon an examination of the findings of research studies on the effectiveness of each type of material in producing increased achievement by students.

In seeking studies which compared the effectiveness of commercially produced materials and teacher-produced materials, this writer was able to find only three studies which made such comparisons (Birch & Seersucker, 1952; Cinnamon, Rayon, & White, 1961; Silver, 1948). He was unable to find any studies which made such a comparison using spelling materials. It appears that there is little or no available research on the relative effectiveness of teacher-produced spelling materials and commercially produced spelling programs.

STATEMENT OF PURPOSE

It is the purpose of this study to examine the extent to which teacher-produced spelling materials help fourth-grade students improve their spelling abilities. This examination seeks to explore the effectiveness of such spelling materials when compared with commercially produced spelling materials. In order to attain this purpose, this writer plans to undertake the following procedures:.

1. He will confer with the administrative council and the superintendent of the targeted school district concerning the nature and purpose of the study in order to obtain the necessary permission to conduct the study.

2. He will obtain a listing of all fourth-grade classes and teachers in the school system. The school system serves a city of 22,000 located near the geographic center of the United States. A total of approximately 400 fourth-grade students in approximately 13 classes constitute the total population of fourth-graders.

3. *Sampling Strategy 1*:
   a. From this pool of fourth-grade classes, he will randomly select four classes.
   b. He will then contact the teachers of these classes, will explain the nature and purpose of the study, and will attempt to persuade these

teachers to participate in the study. If all four teachers agree, he will randomly assign two classes to the experimental treatment (teacher-produced materials) and two classes to the control treatment (commercially produced spelling program).

4. *Sampling Strategy 2:*
   a. If this writer finds that one or more of the teachers of the fourth-grade classes randomly selected declines to participate in the study, he will then contact the teachers of each of the other fourth-grade classes in the school system. He will explain the nature and purpose of the study to each teacher and will identify fourth-grade teachers willing to participate in the study. He will then randomly select four classes from this pool of voluntary participants.
   b. He will then randomly assign two classes to the experimental treatment and two classes to the control treatment.

5. To eliminate possible differences between treatments due to training of the teachers, this writer will hold workshops to help both sets of teachers become familiar with the methods and materials to be employed in their classes.

6. Once two classes of fourth-graders have been assigned to each treatment, this writer will hold a meeting (workshop) with the two teachers involved in the experimental treatment of the study. At this meeting, he will explain how these teachers are to design their own spelling materials. Using a book of ideas, suggestions, and guidesheets prepared by this writer, the teachers will design materials for teaching spelling. Following this meeting, the teachers will exchange materials and will discuss how each material could be used or improved. At a second meeting (workshop), these teachers will determine which of these materials will be used. They will agree to use the same materials in both classes.

7. This writer will also call a meeting of the two teachers in the control treatment. He will present them with the commercially produced *Lizard and Swan Spelling Program* (1980). He will explain how the materials are used and will familiarize the teachers with the procedures used in assigning students to appropriate levels. Each teacher will then take a boxed copy of the Lizard and Swan Spelling Program with him or her. At a second meeting, this writer will work with the two teachers to make certain that they understand how to use the materials. At this meeting, he will present simulations of student spelling skills, will assist the teachers in placing and evaluating students, and will answer any questions which they may have.

8. Using Dolch lists, spelling workbooks, and conferences with fourth-grade teachers, this writer will synthesize a list of two hundred spelling words which fourth-graders commonly misspell.

9. He will prepare a series of ten tape-recorded spelling tests each of which randomly samples twenty of these two hundred spelling words.

10. This writer will then select five of these tests randomly, and these will constitute the composite pretest which will be administered to all four classes during the first week of school.

11. He will also select five tests randomly from the pool of ten tests and these will constitute the composite posttest which will be administered to all four classes at the conclusion of the two month study.

12. This writer will call a meeting at which he will explain to the four teachers in the study how to administer the tests and will address the handling of absences and other problems.

13. The study will be conducted for eight weeks.

14. During the period of the study this writer will confer with each teacher once every two weeks.

15. At the midpoint of the study, this writer will administer a questionnaire to each teacher to determine the extent to which he or she felt that the training meetings (workshops) prepared him or her to work with the materials he or she is using.

16. At the conclusion of the study, this writer will compare achievement between treatments.

STATEMENT OF THE HYPOTHESIS

The hypothesis for this study is stated below in null form. That is,

> There will be no significant difference in spelling achievement (as measured by a pretest-posttest comparison of scores on tests of words commonly misspelled by fourth-graders) between fourth-grade students who receive spelling instruction using teacher-produced materials and comparable fourth-grade students who work with a commercially available, nationally produced spelling program.

REFERENCES

ALLIGATOR, Y. D. (1979). A spelling workbook for 3rd graders. New York: Depression Brothers.

ALLSPICE, A. K. (1972). The three r's: Return to the basics. English Progress, 15, 56–64.

APPLE, T. L. (1961). Spelling achievement of elementary students: Some scores: A discussion. Journal of Measures, 2, 136–144.

BAYLEAF, F. F. (1980). The sad state of standardized test scores: It's even worse than it looks. Journal of Measures, 21, 14–29.

BIRCH, D., & SEERSUCKER, G. (1952). Which should you choose: Theirs or yours? A study of instructional effectiveness of classroom materials. Journal of Instructional Design, 2, 143–147.

BLACK, D. D. (1958). Persistent spelling errors: Reduced literacy component correlations. Researcher Issues, 32 (6), 11–23.

BLUE, L. P. (1954). The art of writing. New York: Aardvark Press.

CARAWAY, M. N. (1980). Teaching writing: A guide to better composition instruction. New York: Harbor Publishing Co.

CINNAMON, R., RAYON, P., & WHITE, O. (1961). Do ninth grade students learn more when working with commercial materials? Journal of Instructional Design, 11, 133–137.

The complete program in spelling for elementary students: Grades 3–4. (1979). New York: Bourbonn Press.

COTTON, A., & DENIM, B. (1969). More good ideas. New York: Goodrich Press.

COYOTE, W. T. (1980). Spelling. New York: Accomplishment Press.

CURRY, U. (1983). Declining spelling scores: Finding or artifact? Journal of Measures, 24, 157–161.

DILL, O. P. (1961). Elements of written expression. Boston: Nob Hill Press.

DOUBLEKNIT, T. (1976). A teacher's resourcebook of games and activities that really work. New York: Success Press.

FLANNEL, L. J. (1976). One hundred good ideas for teaching. Lamar, CO.: Rocky Mountain Press.

GINGER, B. (1976). Sure Johnny can't read, write, or figure: Who teaches those skills? Educational Concerns, 6, 162–169.

GREEN, S. N. (1979). It isn't just the ability to write that is being lost: Spelling's gradual decline. English Progress, 22, 53–57.

INSECT, B., & KANGAROO, M. T. (1978). A student workbook of spelling and vocabulary. Boston: Uniroyal Press.

LINEN, R. R. (1978). The bubblegum and string book: Learning can be fun. New York: Applepound, Decade, Seals.

LION, K. J. (1982). Spelling: Level IV. New York: Rumm Publishing Co.

The Lizard and Swan Spelling Program. (1980). New York: Lizard & Swan.

MAGENTA, R. (1980). How can we do it all? Teaching, 42, 69–70.

MAGNOLIA, S. O. (1977). Decline in standardized test scores in the area of spelling for the years 1969–1976. Journal of Measures, 18, 24–30.

MARJORAM, P. R. (1932). How to write. New York: Sanderson Pub.

MAPLE, C. G. (1963). The relationship between spelling and writing skills. English Progress, 6, 209–212.

The Mucmallin spelling program: Levels 3 and 4. (1980). New York: Mucmallin.

NYLON, A., & GINGHAM, R. (1972). Ideas, games, and activities for elementary classes. Boston: Nob Hill Press.

OAK, C. L. (1979). Parental concern in the basics: A nationwide survey of parental involvement in the return to the "3 r's." (Doctoral dissertation, Hallett University, 1979). Dissertation Abstracts International, 40, 3112A–3113A. (University Microfilms No. 666–62,001).

OREGANO, D. (1984). The basics aren't new or old; they're just necessary. English Progress, 27, 112–119.

PAPRIKA, H. T. (1979). Helping your teachers manage their time better. Elementary Leadership, 28, 79–81.

PEAR, P. P. (1974). The longest 180-days-a-year job in the world. Teaching, 36, 89–90.

PINE, E. (1974). Reading is the only one of the 3 r's receiving enough attention: Some suggestions. Journal of Future Needs, 3, 96–98.

POLYESTER, W. M. (1980). Novel approaches to learning and teaching. New York: Riptorn Pub.

POPLAR, V. R. (1978). Some newer aspects of testing spelling growth: What standardized scores say to the educational tester. Journal of Measures, 19, 48–52.

RED, F. J. (1978). The basics are back again: Survival skills never go out of style. Journal of Teaching and Learning, 44, 266–273.

SAGE, R. P. (1975). Guidelines for writers. San Francisco: Bayside Publishing Co.

The self-instructive spelling program. (1980). Detroit, MI: Motown Pub.

SILK, S. (1964). The biggest book of teaching ideas you ever saw. New York: Deal & Wheel Pub.

SILVER, A. U. (1948). A comparative analysis of the instructional effectiveness of commercially produced materials and teacher-produced materials on the secondary level. Unpublished doctoral dissertation, Granville University, Pennsylvania.

STEEL, S. (1965). Who knows your students best: So why buy a pig in a poke? Teaching, 27, 6–9.

TAN, B., & ORANGE, V. (1977). An in-service plan to help teachers reduce their out-of-class paperwork. Inservice Teacher, 12, 82–85.

THYME, G. (1976). A plan to help your students develop survival skills. Teaching, 38, 84–88.

TIN, S. N., & IRON, F. E. (1977). Why commercially produced materials really are better than locally produced ones. Innovation, 3, 11–12.

WHITE, O., & WILLOW, W. (1979). Time out: Where did all your free time go? Journal of Teaching Issues, 9, 106–108.

WOOL, S. I. (1973). Matching teaching style with instructional materials. Journal of Teaching and Learning, 39, 212–214.

YELLOW, H. I. (1980). An in-service program on the basics for teachers. Elementary Leadership, 29, 6–10.

STATISTICS SHEET

1. Calculation of raw scores for the composite pretest and composite posttest for all subjects in the study.

2. Descriptive statistics on each composite test for each group: mean, median, mode, standard deviation, variance.

3. Analysis-of-covariance comparison of posttest scores among the four classes using pretest scores to adjust posttest scores to control for initial differences.

4. Scheffé's test to compare adjusted posttest means should the analysis of covariance reveal significant differences among classes.

5. Wilcoxon matched-pairs signed-ranks test to determine if there is a significant difference between pretest and posttest performance for each class.

6. t-test for independent samples to compare the results of the questionnaire for the two treatments to determine if there was a significant difference in perceived effectiveness of prestudy preparation between the teachers in the two treatments.

EVALUATED INTRODUCTORY SECTIONS
FROM SAMPLE PROPOSALS

On the following pages are presented the *introduction to the problem* and *need for the study* sections from five research proposals. The purpose statement, procedural outline, and null hypothesis for the fifth study are also included. These proposals are presented, not as models of excellence, but as examples of typical beginning proposals, replete with grammatical and logical flaws.

The author includes these samples in the belief that someone seeking to write a research proposal can benefit from examining the attempts and errors of others and from observing the nature of evaluative comments which advisors might be expected to apply to these attempts. Samples of such comments are supplied in the right margins and at the end of each sample. The author has not corrected every flaw in these proposals. He contends that an overabundance of criticism on early efforts is more discouraging than enlightening. These sample proposals show promise that with persistence should be realized.

A RESEARCH PROPOSAL FOR A STUDY OF IMPROVING LISTENING AND READING BY TEACHING LISTENING AS A SEPARATE SKILL

Introduction to the Problem and Need for the Study

In recent years, there has been a great deal of attention directed toward the teaching of the language arts (Benson, 1978; Corcoran, 1976; DeHaven, 1979; Devine, 1968, 1978; Donoghue, 1977; Jolly, 1980; Landry, 1974; Lee, 1979; Lundsteen, 1979). Lundsteen (1979) listed the four main language arts as: listening, speaking, reading, and writing. To teach students to communicate with others at home, school, and work, all four language arts **need** to be included in the school curriculum (Lundsteen, 1979). **Language is used in nearly everything that is done in the classroom throughout the day (Landry, 1974). Lundsteen (1979) stated that an integrated language arts program is a program in language and thinking.**

Reading and listening are considered to be alike because they both are receptors of language (Devine, 1976; Hollingsworth, 1968; Jolly, 1980; Lundsteen, 1979; Thompson, 1971). There are similarities between reading and listening; they both involve comprehension, interpretation, and evaluation (Devine, 1976; Duker, 1965; Hollingsworth, 1968). There is evidence that instruction in listening may bring improvement in reading skills (Devine, 1978; Duker, 1969; Lundsteen, 1979; Patterson, 1979; Schneeberg, 1977; Thompson, 1971). Duker (1965) **wrote** that it is impossible to effectively plan reading instruction if the interrelationships between reading and listening are ignored.

Listening **is being called** the primary language skill by educators and researchers (Duker, 1965; Gigous, 1974; Goddard, 1976; Hardy, 1976; Jolly, 1980; Lundsteen, 1979). Miller (1968) argued that listening is one of the

---

"Need" is arguable. Others might not agree. Why not let Lundsteen argue that . . .?

How are these two sentences related?

A transition sentence would help here.

"argued" would be better here since this is a strong statement.

Avoid the passive. Try "Some educators and researchers name listening as the primary language skill (Duker . . ."

most common ways of acquiring knowledge. **Listening is a very important beginning link in the chain of subskills that children need in learning how to think (Lundsteen, 1979).**

Smith (1975) stated that while reading (has) always (been) an integral part of the school curriculum, listening (is) not. Landry (1974) (found) that listening has been neglected because educators and parents assumed that if a child had the ability to hear, he also had the ability to listen. Definitions of listening (show) that listening differs from hearing. Landry (1974) defined hearing as a "relatively simple registration of sound stimuli which uses the ears as the receptors and the brain as the area of registration" (p. 74). Landry wrote further that listening "involves giving active and conscious attention to the sounds for the purposes of gaining meaning" (p. 74). Another definition of listening is "listening means structuring what you hear" (Paterson, 1979, p. 19).

Landry (1974) wrote that the teaching of listening has been neglected. In the classroom and in school (curriculum) there is little being done in the training of listening skills (Geeting, 1976; Lundsteen, 1979). **Research has shown that listening can be taught (Thompson, 1971; Tutolo, 1977; Weaver, 1976).** Even a short period of listening training can improve listening skills. (*The Skill Building*, 1976). **Educators and researchers** believe the need for students to become effective listeners is more significant today than ever before (Duker, 1965; Geeting & Geeting, 1976; Gigous, 1974; Goddard, 1976; Hardy, 1976; Lundsteen, 1979; Smith, 1975; Wagner, Hosier, & Blackman, 1975). Also there (is a need) for classroom teachers to help students to develop, reinforce, and refine listening skills (Myers, 1979; *Listening and Speaking*, 1975). **Since improving a child's listening is also likely to result in improved reading abilities,** this researcher argues that there is a need to improve the teach-

---

Let her argue this. You keep saying things as if no one could disagree.

verb tense

Is the reason that you present here the only one possible? If not, how can Landry have "found" it? Try "suggested"

This implies that you agree. Try "make a distinction between listening and hearing."

plural? "curricula"

You need to present some of these studies.

Not all. Try "Many educators and researchers . . ."

Let your references argue this for you!

How can you make this statement? Where is your supporting evidence?

ing of listening (*The Skill Building,* 1976; Thompson, 1971).

General Comments About This Introductory Material

You need to get your references up front and let them argue, propose, contend, and suggest for you. You've made it look as if they just happened to agree with you and that you decided to note that fact in parentheses after you wrote your thoughts.

You need to use some connecting phrases like "in agreement," "additionally," "on the other hand," "in contrast," "in comparison" and the like. As is, your text reads somewhat stiffly. Such phrases help improve the flow of a piece of writing by helping the reader see how one thought or sentence flows into another.

Too often you say things as if no one could dispute that they were true. Don't do that. If a statement is open to dispute, support it with evidence.

A RESEARCH PROPOSAL FOR A STUDY OF THE EFFECTS OF DIVORCE ON THE ACADEMIC ACHIEVEMENT AND SELF CONCEPTS OF FOURTH-GRADE STUDENTS

Introduction to the Problem

Purkey (1970) defined self concept as a complex and dynamic system of beliefs which an individual holds true about himself. He wrote, "Academic success or failure appears to be as deeply rooted in concepts of the self as it is in measured mental ability, if not deeper." Several (p. ?). researchers have found a significant relationship between positive self concepts and academic achievement (Bledsoe, 1967: Brownfain, 1952; Campbell, 1967; Wattenberg & Clifford, 1964; Williams & Cole, 1968). Other researchers have found significant relationships between negative self concepts and academic failure (Bruck & Bodwin, 1962; Durr & Schmatz, 1974; Taylor, 1964).

Purkey (1970) wrote that the home — insert "further" environment plays a vital role in the development of self concept in children. A number of studies have found that divorce, **which** } How may it change the **changes the home environment**, affects the } home environment? Take a self concepts of children. Kelly and Wallerstein sentence or two to describe (1975) found that preschool children of divorced some of the changes.

parents had lower self esteem than preschool children whose parents had not divorced. Landis (1960) studied college students whose parents had divorced and found that the effect of divorce was to lower self concepts and make the students feel less secure and less happy than before the divorce. Munger and Morse (1979) found that self concepts of children of divorced parents were more negative than self concepts of children from intact families.

Combs and Snygg (1959) studied the effects of self concept on behavior and identified characteristics of positive concepts as well as negative concepts. Characteristics of positive self concepts (are) effective and efficient behavior, optimistic attitudes, well-adjusted personalities, feelings of security, broad and deep relationships, fluidity of perception and action, and acceptance of self and others. Characteristics of negative self concepts are exaggerated and defensive behavior, pessimistic attitudes, inability to accept perceptions, aggressiveness, fear and distrust of others, and feelings of anxiety, inadequacy, and threat.

Try "which were identified were" instead.

insert "They identified as"

Some of these characteristics of negative self concepts as described above have been found in children of divorced parents. Kelly and Wallerstein (1975) studied the behavior of preschool children of divorced parents and found a higher incidence of regression, whining, irritability, aggression, and fear of aggression, and anxiety than in children whose parents had not been divorced. McDermott (1968) found that preschool children reacted to their parents' divorce with angry, sad, or detached responses, or constricted and bossy behavior. Children of divorced parents were found to rank high among juvenile delinquents and low achievers in studies done by Bowlby (1961). Children who in latency experienced the divorce of their parents displayed acute behavioral changes visible in the form of declines in school performance, newly troubled peer relationships, and moody irritable behavior (Kelly & Wallerstein, 1975).

insert comma

"divorces"

"with"

There is not complete agreement (between) researchers that divorce affects the self concept, academic achievement, or behavior of children. Hammond (1979) found no significanct differences in self concept, mathematics and reading achievement, immaturity, withdrawal, or peer relations between children from divorced and intact families. Hodges, Wechsler, and Ballantine (1979) found that preschool children of divorced parents did not manifest greater problems of aggression, withdrawal, dependency, and inadequacy than children whose parents had not been divorced. Barry (1979) studied (successful) single-parent families and found that divorce did not affect the self concepts of the children in these families.

"Between" is used to compare 2 things. "Among" is used to compare 3 or more things.

What does this mean? You need to be specific about what constitutes success.

∧The divorce rate in the United States is on the rise. The *Statistical Abstract of the United States* (1979) reports that in 1965 the divorce rate in the U.S. was 2.5 in 1000 marriages; in 1977 the rate jumped to 12.6. Kansas divorce rates were (comparable,) rising from 2.6 in 1000 marriages in 1965 to 5.4 in 1977. Divorce involves not only husbands and wives but the children as well. It has been estimated that more than sixteen percent of all children in the United States under the age of eighteen have experienced the divorce of their parents (Westman, 1972).∧The researcher suggests that, with the divorce rate on the rise, it is likely that divorce will have an increasing influence on the schools.

A transition sentence would help here.

These figures aren't "comparable." What they evidence is a similar trend.

Add "In light of the research presented earlier,"

Need for the Study

Considering that the divorce rate is on the rise and the evidence that divorce may have an influence on the self concept of children, and∧self concept may influence academic achievement, the researcher (believes) that there is a need for more studies to determine the effects of divorce on the self concept and academic achievement of children. This need is compounded by the fact that there already are conflicting findings in previous studies of these relationships.

insert "that"

"argues"

General Comments Regarding These Sections

Good use of references and use of connecting phrases. Need for the study could have been stronger.

A RESEARCH PROPOSAL FOR A STUDY TO COMPARE THE EFFECTIVENESS OF PICTURE RECIPE FORMS AND STANDARD RECIPE FORMS WITH THE HEARING-IMPAIRED

Introduction to the Problem and Need for the Study

A hearing-impaired person has many problems that a person without a handicap may not understand. Speaking and listening are used many times during a routine day. But the hearing-impaired person cannot hear what is going on in the world around him or her and may not be able to tell someone verbally what he wants. **Newby (1979) stated "A hearing handicapped person is confronted with an unusual situation."** ⟵

These first two sentences should be combined into one.

This seems like a totally useless quotation.

(p. ?)

In school systems, the hearing-impaired students are in an unusual situation. Many students <u>have been</u> **mainstreamed.** Vernon (1979) (discussed) in his editorial in *American Annals of the Deaf* that even the strong proponents of (PL 94-142) say that mainstreaming is not working effectively for many of the handicapped children, especially for the majority of the deaf or hearing-impaired. Teachers may have some effect on **mainstreaming** because they may not have the special training such as (sign language) that may be needed to work with some hearing-impaired students. Halchin (1976) (contends) that teaching the deaf is a profession that requires highly specialized preparation.

The teaching techniques and sensitivity to the student's unique problems should be considered by the teacher (Yost, 1980). If sensitivity is not considered, then the teacher may lose the confidence of the student before he or she even

Weak sentence.
Add "s".

You need to discuss what "mainstreaming" is.

He seems to have "suggested" rather than "discussed."

You need to explain what PL 94-142 is.

The effect is not on "mainstreaming." It is on the "effectiveness of mainstreaming."

"Sign language" is a communication system, not "training."

Should be past tense.

In what follows, you do not support your arguments. You slip instead into a biased *I say* argument. You need to support your claims.

gets started teaching the students. Teachers (do) (need) to think about how they (should) plan for the hearing-impaired and what teaching techniques can be used with these students. Educators (need) to be aware of the limitations of handicapped children and devote more effort to planning and preparing educational materials that (will help) overcome such limitations as impaired hearing or total deafness (Garton & Bass, 1974). Beckman (1978) stated, "Because each hearing-impaired student is unique, teaching methods needed for each student will vary. Teachers should try to get to know the student, try a variety of teaching techniques, and test the student to determine which method seems most successful" (p. 37). Some of the problems of teachers were suggested in a study by Martin (1978) who found that, "The greatest **needs** identified by the teachers in working with handicapped students **are appropriate instructional materials and resources and assistance in evaluating academic progress**" (p. 16).

See page 39 for opinion words.

These are things which are needed; they are not needs. Don't confuse the two things.

The researcher found that (most) research studies **(Browns, 1979; Christianson & Silvia, 1978; Crandall, 1979; Pini, 1979; Schmidt & Dunn, 1980; Stauffer, 1979)** have concerned the hearing-impaired student in the regular classroom and the teachers who have to deal with their problems. The studies covered topics of reading, writing, math, science, and physical education for the hearing-impaired. **The researcher found only one study (Garton & Bass, 1974) about the hearing-impaired in home economics.**

Of all types?! No. Tell what type.

You need to discuss what these people studied and found.

This brings about a question for the **hearing-impaired home economics teacher.** How do hearing-impaired students learn differently from "normal" students in food preparation classes? **In an interview Marc Gold (Oppert, 1975)** stated, "With the more limited individuals, the difference may be being able to or not being able to cook. But what it is going to take to get them to learn may be something different" (p. 94). Home economics teachers that

Can't you generalize the results of any of the other studies to the needs and problems of Home Economics?

No! The teacher isn't "hearing-impaired."

This is confusing. Who said what and where?

have hearing-impaired students in their classrooms must understand that they will need to meet the demands of these students and may need to develop a whole new set of skills themselves to do this task. Beckman (1978) found that "Deafness is one more variable among many that teachers must take into account when planning a student's home economics program" (p. 34).

Who says? Why? On what evidence is this must *based?*

There are many tasks and responsibilities for students when they work in a food preparation class. Some of these responsibilities may be cleaning up after cooking, to use the equipment correctly, and follow directions that are both oral and written. Students learn to work in the kitchen by using various kitchen appliances and utensils and understanding kitchen safety (Malsam, 1980). Hearing-impaired students may have problems in the food preparation classes because they may not understand verbal directions, cannot comprehend the language on written tests, or may not be able to read recipes or textbooks.

"are"
"using"
"following"
"given both orally and in writing."

insert "additional"

Hearing-impaired students may have difficulty understanding verbal directions. Teachers may think that students can lip-read the directions. But this is not always true. A survey by Whiteford and Anderson (1977) found that teachers who had not worked with hearing-impaired students preferred not to use visual aids for the students but would rather alter the arrangement of the classroom by having the students sit in front of the class so they could understand better. The experienced teachers used the blackboard or faced the class. If a student does not understand verbal directions, then the teacher should recognize this and take a different course of action.

Replace with "verbal"
Combine with previous sentence.
Which students?
Be specific. How does this help?
How experienced?
Who says?

Another problem that may occur for the hearing-impaired students are grades determined on written tests. Materials used for instruction and grading by **hearing-impaired home economics teachers** should be revised to be appropriate for hearing-impaired students. Grades may be given on products that are pro-

noun-verb problem
Try "teachers of the hearing . . ."

duced by the students so that an evaluation can be made of their skills. Spencer and Lohman (1977) stated that "Written tests should not be the only basis for (their) [the student's] grade" (p. 66).
Omit as unnecessary.

A concern among home economics teachers of the hearing-impaired is the readability of materials used in the classroom. Elliott (1978) found that "Educators of the deaf have long been concerned about the readability of materials" (p. 18). Beckman (1978) found that "Since they are unable to hear, hearing-impaired students do not acquire English as hearing students do. Mastering English becomes a formidable task for them. Even after years in school, hearing-impaired high school students may still read on only a fourth or fifth grade level" (p . 36). Beckman (1978) (contends) that very few commercial curriculum materials have been produced by commercial publishers for home economics teachers to use with hearing-impaired students. Some materials written by commercial publishers are at a lower language level which would help the hearing-impaired but they have too much repetition of concepts which make the materials more appropriate for mentally retarded students.
Use past tense.

This sentence is confusing. It needs rewriting.

County home economists in the state of Kansas make available films, literature, and bulletins to disabled children and adults. Cobe (1978) recommended these materials be used by the handicapped. However, this material contains the problem of a **high language usage level**. Even materials written on a junior high level are often too hard for the hearing-impaired to understand (Beckman, 1978).
Avoid jargon like this. Say it simply and clearly instead.

Dahl, Appleby, and Lipe (1978) stated that "Vision is a hearing-impaired student's primary means of receiving information" (p. 149). Garton and Bass (1974) recommended "Since deaf students are dependent upon visual contact as a means of acquiring knowledge, well-designed visual materials that reinforce words and concepts with appropriate illustration would be invaluable teaching aids" (p. 62). The visual methods could eliminate or minimize the use of language. McDaniel (1980) found that "Once the role of language is minimized or eliminated, the perceptual memory of the deaf is little different from the hearing over a rather wide range of visual tasks" (p. 20).

When teachers have understood the ← Let Elliott argue this.
problems that relate to hearing-impaired
students such as understanding verbal
directions, taking written tests, reading
recipes, and comprehending textbooks,
than they may realize that it is necessary ⟵ Should be "then."
to develop and adapt materials more
appropriate to the needs of the hearing-
impaired students (Elliott, 1978). The
teacher may help the students by presenting
written materials on their reading **level** and ← Add "s" for plural.
provide visual aids in the classroom. A **synop-** ← Incorrect word.
sis of the review of literature tends to indicate to
the researcher that the use of visual aids will
help the hearing-impaired student in the classroom make greater progress.

One type of visual aid that may be used in the food preparation class with hearing-impaired students is the use of a picture recipe cookbook. Cookbooks designed with the use of pictures have been developed for the mentally retarded (Cline, 1969; Kahan, 1974; Steed, 1974). Mankoski (1977) developed a workbook that uses a linguistic approach in helping deaf students to cope with problems of reading in a parallel text. Riggers (1975) suggested that a cookbook using recipes broken down into their simplest components and properly sequenced by the use of pictures and cooking terms is needed for cooking when it is performed by hearing-impaired students. However, the researcher has not found a cookbook that would appropriate for the hearing-impaired. If the needs of the hearing-impaired will be met in the food preparation classes, then the researcher contends there is a need for a research study to determine if the use of a picture recipe cookbook will improve the instruction of hearing-impaired students.

General Comments About This Section

This section is extremely poorly organized. The flow of argument and evidence never comes together. You needed to write a strong outline before you began writing this.

You need to let your references argue for you. You make too many unsubstantiated statements which reveal your biases and make your work seem nonobjective. You needed to present some evidence from previous research studies which you read.

A RESEARCH PROPOSAL ON THE RELATIVE
EFFECTIVENESS OF GROUP COUNSELING
SESSIONS WHICH STRESS PEER SUPPORT
GROUPS AS COMPARED WITH THOSE WHICH
DO NOT

Introduction to the Problem and Need for the Study

The national problem of school dropouts is a serious one. It is serious for the child involved and for the nation. Varner (1967) reported a 15% greater unemployment rate for dropouts. Kostner (1964) reported a loss of job status, savings power, and earnings power. He reported that the decision not to complete the eighth grade cost the average male $52,343 in 1963 dollars. Greene (1966) reported **alienation** "that dropouts tended to be from society. The consequences for the individ- alienated" ual are indeed severe, but there are serious consquences for the nation as well.

~~The nation suffers many consequences as a~~ —Omit sentence. ~~result of the dropout problem.~~ Kostner (1964) reported that those over twenty-five years of age in 1960 who did not complete the 8th grade cost the United States an aggregate loss of 954 bil- Replace with "in" lion dollars (to) the national income. Had they insert completed one to three years of high school, the "He argued that" national income would have increased almost another 380 billion dollars. The combined amount represents approximately 2½ times the national income of the United States in 1962. Kostner went on to report that in addition to this aggregate loss, the United States would dispense a great deal of money for these people in various forms of social aid. Miller (1964) reported a higher incidence of delinquency among dropouts, along with other damaging behaviors such as a high incidence of drinking (16 percent). The consequences of the dropout problem are indeed serious, and the problem has long been a concern in the United States.

The problem of school dropouts in the United States is well over a century old. Over one hundred years ago, in 1872, a paper titled "The Early Withdrawal of Pupils from Schools" was presented at the annual convention of the National Education Association, Schreiber (1968) reported. Kostner (1964) reported President Kennedy's concern over the problem as was expressed by the President in his 1963 State of the Union message to Congress. Bachman (1974) reported a similar concern expressed by President Johnson and his hopes for America's youth in "The Great Society." The problem has long been with us, yet, some **decrease** has occurred. _In what?

Over the years the decline in the percentage of students dropping out of school has been gradual but continuous. Bachman (1971) reported that in 1900, 90 percent of male students did not graduate from high school; by 1920, 80 percent did not graduate; in the 1950s the figure fell below 50 percent. This downward trend continued into the next two decades, with the class of 1959 having a dropout rate of 38 percent and the class of 1969 having a 22 percent dropout rate (Kruger, 1969).

In an attempt to project the future dropout rate, the United States Office of Education conducted a national survey in 1970. Twenty-two thousand teachers filled out questionnaires about eighty-five thousand students in grades two, four, and six. Only nine percent of the students were identified as potential dropouts (Hect, 1975). It appears that the percentage of dropouts has progressively decreased over the years, but it is still a great concern.

As a consequence of concern over the dropout problem, a great many researchers and educational professionals have conducted studies directed at identifying the cause of the problem. The consensus of these professionals is that the problem has many causes (Bachman, 1971; Berkovitz, 1975; Cervontes, 1969; Chansky, 1966; Greene, 1966; Miller, 1963; Smith, 1971). Cervontes (1969) listed three major causes. —"which were . . ."
Miller (1964) cited five major causes, as identified by the dropouts themselves. Varner (1967) —"These causes were . . ." presented a summary of seven studies of the causes of early school withdrawal. The summary identified an average of 7.8 causes per study as having a positive correlation with early school withdrawal. From these and similar studies common themes emerge, and major causes are "may be" identified or stressed. Hect (1975) felt that attitude was the dominant cause. Goodyear (1974) contended that self-concept was primary. Strom (1964) asserted that "the culture of poverty" was the major common element. Lastly, some researchers argue that the schools themselves are the major cause (Drews, 1964; Holt, 1970). The identification of these major themes has served to focus the research for those involved in the area of dropout prevention programs.

One prevention program which seemed to encompass many of these concerns was group counseling (Amos, 1968; Dinkmeyer, 1969; Loughery, 1961; Silverman, 1978). This is reflected in President Kennedy's decision in 1963 to allocate $250,000 out of the Presidential Emergency Fund for the express use of school counselors in their attempt to deal with the dropout problem. There seems to be disagreement, however, as to what method of group counseling is most effective. Witkin (1978) investigated the use of peer reinforcement as a group counseling approach and found that it made no significant difference. Conversely, Goodyear (1973) and Schweisheimer (1976) found that such an approach had a positive effect on attendance.

You probably should make this a separate detailed paragraph on causes.

A summary paragraph on common causes might go here.

Add "may demonstrate . . ."

Casella (1975) had groups visit with community members who counseled with them. This had some positive effects. Randolph (1973) reported that behavioral counseling has some positive effect. Regular class meetings, **claimed Mush-olt** (1974) were helpful. There are many diverse approaches to the dropout problem which report some positive results, but no single one which clearly has greater merit.

— Rearrange: "Musholt (1974) claimed that . . ."

— Insert "demonstrated"

Other researchers and education professionals asserted that the effect of the approach on the student's feeling about **himself** was the major element (Dinkmeyer, 1969; Lefkovitz, 1979; Pickart, 1974; Schleiger, 1972). Hect (1975) felt that a positive attitude was needed on the part of the student. Giles (1975) argued that the increased self-concept incurred by a positive peer culture would bring about the required change in the student. Goodyear (1973), after studying six different group approaches to the problem, concluded that any approach was only effective to the extent that it made the group members feel that they were valuable in and of themselves, that they were cared for, and that they were members of a community. This statement seemed to encompass and accurately express the findings of this group of researchers and educators. This group, which felt that positive self-concept was the key to success in reducing dropouts seemed to have the broadest based support.

— "or herself"

— Remove comma.

With this in mind, this investigator questioned whether the formation of an outside (of school) peer support group, by in-school group members would or would not enhance a group member's feeling of being valuable, cared for, and being a member of a community and thereby reduce **his** potential as a dropout.

— The use of the passive makes this sentence awkward.

— "or her"
Insert final sentence: "For this reason, he undertook this study."

General Comments About This Section

The material was quite good and you included data from relevant studies and appropriate and informative statistical information. You could have included more specifics on studies, as the marginal notes indicate.

You generally connected your thoughts and arguments well.

You should have talked a bit more about support groups—what they are, where they have been used, what their benefits are. That would have strengthened this section appreciably.

A RESEARCH PROPOSAL FOR A STUDY
OF BATTERED WOMEN IN A RESIDENTIAL
SELF-HELP CENTER

Introduction to the Problem and Need for the Study

Davidson (1977) observed that although **battered women are not a new phenomenon,** it has only been within the last decade that much has been written about them and their plight. [For the purpose of this study a battered woman will be defined as any woman who reports herself to be seriously and/or repeatedly physically and/or psychologically abused by her spouse or co-habitee and is therefore admitted into residence at a self-help center. For the purpose of this study a self-help center will be defined as a residential facility which provides temporary shelter to the victims of domestic abuse and is operated by self-governing residents.] Martin (1976) credited Erin Pizzey and her book *Scream Quietly or the Neighbors Will Hear* (1974), which is based on her experiences with the establishment of Chiswick Women's Aid in England, with drawing public attention to the problems faced by battered women. Gelles (1978) suggested that while Pizzey's work was important, it was little known in the United States. He contended that it was, therefore, the formation of a National Task Force on Battered Women/Household Violence by the National Organization for Women (NOW) that brought about in the United States a heightened awareness of the existence of battered women and their problems. Langley and Levy (1977) and Hilberman (1980) supported Gelles' (1978) conclusion that national interest in the problems of battered women was largely inspired by the feminist movement. Hilberman (1980) further sug-

Noun-verb agreement problem. Try "women being battered is . . .".

Add brackets to clarify that these are definitions and not part of the regular text.

Need a comma here after an introductory phrase which states a condition influencing the rest of the sentence.

gested that recent attention to battered women specifically evolved from the concern of the anti-rape movement about female sexual abuse.

No national statistics currently exist that identify the number of women abused annually; however, several estimates have been made (Flynn, 1977; Galles, 1974; Martin, 1976; Straus, Steinmets & Gelles, 1980). While these estimates vary widely, from 1.8 million nationally (Straus, Steinmetz, & Gelles, 1980) to 15 million nationally (Gelles, 1974), they suggest that wife abuse is a serious problem to a great many U.S. women; and therefore an area worthy of further study. Gayford (1978) lent further support to this as an area worthy of study when he postulated that the children who witnessed and experienced abuse are more likely to grow up to be the batterers and/or the victims of batterings.

Should be a comma.

Many opinions were expressed about why battered women stay in violent relationships (Gelles, 1976; Hilberman, 1980; Martin, 1976; Rounsaville, 1978; Straus, 1976, 1977; Walker, 1977, 1979). Gelles cited three factors that increased the likelihood of an abused woman staying in the marriage: 1) less frequent and less severe violence; 2) the frequency with which the woman was struck by her parents as a child; 3) fewer resources and less power. In agreement with Gelles' (1976) first conclusion that the less frequent and the less violent the relationship the more likely the woman was to stay, Rounsaville (1978) found no support for a theory of masochism on the part of the women involved in abusive relationships. Lending support for Gelles' conclusion that the less resources the woman had the more likely she was to stay, Straus (1976, 1977) contended that the economic resources of these women frequently left them no option but to stay. Straus (1976, 1977) further argued that most women are economically dependent on their husbands and have neither the job skills nor the opportunities necessary for financial independence. Walker (1977, 1979) lent support to Gelles'

This sentence seems a bit stilted. Why not get it out of the passive voice? For example: "Many researchers expressed opinions about . . ."

"Fewer" not "less."

(1976) conclusion that the less power a woman possessed the more likely she was to stay in a violent relationship when she suggested that the battered woman stayed because she did not believe she could escape from the domination of the batterer. More specifically, Walker (1977, 1979) postulated that it was this expectation of powerlessness coupled with the expectation of not being able to control her own life, whether real or perceived, that prevents action on the part of the battered wife. Similarly, Hilberman (1980) argued that women have little preparation for independence or assertive problem solving because sex role socialization has reinforced the idea that the needs of (a woman) are fulfilled, and their identities derived indirectly, through their men. Not all researchers supported Gelles' (1976) conclusions, however. Martin (1976) contended that it was fear that kept these women from leaving a battering spouse. More specifically, Martin (1976) suggested that the combination of continuing threats and violence by the husband and the absence of safe shelter deterred these women from leaving.

Change to plural: "women."

Begin new paragraph here. This is a logical division point.

Francle (1976), Gayford (1978), and Gelles (1974), along with other researchers (Langley & Levy, 1977; Leghorn, 1976; Martin, 1976; Roy, 1978; Straus, 1976; Walker, 1979) suggested that in searching for ways out of these relationships, battered women have sought the aid of many community professionals. Previous studies by Gayford (1978), Gelles (1974), and Roy (1978) indicated that the police were frequently contacted either by the battered woman or a concerned neighbor during episodes of violence. A prior study by Gayford (1978) indicated that attorneys were consulted less frequently than were the police. Still other research by Martin (1976) and Walker (1979) indicated that **both the medical profession and the social work profession** were frequently contacted by battered women looking for options to remaining with a battering spouse. Hilberman (1980), Martin (1976), and Walker (1979) argued

Either say "members of" here or rewrite to say "physicians and social workers." The rewrite is preferable.

that not until the "refuge" or "shelter" movement did these women perceive themselves as
having a real alternative to remaining with an
abusive spouse.

In a survey of 150 cases, which were selected
at random from 1000 calls received by the Abused
Women's Aid Crisis Hotline, Roy (1978) found that
100 of the 150 battered women surveyed (had) sought police intervention. Roy (1978) reported
that seventy of the 100 that sought help reported
that they had not found the police to be helpful. Fur-
thermore, she reported that the four most common
reasons given by the other fifty women surveyed for
not calling the police were 1) fear of reprisals by the
husbands to themselves or next of kin; 2) fear of
social humiliation; 3) lack of faith in police as a
helping agency; and 4) desire to prevent their children from seeing their fathers being arrested (Roy,
1978).

Careful here! Say "responded that they . . ."

Gelles (1974) also reported that police
departments were sometimes unsupportive of
battered women because they may have "stitch
rules" which require that a woman receive a pre-
determined number of stitches before she can
file an assault charge against her husband. Similarly, Gayford (1978), who interviewed 89
women from Chiswick Women's Aid and eleven
from a psychiatric practice, found that thirty-two
of the 100 women (had called) the police only to
find that the police were "impotent or reluctant
to intervene in a domestic dispute" (p. 30). Likewise, Martin (1976) presented data indicating
that home disturbance calls were of such low
priority for the police that they took from several
minutes to several hours to respond depending
on the locale of the individual police department.
The findings of the above studies indicated to
this researcher that while many victims of
spouse abuse contact the police, they do not
appear generally to find the police to be supportive or sympathetic to their problem.

Careful! Try "reported that they"

Based on Gayford's (1978) findings, it
appeared that a smaller number of women chose
to seek the help of an attorney. In comparison to
the thirty-two out of 100 sampled that had

sought help from the police, only ten out of 100 had consulted with an attorney (Gayford, 1978). In compiling data for her book, *Battered Wives*, Martin (1976) contended that battered women encounter many roadblocks when trying to obtain legal aid. Both Martin (1976) and Walker (1979) concluded that the legal profession was not only reluctant to assume cases involving marital violence, but also often encouraged the battered woman to reconcile with her husband. Straus, Gelles, and Steinmenz (1980) argued that this position taken by attorneys with regard to battered women has led to "viewing the marriage license as a hitting license" (p. 31). Serveral researchers maintained that although the husband no longer has the right to chastise his wife, the spirit that permeated such laws has lingered on in such doctrines as spousal immunity, which has prevented wives from filing assault charges against their husbands in many jurisdictions (Langley & Levy, 1977; Martin, 1976; Roy, 1977; Straus, 1976; Walker, 1979). Based on the above evidence, this researcher concluded that while fewer battered women sought legal aid than sought police intervention, many still found little if any support or empathy when consulting attorneys.

> A survey response may not be true. Try "responded that they"

> Try "appear to seek" instead of "sought."
> Try "appear to find" instead of "still found."

Gayford (1978), Martin (1976), and Walker (1969) suggested that while battered women frequently consulted both private and/or emergency room physicians, these physicians often failed to diagnose the women consulting them as battered wives. Gayford (1978), Martin (1976), and Walker (1979) argued that private physicians consulted by battered women during the tension building phase of the abuse cycle most often diagnosed the woman's symptoms as being due to depression or nerves and prescribed antidepressants or tranquilizers. Gayford (1978), Martin (1976), and Walker (1979) also contended that the emergency room physician, who was most frequently reported as the one who saw the victim after a physically abusive episode, was too pressured by work demands to question the accident alibis given to him by the

> Move "as battered wives" to clarify modification.

victim or her spouse. Gayford (1978) further concluded, based on the evidence of seventy-eight out of 100 battered women surveyed, that even when the correct diagnosis was made by the physician, **he** was **impotent** with regard to preventing a recurrence. While physicians were frequently consulted by battered women, it appears to this researcher that they afforded little if any support to the battered women consulting them.

Replace with "powerless".

"or she"—Doctors can also be female.

A report prepared by the National Women's Aid Federation (N.W.A.F.) and published in Steinmetz and Straus (1974) suggested that 50 percent of women coming to refuges have had previous contact with a social worker. This report further contended, as did Walker (1979, p. 201) and Leghorn (1976, p. 93), that once the social worker had referred women to refuges, the social worker proceeded either to ignore the client or to use the shelter to overcome the immediate crisis and then to pressure the client to return to her spouse once the crisis was over. The report posited that the case-worker's action was based on the underlying casework philosophy which emphasized the importance of the nuclear family (N.W.A.F., 1974). The report contended that, because of this emphasis, social workers usually defined wife aubse as a marital problem which could be remedied through marriage counseling rather than defining it as a potentially life-threatening situation that called for the immediate separation of the spouses involved (N.W.A.F., 1974). Ball (1977) acknowledged that both the public and the social work profession were changing their expectations with regard to the roles for social workers and the services that should be provided for abused wives and their children. The emerging expectations that Ball (1977) voiced were the provision of both physical and emotional support as well as the removal of the violent spouse or the wife and children from the home after an abusive episode. If the arguments and contentions presented above are valid, then the social work profession appears not always to

have been sympathetic to the problems faced by battered women. Ball's article (1977) suggested that the social work profession was becoming aware of this apparent inadequacy and seemed motivated both to reexamine and to reevaluate the profession's roles ~~as well as the profession's~~   *Replace with "and".*
service in order to (better) meet its clients' needs.   *Eliminate.*   *Add "more effectively" before period.*

Many researchers have observed that battered women living in refuges tend to exhibit common characteristics. **(Ball, 1977; Gayford, 1978; Hilberman & Munson, 1977; Martin, 1976; Pizzey, 1974; Thorman, 1980).**   *Since you discuss these below, you do not need the laundry list here.*

The characteristics most often cited were passivity, inhibition, helplessness, dependency, and low self-esteem (Ball, 1977; Gayford, 1978; Hilberman & Munson, 1977; Martin, 1976; Pizzey, 1974; Thorman, 1980). Leghorn (1976), Martin (1976), and Walker (1980) suggested that the combination of a supportive atmosphere and a reeducation program for the abused women in shelters could change this self-image. While Ball and Wyman (1977), Martin (1976), and Walker (1980) advocated using assertiveness training, O'Leary (1980) along with Bash-Van Vleet and de Velasco (1979) recommended using Effectiveness Training for Women (E.T.W.). Ball and Wyman (1977) defined assertiveness training as a combination of cognitive restructuring and behavioral techniques such as modeling, behavioral rehearsal, coaching, and feedback designed to teach individuals how to express their thoughts without attacking others or denying their own feelings. O'Leary (1980) described E.T.W. as teaching asertiveness skills along with listening and problem solving skills. Bash-Van Vleet and de Velasco (1979) reported that a Coalition on Domestic Violence which is comprised of several Battered Women's Shelters, a Catholic Service agency, and a Community Mental Health Agency has applied for federal funds and is studying the effectiveness of E.T.W. with both the staff and the battered women housed at a residential shelter. This researcher was unable to obtain any findings from this research, although she did call Effectiveness Training, Inc. and talked with the E.T.W. Program Director, who reported that at this time E.T.W. has no valid research data available on the topic of battered women. However, Christensen (1980), Girimonte (1979), and Sands (1980) contended that E.T.W. has been used effectively with such groups as Catholic sisters, teachers, and wives of clergy. This researcher was unable to locate any findings **other than those presented above**. ← Replace end of sentence with "which demonstrated conclusively that . . ." and tell what they failed to demonstrate.

STATEMENT OF PURPOSE

It is the purpose of this study to explore treatment and service alternatives available to battered women in a midwestern community of 40,000. More specifically this study will ascertain how many battered women residing in a local self-help center contacted the police, an attorney, a private or emergency room physician, and/or a social case worker prior to their residency at the self-help center. Secondly, this study will determine if the battered women participating in this study perceived these frequently consulted community professionals as supportive or nonsupportive. Thirdly, this study will compare the use of Thomas Gordon's Effectiveness Training for Women (E.T.W.) with the use of an assertiveness training program to see if either proves to be more beneficial in fostering independence and self-esteem in these women, as measured by the California Psychological Inventory (C.P.I.).

In order to attain these purposes this researcher has undertaken or will undertake the following procedures:

1. This researcher contacted the executive director of the Family Self-Help Center, to obtain the demographics needed to define this population. The Self-Help Center is located in a midwestern city of 40,000. The women most frequently served by this center are from this city and from the two sur-

rounding counties. While the women housed here in the last three years have ranged in age from 15–81, they most often fall in the range of 20–30. Based on a recent computation of the last three years' data, the mean number of days spent in residence at the shelter is six days. Of the 141 women served in the last three years, all but 4 were Caucasian: 3 were Black, and 1 was American Indian.

2. This researcher consulted Buros (1978), *The Eighth Mental Measurements Year-book*, and selected the California Psychological Inventory (C.P.I.) (to be) the instrument used to measure the subjects' levels of independence and self-esteem. The C.P.I. is made up of 480 items that comprise eighteen scales. Developed by Gough, these scales measure the following characteristics: dominance, self-acceptance, sense of well being, responsibility, socialization, self-control, tolerance, achievement via conformance, achievement via independence, flexibility, femininity, psychological-mindedness, intellectual efficiency, good impression, communality, social presence, sociability, and capacity for status.

"as" Insert "to be".

3. This researcher will work as a volunteer staff person at the Family Self-Help Center. This will be done on a 24-hour a day basis for the two weeks immediately prior to carrying out the research project. The purpose of this will be to observe the daily life and routine of the Family Self-Help Center. Based on these observations this researcher will adjust or modify the research design as needed to (accomo-date) the residents at the center.

"accommodate"

4. This researcher will interview and select two instructors, one to teach an assertiveness training class and one to teach a class in Effectiveness Training for Women (E.T.W.)

5. This researcher will explain the research project and solicit volunteers from among the residents. She will do this on the second morning for each incoming resident.

At this time, each volunteer will be asked to fill out a demographic sheet. (They) will also be asked to fill out a (questionare) asking if they have ever before sought help, if so, in what ways, how often, and did they perceive the professional or agency contacted to be supportive or nonsupportive. At this time they will also be asked to sign a release of information statement.

"These volunteers"

"questionnaire"

6. This researcher will employ a multiple measure nonequivalent control group design to carry out this project. To do this, each volunteer will be given the C.P.I. to help this researcher ascertain whether that volunteer experiences any measurable growth in the areas of independence and/or self-esteem during (their) residency at the shelter.

Should be "her" since this is a *single* volunteer.

7. This researcher will assign by the flip of a coin each volunteer to one of the two classes upon the completion of the first C.P.I. These classes will each meet three evenings a week from 7–9 p.m.

8. This researcher will administer the C.P.I. to each volunteer again on her fourth day.

9. This researcher will administer the C.P.I. to each volunteer again on the day she leaves the center. It is to be understood that in between the testings the volunteers should be attending one or the other of the two classes.

10. This researcher will compare the E.T.W. groups' scores with the assertiveness groups' scores at the end of one year of research. The scores used in this comparison will be compiled from those volunteers who remained in residence at the Family Self-Help Center six or more days. This researcher feels a year would be needed to generate a large enough sample (so as) to provide a sufficiently broad sample from this population.

"so as" is unnecessary. Why not say "a sample which is large enough to be representative of this population"?

11. This researcher will analyze the data collected from the survey given to the volunteers on their second day of residence at the center at the end of one year also. The results of this analysis will be used to

provide feedback to the community professionals that the battered women in this study consulted.

12. This researcher will do a subsample analysis to control for any difference in measured independence and/or self-esteem (**being**) due to maturation rather than to the treatment administered.

"being" is unnecessary.

13. This researcher will mail out a C.P.I. to each volunteer six weeks after (**they**) leave the Family Self-Help Center and then randomly select from each group of respondents. This measurement will help this researcher determine if any measurable difference of independence/self-esteem was short-term and "wore off" after the subjects left the center.

Should be "she" since a *single* volunteer.

STATEMENT OF THE HYPOTHESIS

The hypothesis for this study is stated below in null form. That is:

There will be no significant difference in the measured level of independence and/or self-esteem, as measured by the California Psychological Inventory (C.P.I.), between battered women housed at a community self-help center who receive training in Effectiveness Training for Women, and battered women housed at a community self-help center who receive training in assertiveness.

General Comments About This Proposal

This was an excellent proposal. You used your references well and made a very strong case for the study. Your thoroughness in reviewing the literature left the reader with a sense of confidence in your ability to carry out this study and to draw intelligent conclusions based on the findings.

REFERENCES

AHMANN, J. S., & GLOCK, M. D. (1971). *Evaluating pupil growth* (4th ed.). Boston: Allyn & Bacon.

American Psychological Association. (1974). *Publication manual* (2nd ed.). Washington, D.C.: American Psychological Association.

ARMSTRONG, R. L. (1974). Hypotheses: Why? when? how? *Phi Delta Kappa Research Notes, 56,* 213–214.

ARY, D., JACOBS, L. C., & RAZAVIEH, A. (1979). *Introduction to research in education* (2nd ed.). New York: McGraw-Hill.

ASHER, J. W. (1976). *Educational research and evaluation methods.* Boston: Little, Brown & Co.

BARR, A. J., GOODNIGHT, S., & HELWIG, G. (1976). A user's guide to SAS 76. Raleigh, NC: SAS Institute, Inc.

BORG, W. R., & GALL, M. D. (1979). *Educational research: An introduction* (3rd ed.). New York: Longman.

BRACHT, G. H., & GLASS, G. V. (1968). The external validity of experiments. *American Educational Research Journal, 5,* 437–474.

BRUNING, J. L., & KINTZ, B. L. (1968). *Computational handbook of statistics.* Glenview, IL: Scott, Foresman.

BUROS, O. K. (Ed.). (1972). *The seventh mental measurement yearbook.* Highland Park, NJ: Gryphon Press.

CAMPBELL, D. T., & STANLEY, J. C. (1963). Experimental and quasi-experimental designs for research on teaching. In N. L. Gage (Ed.), *Handbook of research on teaching,* 171–246. Chicago: Rand McNally.

CAMPBELL, W. G., & BALLOU, S. V. (1978). *Form and style: Theses, reports, term papers* (5th ed.). Boston: Houghton Mifflin.

CATES, W. M. (1978). Organized non-activity: A proposed solution to some common classroom problems. *Clearing House, 51,* 220–222.

———— (1982). Do-or-die spelling: Teaching without the struggle. *English Journal, 71,* 45–47.

CRONBACH, L., & FURBY, L. (1970). How should we measure "change"—Or should we? *Psychological Bulletin, 74,* 68–80.

ELASHOFF, J. D. (1969). Analysis of covariance: A delicate instrument. *American Educational Research Journal, 6,* 383–399.

FERGUSON, G. A. (1976). *Statistical analysis in psychology and education* (4th ed.). New York: McGraw-Hill.

GAY, L. R. (1976). *Educational research: Competencies for analysis and application.* Columbus, OH: Charles E. Merrill.

———— (198!). *Educational research: Competencies for analysis and application* (2nd ed.). Columbus, OH: Charles E. Merrill.

GUILFORD, J. P. (1956). *Fundamental statistics in psychology and education* (3rd ed.). New York: McGraw-Hill.

HARRIS, C. W. (1963). *Problems in measuring change*. Madison, WI: The University of Wisconsin Press.

HARRISON, N. (1979). *Understanding behavioral research*. Belmont, CA: Wadsworth.

HOPKINS, C. D. (1980). *Understanding educational research: An inquiry approach*. Columbus, OH: Charles E. Merrill.

HUCK, S. W., & SANDLER, H. M. (1973). A note on the Solomon 4-group design: Appropriate statistical analyses. *Journal of Experimental Education, 42*, 54–55.

JOHNSON, M. C. (1977). *A review of research methods in education*. Chicago: Rand McNally.

KEAN, M. H. (1983). Administrative uses of research and evaluation information. In E. W. Gordon (Ed.), *Review of Research in Education* (Vol. 10, 361–414.). Washington, D.C.: American Educational Research Association.

KENNY, D. A. (1975). A quasi-experimental approach to assessing treatment effects in a non-equivalent control group design. *Psychological Bulletin, 82*, 345–362.

KERLINGER, F. N. (1979). *Foundations of behavioral research* (2nd ed.). New York: Holt, Rinehart and Winston.

MARKEN, R. (1981). *Methods in experimental psychology*. Monterey, CA: Brooks/Cole.

NIE, N. H., HULL, C. H., JENKINS, J. G., STEINBRENNER, K., & BENT, D. H. (1975). Statistical package for the social sciences (2nd ed.). New York: McGraw-Hill.

RATHS, J. (1967). The appropriate experimental unit. *Educational Leadership, 25*, 263–266.

RICHARDSON, M. W., & KUDER, G. F. (1939). The calculation of test reliability coefficients based upon the method of rational equivalence. *Journal of Educational Psychology, 30*, 681–687.

ROSENTHAL, R., & ROSNOW, R. L. (1975). *The volunteer subject*. New York: John Wiley & Sons.

SAX, G. (1979). *Foundations of educational research*. Englewood Cliffs, NJ: Prentice-Hall.

SNOW, R. E. (1974). Representative and quasi-representative design for research on teaching. *Review of Educational Research, 44*, 265–291.

STRUNK, W., JR., & WHITE, E. B. (1959). *The elements of style*. New York: Macmillan.

STUFFLEBEAM, D. L., FOLEY, W. J., GEPHART, W. J., GUBA, E. G., HAMMOND, R. L., MERRIMAN, H. O., & PROVUS, M. M. (1971). *Educational evaluation and decision-making in education*. Itasca, IL: Peacock.

SUDMAN, S. (1976). *Applied sampling*, New York: Academic Press.

TAYLOR, H. C., & RUSSELL, J. T. (1939). The relationship of validity coefficients to the practical effectiveness of tests in selection: Discussion and tables. *Journal of Applied Psychology, 23*, 565–578.

THORNDIKE, R. L., & HAGEN, E. P. (1961). *Measurement and evaluation in psychology and education* (2nd ed.). New York: John Wiley.

VAN DALEN, D. B. (1979). *Understanding educational research: An introduction* (4th ed.). New York: McGraw-Hill.

WALSH, J. M., & WALSH, A. K. (1972). *Plain English handbook: A complete guide to good English* (6th rev. ed.). Cincinnati, OH: McCormick-Mathers.

WARRINER, J. E., & GRIFFITH, F. (1973). *English grammar and composition: Complete course*. New York: Harcourt Brace Jovanovich.

WATKINS, F. C., & DILLINGHAM, W. B. (1979). *English handbook*. Boston: Houghton Mifflin.

WILLIAMS, F. (1979). *Reasoning with statistics* (3rd ed.). New York: Holt, Rinehart and Winston.

WILLIAMSON, J., KARP, D., DALPHIN, J., & GRAY, P. (1982). *The research craft: An introduction to social research methods*. (2nd ed.). Boston: Little, Brown & Company.

APPENDIX

SAMPLE HYPOTHESES FOR RESEARCH PROBLEMS

NULL HYPOTHESIS FOR EXAMPLE 2, p. 18

There will be no significant difference in behavioral change in the desired direction between fifth-grade girls who are exposed to a behavior modification program and comparable fifth-grade boys exposed to an equivalent program. Behavioral change will be measured using a comparison of baseline and poststudy observation. Desired direction of behavioral change will be specified by prestudy teacher objectives.

NULL HYPOTHESIS FOR EXAMPLE 3, p. 18

There will be no significant difference in frequency of injury suffered by male high school basketball players who participate in a flexibility program and by comparable players who do not participate in the program. The flexibility program consists of each subject completing 15 minutes of specified stretching exercises designed to increase flexibility prior to and immediately following each day's practice session.

ALTERNATIVE HYPOTHESES FOR
EXAMPLE 3, p. 21

1. ALT. HYPO.:   Any significant difference (or the absence of a significant difference) in frequency of injury between the two groups of players might be due to previous injuries.

    CONTROL: The subjects will be assigned randomly to each group and information concerning previous injuries will be gathered.

2. ALT. HYPO.:   Any significant difference (or the absence of a significant difference) in frequency of injury between the two groups might be due to injuries sustained by the players who are not in the program "horsing around" during the fifteen minutes when the other group is stretching.

    CONTROL: The players not in the program will be supervised during this period of time.

3. ALT. HYPO.:   Any significant difference (or the absence of a significant difference) in frequency of injury between the two groups might be due to coaches' and trainers' increased awareness of the role of flexibility in injuries leading them to place more emphasis on activities (other than stretching) which develop flexibility and to require all players to do these activities.

    CONTROL: For the period of the study, there will be no change in the normal activities used with the players (aside from the flexibility program employed as the treatment).

TABLE A   T Values Associated With Interpreting Directional and Nondirectional Hypotheses

PROBABILITY LEVELS

For Directional Hypotheses		.40	.25	.10	.05	.025	.01	.005
For Nondirectional Hypotheses		.80	.50	.20	.10	.05	.02	.01
	1	0.325	1.000	3.078	6.314	12.706	31.821	63.657
	2	.289	0.816	1.886	2.920	4.303	6.965	9.925
	3	.277	.765	1.638	2.353	3.182	4.541	5.841
	4	.271	.741	1.533	2.132	2.776	3.747	4.604
	5	0.267	0.727	1.476	2.015	2.571	3.365	4.032
	6	.265	.718	1.440	1.943	2.447	3.143	3.707
	7	.263	.711	1.415	1.895	2.365	2.998	3.499
	8	.262	.706	1.397	1.860	2.306	2.896	3.355
	9	.261	.703	1.383	1.833	2.262	2.821	3.250
D	10	0.260	0.700	1.372	1.812	2.228	2.764	3.169
E	11	.260	.697	1.363	1.796	2.201	2.718	3.106
G	12	.259	.695	1.356	1.782	2.179	2.681	3.055
R	13	.259	.694	1.350	1.771	2.160	2.650	3.012
E	14	.258	.692	1.345	1.761	2.145	2.624	2.977
E								
S	15	0.258	0.691	1.341	1.753	2.131	2.602	2.947
	16	.258	.690	1.337	1.746	2.120	2.583	2.921
O	17	.257	.689	1.333	1.740	2.110	2.567	2.898
F	18	.257	.688	1.330	1.734	2.101	2.552	2.878
	19	.257	.688	1.328	1.729	2.093	2.539	2.861
F								
R	20	0.257	0.687	1.325	1.725	2.086	2.528	2.845
E	21	.257	.686	1.323	1.721	2.080	2.518	2.831
E	22	.256	.686	1.321	1.717	2.074	2.508	2.819
D	23	.256	.685	1.319	1.714	2.069	2.500	2.807
E	24	.256	.685	1.318	1.711	2.064	2.492	2.797
O								
M	25	0.256	0.684	1.316	1.708	2.060	2.485	2.787
	26	.256	.684	1.315	1.706	2.056	2.479	2.779
	27	.256	.684	1.314	1.703	2.052	2.473	2.771
	28	.256	.683	1.313	1.701	2.048	2.467	2.763
	29	.256	.683	1.311	1.699	2.045	2.462	2.756
	30	0.256	0.683	1.310	1.697	2.042	2.457	2.750
	40	.255	.681	1.303	1.684	2.021	2.423	2.704
	60	.254	.679	1.296	1.671	2.000	2.390	2.660
	120	.254	.677	1.289	1.658	1.980	2.358	2.617
	∞	.253	.674	1.282	1.645	1.960	2.326	2.576

This table is abridged from Table 12 in the *Biometrika Tables for Statisticians,* Vol. 1, Third edition (1966), E. S. Pearson and H. O. Hartley, eds. Reproduced by permission of the Biometrika Trustees.

The values in the two right hand columns (.01 and .005, Directional Hypotheses) are drawn from Table III in R. A. Fisher and F. Yates, *Statistical Tables for Biological, Agricultural and Medical Research,* published by Longman Group Ltd., London (previously published by Oliver and Boyd Ltd., Edinburgh) and are reprinted by permission of the authors and publishers.

TABLE B F-Values Associated With The .05 Probability Level

DEGREES OF FREEDOM IN THE NUMERATOR

DEGREES OF FREEDOM	1	2	3	4	5	6	7	8	9	10	12	15	120	∞
1	161.4	199.5	215.7	224.6	230.2	234.0	236.8	238.9	240.5	241.9	243.9	245.9	253.3	254.3
2	18.51	19.00	19.16	19.25	19.30	19.33	19.35	19.37	19.38	19.40	19.41	19.43	19.49	19.50
3	10.13	9.55	9.28	9.12	9.01	8.94	8.89	8.85	8.81	8.79	8.74	8.70	8.55	8.53
4	7.71	6.94	6.59	6.39	6.26	6.16	6.09	6.04	6.00	5.96	5.91	5.86	5.66	5.63
5	6.61	5.79	5.41	5.19	5.05	4.95	4.88	4.82	4.77	4.74	4.68	4.62	4.40	4.36
6	5.99	5.14	4.76	4.53	4.39	4.28	4.21	4.15	4.10	4.06	4.00	3.94	3.70	3.67
7	5.59	4.74	4.35	4.12	3.97	3.87	3.79	3.73	3.68	3.64	3.57	3.51	3.27	3.23
8	5.32	4.46	4.07	3.84	3.69	3.58	3.50	3.44	3.39	3.35	3.28	3.22	2.97	2.93
9	5.12	4.26	3.86	3.63	3.48	3.37	3.29	3.23	3.18	3.14	3.07	3.01	2.75	2.71
10	4.96	4.10	3.71	3.48	3.33	3.22	3.14	3.07	3.02	2.98	2.91	2.85	2.58	2.54
11	4.84	3.98	3.59	3.36	3.20	3.09	3.01	2.95	2.90	2.85	2.79	2.72	2.45	2.40
12	4.75	3.89	3.49	3.26	3.11	3.00	2.91	2.85	2.80	2.75	2.69	2.62	2.34	2.30
13	4.67	3.81	3.41	3.18	3.03	2.92	2.83	2.77	2.71	2.67	2.60	2.53	2.25	2.21
14	4.60	3.74	3.34	3.11	2.96	2.85	2.76	2.70	2.65	2.60	2.53	2.46	2.18	2.13
15	4.54	3.68	3.29	3.06	2.90	2.79	2.71	2.64	2.59	2.54	2.48	2.40	2.11	2.07
16	4.49	3.63	3.24	3.01	2.85	2.74	2.66	2.59	2.54	2.49	2.42	2.35	2.06	2.01

df														
17	4.45	3.59	3.20	2.96	2.81	2.70	2.61	2.55	2.49	2.45	2.38	2.31	2.01	1.96
18	4.41	3.55	3.16	2.93	2.77	2.66	2.58	2.51	2.46	2.41	2.34	2.27	1.97	1.92
19	4.38	3.52	3.13	2.90	2.74	2.63	2.54	2.48	2.42	2.38	2.31	2.23	1.93	1.88
20	4.35	3.49	3.10	2.87	2.71	2.60	2.51	2.45	2.39	2.35	2.28	2.20	1.90	1.84
21	4.32	3.47	3.07	2.84	2.68	2.57	2.49	2.42	2.37	2.32	2.25	2.18	1.87	1.81
22	4.30	3.44	3.05	2.82	2.66	2.55	2.46	2.40	2.34	2.30	2.23	2.15	1.84	1.78
23	4.28	3.42	3.03	2.80	2.64	2.53	2.44	2.37	2.32	2.27	2.20	2.13	1.81	1.76
24	4.26	3.40	3.01	2.78	2.62	2.51	2.42	2.36	2.30	2.25	2.18	2.11	1.79	1.73
25	4.24	3.39	2.99	2.76	2.60	2.49	2.40	2.34	2.28	2.24	2.16	2.09	1.77	1.71
26	4.23	3.37	2.98	2.74	2.59	2.47	2.39	2.32	2.27	2.22	2.15	2.07	1.75	1.69
27	4.21	3.35	2.96	2.73	2.57	2.46	2.37	2.31	2.25	2.20	2.13	2.06	1.73	1.67
28	4.20	3.34	2.95	2.71	2.56	2.45	2.36	2.29	2.24	2.19	2.12	2.04	1.71	1.65
29	4.18	3.33	2.93	2.70	2.55	2.43	2.35	2.28	2.22	2.18	2.10	2.03	1.70	1.64
30	4.17	3.32	2.92	2.69	2.53	2.42	2.33	2.27	2.21	2.16	2.09	2.01	1.68	1.62
40	4.08	3.23	2.84	2.61	2.45	2.34	2.25	2.18	2.12	2.08	2.00	1.92	1.58	1.51
60	4.00	3.15	2.76	2.53	2.37	2.25	2.17	2.10	2.04	1.99	1.92	1.84	1.47	1.39
120	3.92	3.07	2.68	2.45	2.29	2.17	2.09	2.02	1.96	1.91	1.83	1.75	1.35	1.25
∞	3.84	3.00	2.60	2.37	2.21	2.10	2.01	1.94	1.88	1.83	1.75	1.67	1.22	1.00

TABLE B.2 F-Values Associated With The .01 Probability Level

DEGREES OF FREEDOM IN THE NUMERATOR

	1	2	3	4	5	6	7	8	9	10	12	15	120	∞
1	4052.	4999.5	5403.	5625.	5764.	5859.	5928.	5981.	6022.	6056.	6106.	6157.	6339.	6366.
2	98.50	99.00	99.17	99.25	99.30	99.33	99.36	99.37	99.39	99.40	99.42	99.43	99.49	99.50
3	34.12	30.82	29.46	28.71	28.24	27.91	27.67	27.49	27.35	27.23	27.05	26.87	26.22	26.13
4	21.20	18.00	16.69	15.98	15.52	15.21	14.98	14.80	14.66	14.55	14.37	14.20	13.56	13.46
5	16.26	13.27	12.06	11.39	10.97	10.67	10.46	10.29	10.16	10.05	9.89	9.72	9.11	9.02
6	13.75	10.92	9.78	9.15	8.75	8.47	8.26	8.10	7.98	7.87	7.72	7.56	6.97	6.88
7	12.25	9.55	8.45	7.85	7.46	7.19	6.99	6.84	6.72	6.62	6.47	6.31	5.74	5.65
8	11.26	8.65	7.59	7.01	6.63	6.37	6.18	6.03	5.91	5.81	5.67	5.52	4.95	4.86
9	10.56	8.02	6.99	6.42	6.06	5.80	5.61	5.47	5.35	5.26	5.11	4.96	4.40	4.31
10	10.04	7.56	6.55	5.99	5.64	5.39	5.20	5.06	4.94	4.85	4.71	4.56	4.00	3.91
11	9.65	7.21	6.22	5.67	5.32	5.07	4.89	4.74	4.63	4.54	4.40	4.25	3.69	3.60
12	9.33	6.93	5.95	5.41	5.06	4.82	4.64	4.50	4.39	4.30	4.16	4.01	3.45	3.36
13	9.07	6.70	5.74	5.21	4.86	4.62	4.44	4.30	4.19	4.10	3.96	3.82	3.25	3.17
14	8.86	6.51	5.56	5.04	4.69	4.46	4.28	4.14	4.03	3.94	3.80	3.66	3.09	3.00
15	8.68	6.36	5.42	4.89	4.56	4.32	4.14	4.00	3.89	3.80	3.67	3.52	2.96	2.87
16	8.53	6.23	5.29	4.77	4.44	4.20	4.03	3.89	3.78	3.69	3.55	3.41	2.84	2.75

DEGREES OF FREEDOM (denominator)

17	2.65	2.75	3.31	3.46	3.59	3.68	3.79	3.93	4.10	4.34	4.67	5.18	6.11	8.40
18	2.57	2.66	3.23	3.37	3.51	3.60	3.71	3.84	4.01	4.25	4.58	5.09	6.01	8.29
19	2.49	2.58	3.15	3.30	3.43	3.52	3.63	3.77	3.94	4.17	4.50	5.01	5.93	8.18
20	2.42	2.52	3.09	3.23	3.37	3.46	3.56	3.70	3.87	4.10	4.43	4.94	5.85	8.10
21	2.36	2.46	3.03	3.17	3.31	3.40	3.51	3.64	3.81	4.04	4.37	4.87	5.78	8.02
22	2.31	2.40	2.98	3.12	3.26	3.35	3.45	3.59	3.76	3.99	4.31	4.82	5.72	7.95
23	2.26	2.35	2.93	3.07	3.21	3.30	3.41	3.54	3.71	3.94	4.26	4.76	5.66	7.88
24	2.21	2.31	2.89	3.03	3.17	3.26	3.36	3.50	3.67	3.90	4.22	4.72	5.61	7.82
25	2.17	2.27	2.85	2.99	3.13	3.22	3.32	3.46	3.63	3.85	4.18	4.68	5.57	7.77
26	2.13	2.23	2.81	2.96	3.09	3.18	3.29	3.42	3.59	3.82	4.14	4.64	5.53	7.72
27	2.10	2.20	2.78	2.93	3.06	3.15	3.26	3.39	3.56	3.78	4.11	4.60	5.49	7.68
28	2.06	2.17	2.75	2.90	3.03	3.12	3.23	3.36	3.53	3.75	4.07	4.57	5.45	7.64
29	2.03	2.14	2.73	2.87	3.00	3.09	3.20	3.33	3.50	3.73	4.04	4.54	5.42	7.60
30	2.01	2.11	2.70	2.84	2.98	3.07	3.17	3.30	3.47	3.70	4.02	4.51	5.39	7.56
40	1.80	1.92	2.52	2.66	2.80	2.89	2.99	3.12	3.29	3.51	3.83	4.31	5.18	7.31
60	1.60	1.73	2.35	2.50	2.63	2.72	2.82	2.95	3.12	3.34	3.65	4.13	4.98	7.08
120	1.38	1.53	2.19	2.34	2.47	2.56	2.66	2.79	2.96	3.17	3.48	3.95	4.79	6.85
∞	1.00	1.32	2.04	2.18	2.32	2.41	2.51	2.64	2.80	3.02	3.32	3.78	4.61	6.63

DENOMINATOR

TABLE C   Chi-square (x^2) Values Associated With Interpreting Hypotheses

PROBABILITY LEVELS

		.25	.10	.05	.025	.01	.005	.001
	1	1.323	2.706	3.841	5.024	6.635	7.879	10.828
	2	2.773	4.605	5.991	7.378	9.210	10.597	13.816
	3	4.108	6.251	7.815	9.348	11.345	12.838	16.266
	4	5.385	7.779	9.488	11.143	13.277	14.860	18.467
	5	6.626	9.236	11.071	12.833	15.086	16.750	20.515
	6	7.841	10.645	12.592	14.449	16.812	18.548	22.458
	7	9.037	12.017	14.067	16.013	18.475	20.278	24.322
	8	10.219	13.362	15.507	17.535	20.090	21.955	26.125
	9	11.389	14.684	16.919	19.023	21.666	23.589	27.877
D	10	12.549	15.987	18.307	20.483	23.209	25.188	29.588
E	11	13.701	17.275	19.675	21.920	24.725	26.757	31.264
G	12	14.845	18.549	21.026	23.337	26.217	28.300	32.909
R	13	15.984	19.812	22.362	24.736	27.688	29.820	34.528
E	14	17.117	21.064	23.685	26.119	29.141	31.319	36.123
E								
S	15	18.245	22.307	24.996	27.488	30.578	32.801	37.697
	16	19.369	23.542	26.296	28.845	32.000	34.267	39.252
O	17	20.489	24.769	27.587	30.191	33.409	35.719	40.790
F	18	21.605	25.989	28.869	31.526	34.805	37.156	42.312
	19	22.718	27.204	30.144	32.852	36.191	38.582	43.820
F								
R	20	23.828	28.412	31.410	34.170	37.566	39.997	45.315
E	21	24.935	29.615	32.671	35.479	38.932	41.401	46.797
E	22	26.039	30.813	33.924	36.781	40.289	42.796	48.268
D	23	27.141	32.007	35.173	38.076	41.638	44.181	49.728
O	24	28.241	33.196	36.415	39.364	42.980	45.559	51.179
M								
	25	29.339	34.382	37.653	40.647	44.314	46.928	52.618
	26	30.435	35.563	38.885	41.923	45.642	48.290	54.052
	27	31.528	36.741	40.113	43.195	46.963	49.645	55.476
	28	32.621	37.916	41.337	44.461	48.278	50.993	56.892
	29	33.711	39.088	42.557	45.722	49.588	52.336	58.301
	30	34.800	40.256	43.773	46.979	50.892	53.672	59.703
	40	45.616	51.805	55.759	59.342	63.691	66.766	73.402
	50	56.334	63.167	67.505	71.420	76.154	79.490	86.661
	60	66.982	74.397	79.082	83.298	88.379	91.952	99.607
	70	77.577	85.527	90.531	95.023	100.425	104.215	112.317
	80	88.130	96.578	101.879	106.629	112.329	116.321	124.839
	90	98.650	107.565	113.145	118.136	124.116	128.299	137.208
	100	109.141	118.498	124.342	129.561	135.807	140.169	149.449

This table is abridged from Table 8 in the *Biometrika Tables for Statisticians,* Vol. 1, Third edition (1966), E. S. Pearson and H. O. Hartley, eds. Reproduced by permission of the Biometrika Trustees.

INDEX